A   ICS

ELECTRONIC MEDIATIONS

KATHERINE HAYLES, MARK POSTER, AND SAMUEL WEBER
SERIES EDITORS

DATABASE
AESTHETICS

Art in the Age of
Information Overflow

VICTORIA VESNA, EDITOR

ELECTRONIC MEDIATIONS, VOLUME 20

UNIVERSITY OF MINNESOTA PRESS
MINNEAPOLIS • LONDON

An expanded version of this book will be on the Database Aesthetics Web site, http://victoriavesna.com/dataesthetics. This site is a long-term project that will continuously be making connections as a living artistic organism.

Published by the University of Minnesota Press
111 Third Avenue South, Suite 290
Minneapolis, MN 55401-2520
http://www.upress.umn.edu

Library of Congress Cataloging-in-Publication Data

Database aesthetics : art in the age of information overflow /
    Victoria Vesna, editor.
        p. cm. — (Electronic mediations)
    Includes bibliographical references and index.
    ISBN-13: 978-0-8166-4118-5 (hc : alk. paper)
    ISBN-13: 978-0-8166-4119-2 (pb : alk. paper)

    1. Arts—Data processing. 2. Database design. 3. Information
behavior. I. Bulajic, Viktorija Vesna.
    NX260.D38 2007
    776—dc22

                        2007008226

Printed in the United States of America on acid-free paper

The University of Minnesota is an equal-opportunity educator and employer.

15 14 13 12 11 10   10 9 8 7 6 5 4 3 2

CONTENTS

ACKNOWLEDGMENTS

Completing this project became so overwhelming in the midst of all other obligations (including children, chairing the Department of Design I Media Arts at UCLA, and major art exhibitions involving new work) that I often felt like giving up. But I felt a commitment to the contributors in this book and particularly to media arts students everywhere who could benefit greatly from considering this subject from an artist's perspective. Many of the authors in this volume are part of the University of California's Digital Research Network (UC DARnet), and I am grateful for its support in helping to sponsor the editing process. The editing of the book was completed impeccably by Susan Jones, who made sure that every detail was addressed and all essays were consistent. I thank Mark Poster for initiating this effort and Douglas Armato, director of the University of Minnesota Press, who had infinite patience and trusted that I would eventually deliver the manuscript. Most of all, I am indebted to my daughters, Angelica and Aleksandra, for growing into beautiful women who understand and support their mother.

INTRODUCTION

VICTORIA VESNA

In 1999, I compiled a special issue for the journal *AI & Society* titled "Database Aesthetics: Issues of Organization and Category in Art." To work with the authors more efficiently, I replicated the progress of the book on the Web as it was emerging and continually updated the Web site until completed. As with many academic journals, *AI & Society* was printed in limited numbers and distributed primarily in the UK. The working site remained online and was soon discovered by a number of people and cited frequently. Even one of the editors of the Electronic Mediations series, Mark Poster, who approached me to expand the "Database Aesthetics" issue into a book, found the Web site before getting a copy of the printed journal.

With computers becoming smaller, faster, and more ubiquitous, so much had changed that it was impossible simply to redo the issue of *AI & Society,* and thus this anthology became a much larger project than we first envisioned. In the meantime, the human genome had been decoded, biotech had become a new field for artistic engagement, and many more media artists had emerged with online works deliberately manipulating databases.

This compilation is not about the technical aspects of computer databases but, rather, a collection of essays that begins to show how an aesthetic emerges when artists take on the challenge of creating work using the vast amount of information that bombards us daily. As an artist working with networked technologies for the past fifteen years, I have discovered that one has to be conscious of the information overflow and develop a philosophy in relation to handling large amounts of data. This is particularly true with interactive work, which generates even more information because it includes audience participation. As a professor in the field of media arts, I have realized that too often novice media artists and designers develop work first, and then, as an afterthought, turn to thinking about how to store and manage the data. This method of working results in many awkward pieces that use preconceived notions of organization that may actually contradict the meaning of the piece itself. The core message of this volume is that one first has to research, collect, and survey the data needed for the envisioned work and then decide how the database design and engine will appropriately reflect the concept. In other words, artists working with computer technology have to think of the invisible backbone of databases and navigation through information as the driving aesthetic of the project.

During the final stages of compiling this volume, I co-taught a graduate seminar with Mark Hansen.[1] We decided to admit as many people as applied in order to amplify the very problem the class addresses: How does one design a situation that involves too many people and, consequently, too much information? A class that typically would have no more than ten students grew to twenty-seven. To complicate matters even more, we opened the class to disciplines outside the arts and allowed students from information science, geography, statistics, and film studies to participate. The first assignment was to come up with a database of the self using any media. The assignment immediately confronted students with the issues faced when starting to imagine a project that would forefront how information is organized as an aesthetic and philosophical challenge. How does one begin to define oneself in terms of information? The editing process immediately becomes apparent: What do you make public and what do you keep archived and private? Do you use your genome or your Social Security and credit card numbers as part of your identity? Do you use your body parts, clothes, and belongings? Would you include your relations with others as a way to define yourself? Are you an open or closed or semiclosed system? What media do you use and can it be exhibited, archived, and retrieved? Almost all the issues raised in this book surfaced instantly when faced with databasing the self.

Students responded with the widest spectrum of approaches—from a photographic representation of a room that included books and personal belongings, to bar codes on all personal objects, to credit cards, to Power-Point presentations of research in information studies, to traces of daily steps, to cookies that represented the process learned by watching.[2]

Once we surveyed the ideas, we challenged the students to think about how they would create a database of the class projects. We did not go so far as asking them to actually do this because we knew this would be a huge project that would last years and involve teams of people. The goal was to present them with the daunting problem that many are not aware of when designing database systems: How does one represent the information without dehumanizing it? This question is central to this compilation of practicing artists who are consciously addressing this issue in their creative work. Although the preoccupation is not new, it is certainly amplified in the age of ever-increasing speed of computing power, miniaturization, and ample storage availability.

THE PRACTICE OF DATABASE ART

Archives and databases offer artists a vehicle for commenting on cultural and institutional practices through direct intervention. Art itself has been recognized by conceptualists as an institution with all the training of product production, display, and consumption—and in many cases artists themselves have made us conscious of these issues more successfully than historians, anthropologists, or even sociologists. From the beginning of the twentieth century, the art world has been slowly deconstructed and dissembled by the very artists the institutions were promoting. In parallel, communication technologies have reinforced much of this work, and as an entire new generation of artists and audiences emerges, we are bound to witness an acceleration of change. The most promising arena for conceptual work in the twenty-first century is already in place since the archives and database systems are being developed with dizzying speed. It is in the code of search engines and the aesthetics of navigation that the new conceptual fieldwork lies for the artist. These are the places not only to make commentaries and interventions but also to start conceptualizing alternative ways for artistic practice and even for commerce. As new institutions and authorities take shape right in front of our eyes, we must not stand by in passive disbelief, for history possibly could repeat itself, which would leave current and future artistic work on the Internet as marginalized as video art.

Artists have long recognized the conceptual and aesthetic power of databases, and much work has resulted using archives as a deliberate base for artistic endeavors. In view of activities such as those cited above, this is a rich territory for artists—and on many levels. Databases and archives serve as ready-made commentaries on our contemporary social and political lives. Even museums as institutions and the general societal attitude toward art objects can be viewed and dissected from this perspective. The gallery becomes the public face, while the storerooms are its private parts, with the majority of the collection residing there. Artwork resides in storerooms that not only are cut off from the critical arena but also are subsisting in the graceless form of regimented racks. Artists have produced work that comments on these logistics of museum collection and display, a system on which museums have traditionally depended. Let us consider some art practices in this domain before discussing how contemporary artists working with digital technologies are responding to knowledge organization and production.[3]

Marcel Duchamp's *Boîte-en-Valise* is often considered to be the first critique of museum practice: "[It] parodies the museum as an enclosed space for displaying art . . . mocks [its] archival activity . . . [and] satirically suggests that the artist is a travelling salesman whose concerns are as promotional as they are aesthetic."[4] After publishing an edition of three hundred standard and twenty luxury versions of *The Green Box*,[5] Duchamp devised a series of valises that would contain miniature versions of his artwork to be unpacked and used in museums. He commissioned printers and light manufacturers throughout Paris to make 320 miniature copies of his artworks and a customized briefcase in which to store and display them: "In the end the project was not only autobiographical, a life-long summation, but anticipatory as well. As an artwork designed to be unpacked, the viewing of *Valise* carries the same sense of expectation and event as the opening of a crate."[6]

In the 1970s and 1980s, such artists as Richard Artschwager, Louise Lawler, Marcel Broodthaers, and Martin Kippenberger commented on museum practice using archiving and packing practices as an anchor. Ironically, storage of fine art in many cases is more elaborate and careful in execution than the very art it is meant to protect. Perhaps anticipating the art of "containers" of interface to data, Artschwager takes the crate and elevates it to an art form by creating a series of crates and exhibiting them in museum and gallery spaces. Similarly, Andy Warhol (an obsessive collector in his own right) curated a show at the Rhode Island School of Design that consisted entirely of a shoe collection from the costume collection, shelf and all. The show was part of a series conceived by John and Dominique de Menil, who were interested in bringing to light some of the "unsuspecting treasures mouldering in museum basements, inaccessible to the general public."[7]

Artists working with digital media, particularly on the networks, are acutely aware of information overflow and that the design of navigation through these spaces has become a demand of aesthetic practice. One of the first artists who used the World Wide Web with the now-obsolete Mosaic browser was Antonio Muntadas. Muntadas's project *File Room* was devoted to documenting cases of censorship that frequently are not available at all or exist somewhere only as dormant data.[8] Similarly, Vera Frankel created an installation, *Body Missing*, that extends onto the Web and addresses issues of art collection, specifically of Hitler's obsession:

A particular focus of these conversations has been the Sonderauftrag (Special Assignment) Linz, Hitler's little publicized but systematic plan to acquire art work by any means, including theft or forced sale, for the proposed Führer-museum in Linz, his boyhood town. Shipped from all over Europe to the salt mines at the nearby Alt Aussee, the burnt collection was stored in conditions of perfect archival temperature and humidity, until found by the Allies after the war: cave after cave of paintings, sculptures, prints and drawings destined for the vast museum that was never built.[9]

Frankel invites other artists to contribute their own narratives and bibliographies to the work, thus making the piece itself become a kind of archive whose content does not belong to only one artist. Fear of the loss of originality and the revered artist personae are frequently connected to the endless reproductions that the digital media affords. Another source of fear for artists confronting the new technologies is the integration of individual artists into the context of other works or the creation of metaworks. Of course, this is not a fear for those who have taken on a broader view of what "originality" might mean. Ultimately, artists working with digital media necessarily work in collaborative groups and are context providers. Indeed, the development of context in the age of information overload is the art of the day. This is particularly true of the current artistic practice on the Internet in which artists frequently co-opt and summon the work and data of others. One by-product of a "global culture" is the emergence of meta-structures that include physical architectures, software such as the browser technology that allows us to view information on the Internet via the Web, and artworks that are meta-art pieces, including work not only by other artists but by the audience itself.

Artists working with the Internet as a medium are concerned essentially with the creation of a new type of aesthetic that involves not only a visual representation but invisible aspects of organization, retrieval, and navigation as well. Data are the raw forms that are shaped and used to build architectures of knowledge exchange and serve also as an active commentary on the environment they depend on—the vast, intricate network with its many faces.

In an age in which we are increasingly aware of ourselves as databases, identified by Social Security numbers and genetic structures, it is imperative that artists actively participate in how data are shaped, organized, and disseminated. The collapse of the Berlin Wall, broken with the help of communication technologies, marked the beginning of the breakdown of many walls of categories. In this context, artists become information architects who help to usher in this new way of working, thinking, anticipating, and helping to visualize new structures.

My purpose in this book is to show not only how practicing artists think in relation to databases but also to raise the awareness of a wider audience about the importance of considering how our social data are being organized, categorized, stored, and retrieved. Too often this process is an extremely dehumanized system, even though societies are defined by the way we organize our information. This book is precisely concerned with accomplishing this end through its focus on both how data are given life and how information is shaped into knowledge. Implicitly, this is also about the need for us all to realize that artists should be increasingly involved in this work, or, at minimum, have an awareness of database construction and their placement. All who have contributed are not only contextualizing themselves from this point of view but are also actively participating in practice.

While compiling this book, I realized that there is a large body of work by digital-media artists who consciously employ databases and use them for aesthetics and the critique of established systems of organization. It also became clear that many artists like me are almost forced to write about our work because it changes so quickly that it is difficult for humanities scholars to keep track and gain an understanding of what it is that we do. This is another reason that the majority of authors in this volume are practicing artists, with the exception of two curators, who actively work with artists engaged in digital media in its many forms.

Part I consists of a series of essays from artists working with information overflow, beginning with my own experience. In "Seeing the World in a Grain of Sand: The Database Aesthetics of Everything," I show how my work increasingly became informed by my realization of how databases are shaping our collective reality. As soon as I started exploring the Internet as a creative space in 1993, I was confronted with large sets of data. Ten years later, when I started spending time in a nano lab, I found vast amounts of data generated in the invisible realm. My goal is to give a sense of context that artists respond to by observing, critiquing, and directly engaging the infrastructures of databases in our creative work, exposing the invisible realm that is rarely connected to the idea of creativity and even less to any kind of aesthetics. Part of that context is the work of my peers in the media arts community who equally contributed to my thinking on the subject. My narrative is followed by Lev Manovich's essay "Database as Symbolic Form," published in the *AI & Society* special issue but later developed into a chapter of his much celebrated book, *Language of New Media*, in which he discusses the relationship of database and film and puts forward that notion that the new language of the computer age is indeed the database. Manovich goes on to make a connection to an emerging new narrative that has a direct relationship to databases. His text is essential for anyone who wants to understand why an artist would take the time to ponder databases, which at first glance seem so uninteresting. He states that "new media artists working on the database/narrative problem can learn from cinema as it is; cinema already exists right in the intersection between database and narrative."

With this poignant connection of the importance of database and cinema, it only made sense to invite Grahame Weinbren, a pioneer interactive artist and theorist who has worked with cinematic issues in his installations since the early 1980s. Weinbren is also the editor of *Millennium Film Journal*, which publishes articles on experimental and avant-garde cinema, video, and more recently works that use new technologies. In his essay, "Ocean, Database, Recut," he uses Salman Rushdie's *Haroun and the Sea of Stories* as an example of literature that uses nonlinear structures as cinema should, instead of the tyranny of linear thinking that we have been subjected to since the nineteenth century in both literature and cinema. Thus, at the outset we have a dialogue developing between authors in this volume. Weinbren disagrees with the introductory stand of Manovich where he puts forward that narrative is replaced by database. Instead, he proposes a less radical approach that would reconsider the narrative in light of the database. To prove his point, he once again returns to Rushdie's story, in which he sees the ocean as deep, changeable, and fluid—a giant library that is always in flux. He also uses the tragic day of 9/11, which he felt powerfully living in downtown New York, as an example of how an event can take on many narratives depending on the person retelling the story, as well as that person's background, placement, and attitude. Each person presents one facet, and only the collection of stories from different perspectives can give us a relatively accurate picture of what really happened. And so it is with the idea of databases and aesthetics. These two authors follow my narrative with a cinematic perspective, from a very different point of view, offering the reader not only a choice but also much to consider.

Norman M. Klein continues this literary/cinematic thread with his own brand of nonlinear thinking and writing, which makes unusual connections and observations that are at once satisfying and sobering. "Data remind us that we are being colonized by our own economy, outsourced and psychologically invaded," he writes in "Waiting for the World to Explode: How

Data Convert into a Novel." A writer who works with memory, presence, and absence, Klein quickly discovered that the book does not suffice as a database narrative. In the early 1990s he began collaborating with media artists on developing works on CD-ROM and DVD that include the endless images accompanying his complex thoughts. *Bleeding Through* is one such project that he describes in his essay as he links to Virginia Woolf, Charles Baudelaire, and Gabriel García Márquez's *One Hundred Years of Solitude,* among others. To me, Klein represents a true contemporary writer who is able to make connections between myriad, seemingly unrelated people, events, and facts in an almost poetic way. He too mentions Manovich, although in passing.

Christiane Paul continues the discussion on narratives in her essay "The Database as System and Cultural Form: Anatomies of Cultural Narratives." After clearly defining her database aesthetics, she goes on to present different data models that will prove helpful to the reader as artists discuss their work later in the volume. She puts forward the tension between the linear and hierarchical structures of databases and the seemingly infinite possibilities of reconfiguring the information within these structures. As a curator and theorist, she has been attracted to artists who work consciously with this tension, such as the Radical Software Group (RSG), Matthew Fuller, and Maciej Wisniewski. Paul gives a good overview of a group of artists— some of whom are represented in this volume—who largely work outside the established museum system and use the Internet as a creative field. She also brings up Manovich's claim that "narrative and databases are natural enemies" and instead offers that computer games are often narratives whose constituent elements are still organized in a form of database structure. By now the reader will most likely agree that databases are another form of narrative and not "competing for the same territory of human culture, each claims an exclusive right to make meaning out of the world." As we discover the vast possibilities presented to us by the World Wide Web database alone, it is easier to envision the ocean, forever in flux, vast, and endlessly deep as the metaphor of choice. Still, it is useful to start with the polarities, lest we drown by plunging into the information ocean first.

Steve Dietz, another curator of media arts whose interest centers largely on network-based artworks, continues the narrative with a short historical background and then presents another group of artists who work with databases. Dietz established himself as the director of New Media Initiatives at the Walker Art Center in Minneapolis, a building with eight floors. He was in charge of the online *Gallery 9,* which resided, famously, on the "ninth floor." He eventually left the museum institution to be a freelance critic and curator. In his essay "The Database Imaginary: Memory_Archive_Database v 4.0," he provides an overview of artists who have approached the subject of archiving and databases, such as the *Unreliable Archivist* by Janet Cohen, Keith Frank, and Jon Ippolito, who directly shake up ideas of purified categories to which museums tend to cling. He also discusses Muntadas's historical *File Room,* an artwork that set a precedent for database works that are politically based by allowing free input of information in relation to censorship. Dietz also notes the important relationship of databases and bodies as "memory archives" by commenting on Eduardo Kac's "Time Capsule," presented by the artist later in this volume.

Memories and embodiment are of central concern to Bill Seaman, who titles his essay "Recombinant Poetics and Related Database Aesthetics." He spent a number of years developing a work called the *World Generator / The Engine of Desire*—a virtual world generating system that specifically draws on the potentials of the database aesthetic. Much of the conceptual work was influenced by his research of the *Memory Theatre* by the sixteenth-century thinker Giulio Camillo, and with research on how DNA works.[10] In other words, Seaman created an artwork with an endless set of potential stories, as do Weinbren and other artists who work consciously with large data sets of information.

Seaman is followed by the essays of the artists Sharon Daniel, Warren Sack, and Robert F. Nideffer, who are theoreticians in their own right and contextualize their work with philosophical and socially conscious stances. All three come from different backgrounds—which is evident in their intellectual approaches to the work they do. Daniel's earlier work focused on performative and experimental video, and as she moved to exploring the Internet as the creative space of choice, her work became progressively socially activist. Appropriately, her approach to database is influenced by reading Michel Foucault's interpretation of the "work" and the "author." Daniel's approach to narrative questions the idea of the author as the sole creator: "The individualization of the author provided a context for the objectification of the work as both unity and commodity." She makes an intense argument for a fluid, complex, and nonlinear narrative in her introduction and then elaborates on her works that show her attitude toward narrative in action. In "The Database: An Aesthetics of Dignity," she repeatedly brings up the tension of the individual and the collective, the illusion of a solitary author, and the importance of the collaborative process, preparing us for Warren Sack's "Network Aesthetics."

Warren Sack is a software designer and media theorist who creates systems in information architecture and the topology of social relations. In other words, he develops ways to visualize the invisible tracks left behind by people connecting and interacting—directly and indirectly—on the Internet. As vast and deep as the Internet is, we still have a flat and, to a large degree, linear access to information. Sack's research moves away from network architecture (connections between machines) and information architecture (connection between people and machines) to discourse architecture, which connects people to people via the networked public space powered by computers. Again, we return to the idea of narrative, but this time in a more expanded manner. He brings into the discussion the use of Artificial Intelligence (AI) in designing systems that allow for discourse architecture to emerge and introduces the reader to the background and core concepts of AI before going further into how one may design systems with "common sense." He continues with a similar philosophical base that we encountered in Daniel's essay, elaborating on AI using Immanuel Kant, Gilles Deleuze, Edmund Husserl, and Martin Heidegger, among others, as his philosophical underpinning. It is interesting to see how this philosophical influence comes to life with work that considers and takes it into action with the creation of spaces that actively engage and expose the dialectics.

Sack's network aesthetics is followed by Robert F. Nideffer's exposure of the game engines that power the experience of playing computer games. Christiane Paul brought up games as an example of a new type of narrative, and Nideffer demonstrates how the engine and the player work together as indexical pointers to a significantly extended notion of database. Nideffer received his doctorate in social sciences before shifting to media arts with a focus on computer games. In "Game Engines as Embedded Systems," he makes a strong point of the importance of designing systems that allow flexibility and structural changes of game worlds and game engines. Even though computer games are a relatively new phenomenon, the market for these games developed with dizzying speed but with the unfortunate consequence of formalizing the aesthetic at a very early stage. The dissatisfaction that Grahame Weinbren voices over cinema remaining in the linear realm (except for the few examples in the artist and avant-garde film and video) is already felt with the gaming industry. Many artists became interested in games as a creative space but find themselves confronted with equally monstrous market machines, as did the film industry. Nideffer's essay offers a solid background in the evolution of games before he leads the reader behind the scenes, exposing the invisible aesthetic of the gaming engine.

In Part II, artists give a more descriptive accounting of their works. Nancy Paterson describes her wonderful *Stock Market Skirt,* which is at once funny and disturbing in its many layers of meaning; Lynn Hershman-Leeson gives a retrospective accounting of her database work with identity that moves from analog to digital media; George Legrady describes his long-term project *Pockets Full of Memories,* in which he designed a system for the audience to add continuously to the memory database by scanning in their objects. Eduardo Kac plunges us into the animal database with implanted chips through his "Time Capsule"; and John Klima gives us an example of his work *ecosystm* as a database aesthetic. Finally, Marko Peljhan discusses his work *Polar,* a piece that combines the biological and physical with the abstract and the immaterial using the computer network and database. These essays come full circle from Weinbren's metaphor of database as an ocean. Indeed, Peljhan says that "the work was inspired by the notion of the cognitive 'ocean' as described respectively in Stanislaw Lem and Andrei Tarkovsky's *Solaris.*"[11]

Working on this book has been difficult because it was almost impossible to pin down the meaning of database art while the technological/social/ global context keeps shifting. At some level, the vastness of human knowledge and experience encoded in some sort of information that is in some way or other organized and then networked is beyond comprehension. It is more than we can grasp as individuals, so it is important to collaborate and to recognize the collective network we are all part of. In light of this, an accompanying Web site will become a database emerging from this collection of essays, and we will continue and no doubt expand the dialogue in many more ways.

NOTES

1. Mark Hansen is a statistician who joined the UCLA faculty in the Department of Statistics and Design I Media Arts after working at Bell Labs. His collaborative database art project, *Listening Post,* with artist Ben Rubin, won a Golden Nica at the 2004 Prix Ars Electronica.

2. More information about the class can be accessed through the Database Aesthetic Web site, http://victoriavesna.com/dataesthetics.

3. Curators who responded and understood artists' comments on the culture of storage, archives, and the preservation of art have the opportunity to participate in and remark on this practice. One of the most impressive examples of this kind of work is a recent exhibition titled Deep Storage, organized by Ingrid Schaffner and Matthias Winzen. This show perhaps marks the end of the era of analog archiving and the beginning of an era of digital archiving. A few projects included in this show point to the next step of artwork generated by digital archiving and databasing.

4. Jackie McAllister and Benjamin Weil, "The Museum under Analysis," in *In the Desire of the Museum Catalogue* (New York: Whitney Museum of American Art, 1989), 10.

5. The formal title of *The Green Box* is *The Bride Stripped Bare by Her Bachelors, Even.* The nickname is coined to distinguish *The Box* from Duchamp's masterpiece, a sculpture of the same title produced between 1915 and 1928 and known simply as *The Large Glass.*

6. *Deep Storage: Collecting, Storing, and Archiving in Art,* ed. Ingrid Schaffner and Matthias Winzen (Munich: Prestel-Verlag, 1998), 11.

7. David Bourdon, "Andy's Dish," in *Raid the Icebox 1 with Andy Warhol Catalogue* (Providence: Museum of Art, Rhode Island School of Design, 1970), 17.

8. *File Room* is located at http://fileroom.aaup.uic.edu/FileRoom.

9. Vera Frankel's project on the Web site, *Body Missing,* is an extension of a video installation presented at P.S. 1 Museum, New York. See www.yorku.ca/BodyMissing.

10. *Memory Theater* was a work by the sixteenth-century thinker Giulio Camillo.

11. *Solaris* is a film adaptation of Stanislaw Lem's science-fiction novel of the same name, produced by Andrei Tarkovsky (1972, USSR, 165 minutes).

PART I

DATABASE AESTHETICS

1. Seeing the World in a Grain of Sand: The Database Aesthetics of Everything

VICTORIA VESNA

From Human Flesh to Human Databases

Some thirty years ago, as a young artist to be, I was being trained in a most classical way at the Academy of Fine Arts in Belgrade. The painting program was designed to follow the European tradition of having anatomy at its core. We spent many hours for over two years drawing every bone, every muscle, of the human body, and stopped just short of dissection. We spent the rest of the time in front of nudes or doing portraiture. Looking back, I realize that this was the beginning of my journey to delve deeper into the human body and mind as I kept expanding the idea of the body from the physical bones, muscle, and nervous system to the vast collective body of information of bits to molecules and atoms.

We human beings represent a natural system that evolves progressively from the apparently simple to the very complex—from a sperm and egg to the amazingly complex intelligent living being we call "human." Yet our tendency is to look "top down" and put ourselves at the center of the universe—which was easier to do when our knowledge was more limited and we were unaware of the vast ocean of information that is nonlinear, ubiquitous, and immersive, information that was always there but was out of our view. Today, because of technological advances, we are instead progressively and collectively experiencing a new way of being and it is not orchestrated from the center by a single authority.

Molecular and cellular biosciences have particularly flourished as the speed, power, and storage capabilities of computers have rapidly advanced. Biomolecular, cellular, gene, and genome studies have become major research areas that have already influenced our lives and have the potential to completely change our perception of ourselves and how we function in society. The most popular example is the mapping of the genome and the completion of the human DNA sequence, which has been celebrated and debated in practically all public domains. Completed in 2003, this event coincided with the fiftieth anniversary of James Watson and Francis Crick's description of the fundamental structure of DNA. This discovery was not without controversy as it was preceded by Rosalind Franklin and Maurice Wilkins's meticulous studies using X-rays to probe the structure of DNA, and these images were the key to solving the puzzle. Their discovery also foreshadowed the importance computers would play in future research—even with the way they used the language of computing to describe the structure, genetic code, and sequencing. Molecular biology, gene therapy, and cloning are the grandchildren of this monumental discovery.[1]

A genome is all the DNA in an organism, including its genes. Briefly, genes carry information for making all the proteins required by all organisms. These proteins determine, among other things, how the organism looks, how well its body metabolizes food or fights infection, and sometimes even how it behaves. DNA is made up of four similar chemicals (called "bases" and abbreviated A, T, C, and G) that are repeated millions or billions of times throughout a genome. Although the vast majority of our DNA sequences is the same, scientists estimate that humans are 99.9 percent identical genetically. Yet these DNA sequence variations can have a major impact on how our bodies respond to disease and environmental insults such as bacteria, viruses, toxins, drugs, and various therapies. DNA is probably the most beautiful example of database aesthetics and certainly points to the importance of grasping the efficiency and beauty of design that nature employs in all of life.

Even the DNA molecule for the single-cell bacterium *E. coli* contains enough information to fill all the books in any of the world's largest libraries. More than 95 percent of all DNA was called "Junk DNA" or "molecular garbage" by molecular biologists because they are still unable to ascribe any function to it. But if it were "junk," the sequence of the "syllables"—the nucleotides in DNA—should be completely random. All this is to say that we have the letters but not the language, and there is so much more to be discovered. Yet, even with this first step in understanding DNA, we are poised to think of ourselves in a different way. Consider the fingerprint versus DNA testing, which has revolutionized forensic science. From identifying the remains of soldiers, to deciding paternity cases, to eliminating (and often convicting) criminal suspects, DNA testing has become a powerful new weapon in the lawyer's arsenal. A DNA fingerprint is constructed by first extracting a DNA sample from body tissue or fluid such as hair, blood, or saliva. In the United States, the Federal Bureau of Investigation has created a national database of genetic information called the National DNA Index System. The database contains DNA obtained from convicted criminals and from evidence found at crime scenes. Some experts fear that this database might be used for unauthorized purposes, such as identifying individuals with stigmatizing illnesses.

It is more than a decade since the U.S. genetic engineering company Genentech made both medical and legal history—first with the discovery of the gene that produces insulin, and then by persuading a series of U.S. courts that it had earned the right to patent its discovery. Just as digital libraries funded by governments and developed by university consortiums have their counterparts in the corporate sector, so it is also in the sphere of biotechnology. The Human Genome Project, completed in 2003, was funding thousands of scientists working at universities and research labs with generous budgets in the billions of dollars. But the biotech world has become a kind of battlefield, with certain private companies refusing to share the genetic codes they identified and therefore claim. The case of the *Staphylococcus aureus,* a deadly bacteria that resists the strongest antibiotics, is an example of this conflict. Biotechnology and drug companies have spent huge amounts of money decoding the genome of the *Staph,* hoping to design new drugs to combat it. But they refuse to share their discoveries or to collaborate with federal health officials, forcing them to duplicate the work at a cost of millions of dollars to taxpayers. The question is still open and mirrors the one that is always looming over all data about us: Will information be available and free in the public domain, or will it be patented and owned by the large corporate sector?[2]

Many artists have been inspired to create work that addresses issues raised by biotechnological manipulation, but those working with technological media address these issues in the most direct ways by using the same tools, and the same language, that the scientists do. A few examples of such works include *Eighth Day* by Eduardo Kac, *Microvenus* and *Audio Microscope* by Joe Davis, *GenTerra* by the Critical Art Ensemble, and *One Tree* and the synthetic skin culture work of Natalie Jeremijenko.[3]

BODY DATABASES

Dissecting and analyzing bodies has been ever-present since the Enlightenment, when the problem of imaging the invisible became critical in the fine arts and natural sciences.[4] The Visible Human Project was initiated in 1986 by the National Library of Medicine (NLM), which foresaw an era in which NLM's bibliographic and factual database services would be complemented

by libraries of digital images distributed over high-speed computer networks and by high-capacity physical media. The aim of the Visible Human
Project was the acquisition of transverse CT, MRI, and cryosection images
of a representative male and female cadaver at an average of one-millimeter
intervals. Here is how data of the male body are represented on the Visual
Human Project Web site:

> The male data set consists of MRI, CT, and anatomical images. Axial MRI
> images of the head, neck, and longitudinal sections of the rest of the body
> were obtained at 4 mm intervals. The MRI images are 256 pixel by 256 pixel
> resolution. Each pixel has 12 bits of grey tone resolution. The CT data consists
> of axial CT scans of the entire body taken at 1 mm intervals at a resolution
> of 512 pixels by 512 pixels where each pixel is made up of 12 bits of grey tone.
> The axial anatomical images are 2048 pixels by 1216 pixels where each pixel is
> defined by 24 bits of color, about 7.5 megabytes. The anatomical cross sections
> are also at 1 mm intervals and coincide with the CT axial images. There are
> 1871 cross sections for each mode, CT, and anatomy. The complete male data
> set is 15 gigabytes in size. The data set from the female cadaver will have the
> same characteristics as the male cadaver with one exception. The axial ana-
> tomical images will be obtained at 0.33 mm intervals instead of 1.0 mm inter-
> vals. This will result in over 5,000 anatomical images. The data set is expected
> to be about 40 gigabytes in size.[5]

It is not easy to find on the site that the male body was a thirty-eight-year-
old prisoner who died in Texas by lethal injection, or that the female model
was a fifty-nine-year-old Maryland resident who died of a blockage in the
aorta caused by a small piece of calcium. Dr. Cathy Waldby is one of the few
theoreticians who has attempted to analyze the fascination with the Visible
Humans online, linking it to our society of spectacle and the medical world's
practice of unemotional databasing. She writes: "Medicine's use of data and
data space is itself uncanny, drawing on the peculiar vivid, negentropic qualities of information to (re)animate its productions."[6] Dissecting the human
flesh into millimeter pieces, digitizing, and posting on the Internet is at
once useful for research and also a portrait of the way the Western medical
community has removed itself from the human soul behind the body, which
all too frequently is viewed as a machine. And yet, there is no denying that
this is a quantum leap from the way human anatomy traditionally has
been taught, and it certainly opens the door to new ways of thinking about
the body.

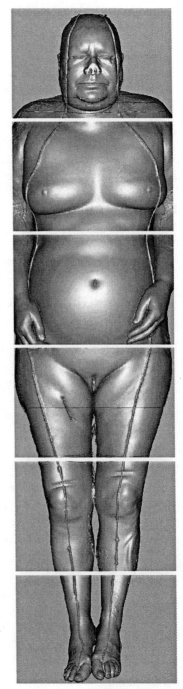

FIGURE 1.1. VISUAL HUMAN PROJECT:
MARCHING THROUGH THE VISIBLE WOMAN.
FULL-BODY SURFACE MODELS. COURTESY
OF WILLIAM E. LORENSEN. AVAILABLE AT
HTTP://WWW.CRD.GE.COM/~LORENSEN/VW/.

In the computerized paradigm, humans are perceived as information, as evidenced by both the Visible Human Project and the Human Genome Project, or as information-processing entities. In both cases the "human" is abstracted from the larger social conditions we occupy. If we juxtapose these assumptions with late capitalism, moving away from durable product to information, we can easily translate this to the art world's dematerialization of the object. We could celebrate this event as a victory of conceptual movements or see it as a dangerous intersection where information about us is being collected, stored, and databased without the opportunity for us to choose, or to know, or to accept either its worth or its consequences.

BODIES INCORPORATED

> In contemporary capitalism, in the society of the simulacrum, the market is "behind" nothing, it is in everything. It is thus that in a society where the commodification of art has progressed apace with the aestheticization of the commodity, there has evolved a universal rhetoric of the aesthetic in which commerce and inspiration, profit and poetry, may rapturously entwine.
>
> —VICTOR BURGIN

Artists have always been concerned with the representation of the body as a mirror or our collective state of consciousness. And I believe our artistic perspective is worthy of consideration—or at least is useful as another viewpoint for ongoing public debates regarding identity and the rights of individuals. This is especially important in light of the inherent assumptions in the media of what constitutes a "body," how biological "life" is defined, and how political answers are separated from larger philosophical issues of the ways in which we, as a society, may be changing our perceptions of self.

My own work with networked bodies and identity led me to think deeper about database aesthetics. In 1995, the World Wide Web was starting to become the center of public attention—both as a promise and a threat—and the Visual Human Project had just been initiated.

Virtual Concrete, completed in 1995 and exhibited in a show of artists working with scientific concepts entitled "Veered Science," was my first artistic response to the potential of the Internet and my introduction to the relationship of the body to online databases.[7] The work was a reaction to the notion of the virtual as somehow being separate from the "real" and directly explores the mind/body split between the conscious and unconscious in relation to a "disembodied" realm of communication. It was also an attempt to question the "real" art experience when the viewer was removed from the art being viewed. At the time, the press was actively promoting the notion that the Internet was being used to proliferate pornography, thus raising serious concerns about possible censorship and the control of information flow. As a response to these fears, the electronic blocking device known as the V-Chip (the "V" standing for "violence") was being promoted and debated widely and the PGP (Pretty Good Privacy) encryption software developed by Philip Zimmerman was under investigation for alleged violation of export regulations.

But the real inspiration for *Virtual Concrete* occurred during the Los Angeles Northridge Earthquake in 1994. Residents and remote television audiences alike were horrified as freeways collapsed within seconds into large pieces of concrete. Communication moved into the "virtual" realm as the Internet and cell phones became the established connection to the "real" world when the wire lines failed. I was also fascinated with the fact that the element silicon is found in concrete as well as in the chip that propels cyberspace.

The first step I took in creating *Virtual Concrete* was to photograph images of a male and female body, each covered with computer chips (no nipples or genitals exposed) and further overlaid by the names of sex chat rooms from the Internet.[8] The photos were printed larger than life—each one eight feet long—and the pigment from the photos was then bonded to huge concrete blocks (without any remains of the paper) using electrostatic output.[9] The end result unexpectedly (but fortuitously) resembled frescoes, lending an aura of classical respectability to the concretized images.

The text on top of the images, almost unnoticeable, was erotically charged, and in order to read it the viewers had to bend over, or crawl over, the concrete.[10] As people moved around the work, these chat-room "destinations" were announced in a matter-of-fact voice by a recording that was triggered by the shadows of people moving over the installation. The shadows also activated compositions of randomly cycling sound and included an occasional mention of habeas corpus in order to provide proof of corporeal presence.[11] With the inert bodies bonded to the concrete and the live bodies walking atop it, a camera mounted on the wall watched silently and, using CU-SeeMe technology, dynamically projected both "bodies" onto the Internet for wider viewing.[12]

Images of the bodies on concrete were thus captured in a photograph, converted into digits, manipulated, printed, and placed onto concrete. Once concretized, the bodies—now granted physicality—could be accepted by the art world and enter into the gallery or museum space, a space where the object is usually considered sacred and untouchable. I wanted the audience

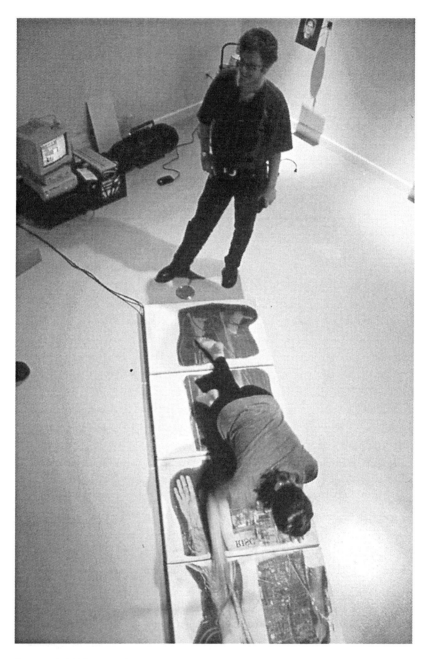

FIGURE 1.2. VIRTUAL CONCRETE: PEOPLE WALKING ON BODIES COVERED WITH TEXT LISTING CHAT ROOMS ONLINE. UC SANTA BARBARA GALLERY, 2003.

to walk on the bodies in pure irreverence, to trespass as they moved on the piece, which uncannily resembled a "sacred" fresco.

The interactivity with the physical piece was successful: people walked, crawled on the concrete, sparked off sounds, and waved at the camera. On the Web, however, I felt that watching the activity of people in the gallery through the camera was not enough. Because the core idea of the project was the idea of a "real" and "virtual" body in cyberspace, I decided that a good way to extend the interactivity would be for the audience to create a body at a distance. Therefore, I put a simple CGI questionnaire on the same page on which the video of the installation was being projected and asked participants to give us a name for their body, assign it a gender, and make a statement about what the body meant to them.[13] To my surprise, there were more than a thousand bodies on order in two weeks—and before long people were asking to "see" the bodies they had "ordered":

> Date: Wed, 08 May 1996 09:12:41
> From: [Body name]
> To: concrete@arts.ucsb.edu
> Subject: body order 3803
> Re virtual body order #3803. I definitely got the idea that at some point there would be a 3d drawing of my body order. Where is it? Or was this simply a concept?

This demand persisted and made me reconsider the meaning of online identity. I decided to respond by creating a new dystrophic project that would "take over" the *Virtual Concrete* and, with it, the database of people who participated. I composed a message to all those who were waiting for their bodies:

> ——————— Forwarded message ———————
> Date: Mon, 12 Aug 1996 15:35:45 -0700 (PDT)
> From: Victoria Vesna <vesna@arts.ucsb.edu>
> To: [Body name]
> Subject: Re: My Body
> Dear [Body name]
> Virtual Concrete was recently acquired by Bodies© INCorporated. Your body is in Limbo INC (a subsidiary of Bodies INC). Please go to our new site and reorder. We are sorry for any inconvenience this delay may have caused.
> Sincerely, Bodies© INC.

Bodies© INCorporated was conceived as a response to the need of the *Virtual Concrete* online audience to "see" their bodies and it was informed by my research of MOOs, multiuser worlds, cyborgs, and avatars. I did not simply want to send back what was demanded, but to answer in a way that would prompt the participants to consider their relationship to the Internet as a corporate machine and understand the meaning of online representation.

When I uploaded the questionnaire in *Virtual Concrete* asking the participants to "order" their imaginary body, it never crossed my mind to take it further than the realm of the conceptual. But I was intrigued by the need to be represented graphically and, further, to have these bodies somehow enact a life of their own.[14] This need is one that could easily be manipulated into a convenient way to gather personal data for other purposes. As we become incorporated into this seemingly democratic space, we also enter a collective state that could mean the loss of identity as we know it. It is a marketplace where your data is the currency.

BODY CONSTRUCTION

The title Bodies© INCorporated is a play on words. "Bodies" is accompanied by a copyright symbol and "INCorporated" draws on the Latin root "corpus," while alluding to a corporation—bodies are incorporated into the Internet and their information is copyrighted. The logo of the project is a bronze head with a copyright sign on its third eye, signifying the inherent contradiction of efforts to control information flow with the New Age idealism of interconnectedness.

Once the participants enter the project, they click through a series of legal notifications. My goal was to create a controlling space where the signing of legal documents and the inputting of personal data would become an emotional experience. These legal announcements were taken from the Disney Web site and edited to become nonsensical when read carefully. The assumption is that no one is reading these documents, despite the fact that they take away all rights—a tactic designed to alert participants about the legal issues attached to their navigation through information space.

Upon entering the main site, participants are invited to create their own bodies and become "members." They have a choice of twelve textures with attached meanings, which are a combination of alchemical properties and marketing strategies. The body parts are female, male, and infantile, left and right leg, and arms, torso, and head. The bodies themselves are wire frames that were donated by Viewpoint Datalabs. The 3D wire-frame database of bodies echoes the Visual Human Project in the way actual anatomical parts or live human bodies are scanned in and each section is sold separately for medical imaging, game design, or animation. Higher-resolution bodies or body parts are of course much more expensive.

There are also twelve sounds attached to the body that can be viewed as an image as well. Participants also complete a more elaborate questionnaire than the one used in *Virtual Concrete* by naming their body and choosing handling directions and comments. Once submitted to the system, the information is incorporated into the database and a message is automatically sent to members via their e-mail addresses.

ARCHITECTURE

Once they have created their bodies, participants may move through four different spaces: "Home," "Limbo," "Necropolis," and "Showplace." I created Limbo as a way to deal with the thousands of bodies in *Virtual Concrete*. We had to move them to the new project, but because of the standards problem, their information could not be moved in an active form. Their information was dormant in Limbo. To activate it, people would have to log on to Bodies© INCorporated and reinvent themselves using the newly established parameters. To alert the previous participants, we sent an e-mail message to each *Virtual Concrete* "body" notifying them of the "corporate takeover" of *Virtual Concrete* and inviting them to become members of Bodies© INCorporated. As an incentive, we promised "50 shares" of the new project.

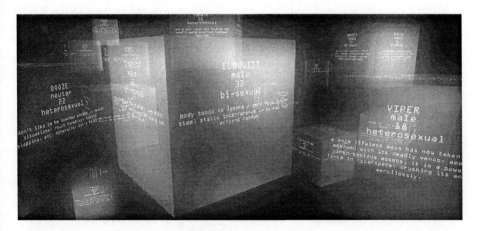

FIGURE 1.3. DATA OF PEOPLE IN LIMBO 3D SPACE IN BODIES© INCORPORATED. 1998. COURTESY OF VICTORIA VESNA.

Later, the idea of Limbo was expanded to denote a space where bodies that do not follow the strict rules and regulations are reduced to text files.

Next, I took this a step further and gave the participants that were sent to Limbo an option to move out in forty days by responding to a series of "legal" e-mail messages (a spam) that required their signatures. "Home" is represented by a large computer "motherboard" with rules and regulations drawn from Irvine, California—a tightly ordered, planned community.[15]

"Necropolis" was devised for the deletion of bodies. This space was not originally part of my plan but emerged from the many requests from people who wanted their bodies deleted. Initially I would respond with a short e-mail:

> Dear (Body name),
> Bodies© INCorporated received your request for body deletion on (date).
> Unfortunately, once you have committed yourself, it is not possible to delete your body. Thank you very much for using our services.

Although occasionally I would manually delete a body because I felt bad for people who were embarrassed by the sexuality of their imaginary body, or who expressed fear that someone they know might discover it, for the most part I remained strict about refusing deletions. There were repeated requests, however, and even an incident when one person contacted the university and threatened legal action. To resolve what had become an uncomfortable position, I decided that we should create a space that made deletion difficult, thus making a point about how posting personal information, even if it is fantasy, can affect our lives.

During this time, I was collaborating with an artist and colleague from UC Irvine, Connie Samaras, on a book/CD-ROM entitled *Terminals*. This project was part of a larger exhibition that we organized in 1995 that included museums of four UC campuses and physical exhibitions and Web sites from each site. Artists and theorists were invited to contribute work that explored the idea of the cultural construction of death, and, in particular, death in relation to technology.[16] As a result, I was surrounded by materials dealing with the meaning of death. Also, I found a now-defunct Web site called *The Crime Archives*, where graphic descriptions of murders were detailed, and I located sites describing cancer and other diseases. From these gruesome resources I compiled a list of "methods of death" that those who chose to delete their bodies had to select from in order to "die." I also mixed in some simple deaths, such as "died in sleep" (though the participant had

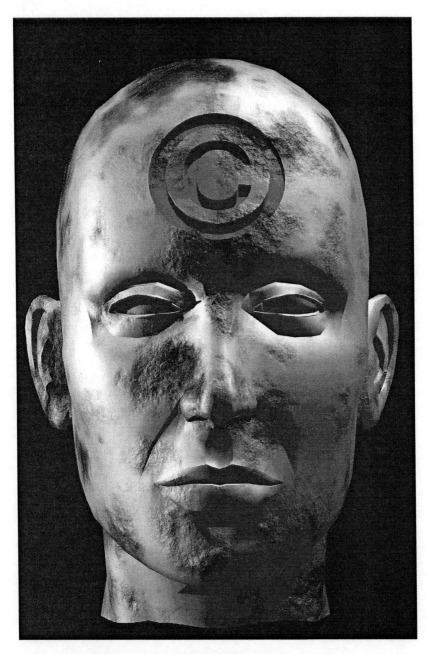

FIGURE 1.4. BODIES© INCORPORATED LOGO: COPYRIGHTED THIRD EYE OF A
BRONZE HEAD, 1998. COURTESY OF VICTORIA VESNA.

to look very hard to find that one). To complete the deletion of a body, the participants had not only to choose a method of "death," but they had to write an obituary and construct a grave.

EXHIBITION IN PHYSICAL SPACES

I soon received invitations to exhibit the project from people who noticed it via the Web (and not through the usual art-world channels). But my problem was to discover ways in which a project designed to exist on the Internet could be exhibited in a gallery space and not be compromised.

I arrived at a solution to this problem during an early installation of Bodies© INCorporated at the Santa Barbara Museum, when I invited local people who had previously created "bodies" to the opening and projected them onto the museum ceiling.[17] To my delight, they treated this as a special event, bringing their friends and families to see "their" body exhibited in a privileged cultural space. Thus the audience was moved out of the background and became part of the exhibition. I realized that this could be a new form of portraiture and decided to develop the approach further.

For the exhibition at the San Francisco Art Institute in 1997, I searched for e-mails with domains based in San Francisco to identify people in the city who had created bodies and notified them of their participation in this event. I output the selected bodies onto slides and projected them on the walls and columns of the gallery and also projected the Web site on the main wall. These bodies were privileged by their location and, as a reward, were given more shares in the project.

This strategy proved successful and I decided to take it a step further while in residence at the Art House in Dublin the following year. I asked the curator to set up appointments with people he found important in his professional life and then met with these people in the gallery and helped them build a "body." At the end of my stay, these bodies were output to slides and projected on the outside of the building during the opening. Although I was not able to attend this event, I heard later that it was successful. This approach became at once performative and participatory while localizing a medium that is inherently about distance and globality.

I devised "Showplace" to address the exhibition not only online but also in privileged physical spaces such as galleries and museums. I asked Peter Weibel, who curated the "net condition" exhibition at the ZKM, to compose a list of people he considered important to his immediate environment. I came to Karlsruhe to meet with everyone in person and helped each one build a body.

In addition to the four spaces, I added a chat as well as a newly emerging "Marketplace." The chat was never meant to have people communicate with one another, but, rather, had a simple bot that responded to all queries with random quotes from dead philosophers. Whatever a participant typed, he or she received an automatic response.

Marketplace is a space that takes the idea of exchanging data and marketing "products" such as T-shirts and caps emblazoned with a copyright logo. Here participants have the illusion of gathering more shares in the project by participating:

- Every time you log on as a member, you receive one share.
- Every time you create a body that receives the approval of the Bodies© INCorporated Board of Directors and Advisory boards, you receive a minimum of ten shares.
- Every time you submit a "dead philosopher quote" that receives the approval of the Bodies© INCorporated Board of Directors and Advisory boards, you receive a minimum of ten shares.
- Every time you submit an idea that is used in the project, you receive ten shares.
- If your body is chosen to be exhibited in Showplace, you will receive a generous compensation of shares. (Value dependent on the institutional prestige).
- When you acquire 500 shares, you are promoted from a Bodies© INCorporated member to the status of an Adept—you will gain building permissions (proposals are submitted to the Board of Director Architexts for review).
- When you have acquired 1,000 shares, you are promoted from a Bodies© INCorporated Adept to an Avatar—this allows you direct communication with the Board of Directors.

DATAMINING BODIES

In many ways, Bodies© INCorporated was a tongue-in-cheek project and, although successful as a critique of the corporate mentality, I began to wonder what the alternative could be. I became obsessed with thinking how online "bodies" could be represented in the vast networked information space without losing identity or becoming static pages on the Web. When we datamine the data of a person, how do we connect to the fact that this is a flesh-and-blood individual?

When I was commissioned to do a piece for an old mine in Dortmund,

Germany, "Zeche Zollern II/IV," I decided to take the opportunity to explore the idea of mining bodies, or "datamining" bodies. I felt that the site of the now-defunct coal mine was ideal for delivering a message of warning about the dangerous aspects of "mining" bodies for data. This project was inspired by the DNA decoding story, the Visible Human Project, and the corporate body we are all increasingly a part of.

"Datamining" is a term used in computer science, traditionally defined as "information retrieval." Many metaphors that refer to the physical act of mining, such as "drilling" or "digging," are commonly used when discussing the activity of accessing information. What is striking, if not disturbing, when researching the practice of "datamining" information (whether it be medical, statistical, or business) is the dissociation from the people who actually carry or contribute this information. With this in mind, my aim was to create a work that commented on the abstraction of information by looking at the notion of mining data in connection to the metaphorical representation of the human body, and the false notion that there had been a clear-cut shift from the Industrial to the Information Age. I wanted to get away from the human-looking "avatar" and abstract the body by using principles of "tensegrity." R. Buckminster Fuller coined the word "tensegrity" by combining tension and integrity to describe a structural system that is composed of a triangulated tension and compression network. Although almost always attributed strictly to Fuller, it should be noted that this system was developed by a student of his, sculptor Kenneth Snelson, at Black Mountain College in North Carolina in the summer of 1948.

I considered a tensile system ideal for the construction of this piece because of the connection to the biological "architecture of life" elaborated by Donald Ingber. He identifies tensegrity as a universal set of building rules that seem to guide the design of organic structures—from simple carbon compounds to complex cells and tissues. In a *Scientific American* article that was highly inspiring and influential to me, he writes: "What does tensegrity have to do with the human body? The principles of tensegrity apply at essentially every detectable size scale in the body. At the macroscopic level, the 206 bones that constitute our skeleton are pulled up against the force of gravity and stabilized in a vertical form by the pull of tensile muscles, tendons and ligaments (similar to the cables in Snelson's sculptures). In other words, in the complex tensegrity structure inside every one of us, bones are the compression struts, and muscles, tendons and ligaments are the tension-bearing members. At the other end of the scale, proteins and other key molecules in the body also stabilize themselves through the principles of tensegrity. My own interest lies in between these two extremes, at the cellular level."[18]

I came to the conclusion that if tensegrity structures work in physical architectures (as in Fuller's domes and Snelson's sculptures), it should be possible to apply the same principles to networked information spaces. However, I was having enormous difficulty finding someone who could both program and understand this type of system—until I "ran into" Gerald de Jong, a programmer working in Holland while I was doing research on the Web. De Jong had developed a system called "struck," which later morphed into "fluidiom" (fluid idiom), and was actively engaged in programming dynamic tensegrity structures. In this system, synergetic geometry or "elastic interval geometries," as De Jong calls them, are used to model arbitrary database information for visualization and decision-making purposes, as well as for the creation of effective and aesthetic presentation graphics and Web applications. The Fluidiom Project's inspiration was directly linked with Fuller's comprehensive scientific philosophy, Synergistics.

As Bodies© INCorporated continued to evolve with people independently creating their bodies and adding data to the project, I began researching visualization of networks and learning about the principles of tensegrity in relation to natural systems. I was inspired to somehow use these principles for envisioning a different type of body, an "energetic body," meaning a body that is networked and built from information but not dehumanized. This led me to consider some of the Eastern representations of the energy centers in the body, specifically the chakra system. "Chakra," which mean "wheels" in Sanskrit, are points of energy believed to run along the spine. Ancient Hindus believed that there were seven of these energy wheels, each a different color and spinning in a clockwise direction. Interestingly enough, the spacing of chakras actually matches major nerve or endocrine centers, while the colors correspond to the electromagnetic spectrum. I decided to borrow the chakra structure loosely, using the colors of the electromagnetic field and shapes constructed from tensegrity.

Each one of the abstracted shapes/structures representing the body is linked with strands suggestive of the DNA helix, playing on the desire to "descend" into the body and discover and mine for deeper levels of information. Levels are seen one at a time, starting at the top, each one programmed to be viewed for a specific amount of time before the next one is exposed. The text of Datamining Bodies consists of fragments of news about the Human Genome Project, news about the thousands of miners dying in the mines in China (attesting to the falsehood of the Western, industrial nations' proclamation of the "end of the Industrial Age"), and fragments of the essay "Mine Too," written by cultural theorist and professor of German literature at UC Santa Barbara, Laurence Rickels.[19] As one "descends" from one layer to the next, there is less and less time and more and more information. The entire sequence lasts for 333 seconds, with all navigation connected to sound.

The physical installation for Datamining Bodies consisted of a large control table, which was part of the original mine equipment, and a large projection screen hanging from the ceiling in front of the table. Only the title of the project is initially visible. As participants approach the table, motion sensors activate the sound. The only visible clue to the project is a large trackball mouse on the table. A video camera mounted above the installation is used for tracking audience movements. All the other equipment is hidden in the basement below the installation proper. The only option is to touch the trackball—which then activates the journey through the abstracted body geometries. The audience uses the trackball to explore the geometric structures and to move around the various levels. Each structure has nodes, which, when rolled over with the mouse, trigger a unique MIDI sequence, modifying the sound environment. As mentioned, after a set period of time the program automatically moves on, whether or not the person viewing it is ready. The images one "mines" are fragments of the human body culled from eighteenth-century representations, MRI and CAT scans, and historical and contemporary images of the Ruhr mine itself.

The idea of descending was magnified by the audio aspect that was created by composer David Beaudry, who used audio samples taken from the

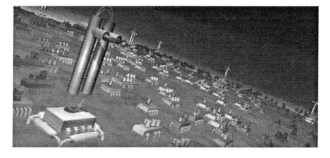

FIGURE 1.5. "DELETED" DATA OF PEOPLE IN NECROPOLIS 3D SPACE IN BODIES© INCORPORATED, 1998. COURTESY OF VICTORIA VESNA.

streets of Los Angeles, Dortmund, and fragments of text written by Rickles. As one descends, a processed elevator sound accompanies the downward movement and each transition is marked with the recorded words "keine zeit" (no more time). As the viewer traverses through the visuals, the sound becomes increasingly layered and, in the end, almost cacophonous. Along with the visual cue of the abstracted DNA helix that connects the embodied information, a "camera" tracks the growth/drill-down process of the viewer. Once at the bottom, the viewer is free to navigate around for a few minutes. After a period of inactivity, the program returns to the uppermost level and the process begins again, with time being the central driving mechanism.

TIME AND DATABASES

Datamining Bodies made me keenly aware of the importance of sound and time in relation to large amounts of data. With the ever-increasing speed of computing, we have moved away from biological/analog measurements of change to nanoseconds, and are overwhelmed with information, processed much faster than we ever were built to absorb. As our bodies are reduced to large data sets, we are entering into an entirely different age and we need to rethink the industrial model of time. Whether digital technologies can help us solve some of those mysteries is an open question. I explored these issues with a project called "n0time" (Building a Community of People with No Time). It was conceived to raise questions about perceptions of time and identity as we overextend our personal networks through communication technologies. The project is manifested in two ways—as a physical installation and as a performance involving cell phones and a networked screensaver, which allows people to share time while away from their computers. In this project, I reduced the time of creation of the "body" to a few minutes and moved away completely from a realistic, physical representation of human data to an initial structure of a tetrahedron that grows as a tensile structure in relation to time and attention.

The project n0time also points to a more collective approach to dealing with the information overflow that results in feeling overwhelmed and having a sense of no time. In fact, there truly is no time, except for our collective construction of a relationship to the ever-present change. And this makes it important to look at how we ourselves document our individual lives in relation to time and space. How do we differentiate ourselves and leave behind a trace of our existence on this planet?

PERSONAL DATABASES

Much of my work has been inspired by R. Buckminster Fuller, whose work I studied for my doctoral research. I had the good fortune to be in Santa Barbara, where his archives resided, and to meet his daughter, Allegra Fuller, who graciously granted me full access to the archive. There I accessed Fuller's Chronofiles, one of the largest databases in the world of a single individual.

The sheer volume of materials that Fuller left behind is staggering, and one cannot help wondering what compels people to collect, organize, and document proof of their existence and particular actions. Fuller began a chronological record of his life in 1907, and in 1917, at the age of twenty-two, he named it Chronofile.[20] It is interesting to see how he starts with himself and, as he progresses through life and evolves as a human being, progressively expands to collecting data of the entire "Starship Earth."

Fuller conceived of Chronofile during his participation in World War I, when he served in the navy as a secret aide to the admiral in command of cruiser transports that carried troops across the Atlantic. After the war, he was charged with amassing the secret records of all movements of the ships and the people on them. He was impressed that the navy kept records chronologically rather than by separate categories such as names, dates, or topics. Inspired by the navy's cataloguing system, Fuller decided to make himself the "special case guinea pig study" in a lifelong research project of an individual

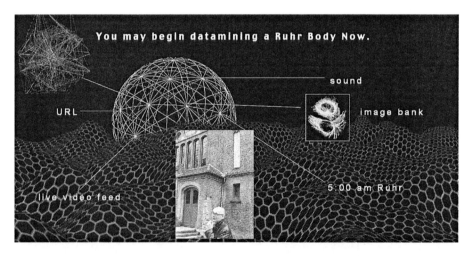

FIGURE 1.6. DATAMINING BODIES IN RUHR, GERMANY, 2001. COURTESY OF VICTORIA VESNA.

born in 1895, the year "automobiles were introduced, the wireless telegraph and automatic screw machine were invented, and X-rays discovered."[21] Along with his own documentation, Fuller was keenly interested in keeping a record of all technological and scientific inventions of the time. He thought it would be interesting not just to cull the attractive sides of his life, but to attempt to keep everything: "I decided to make myself a good case history of such a human being and it meant that I could not be judge of what was valid to put in or not. I must put everything in, so I started a very rigorous record." He dubbed himself "Guinea Pig B."[22]

In 1927, Fuller became even more ambitious. He decided to commit his entire professional output to dealing with planet Earth in its entirety, its resources and cumulative know-how, rather than harnessing his output for personal advantage. He undertook, in his own words, "to comprehensively protect, support, and advantage all humanity instead of committing my efforts to exclusive advantages of my dependants, myself, my country, my team."[23]

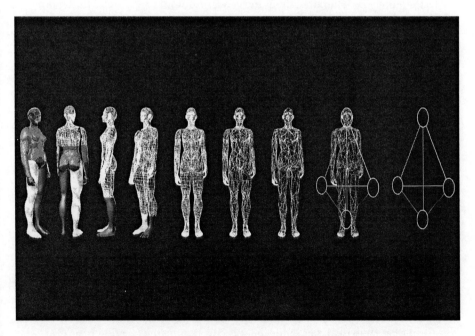

FIGURE 1.7. GRAPHICAL BODIES REDUCED TO WIRE FRAMES AND THEN A TETRAHEDRON IN "N0TIME: BUILDING A COMMUNITY OF PEOPLE WITH NO TIME," 2001. COURTESY OF VICTORIA VESNA.

Fuller knew that few, and perhaps no one, would understand his professional commitment to be a practical one, but because he firmly believed
that it was, he worked to leave proof behind affirming this belief, and he
proceeded to do so in a scientific fashion. At the end of his life, in addition
to the Chronofile, which is considered to be the heart of his archives, he left
behind the Dymaxion Index, blueprints, photos, patents, manuscripts, and a
large amount of random elements. He saved all his correspondences, sketches,
doodles made during his meetings, backs of envelopes, and newspaper-edged
notes—everything possible that was a record of his thought. He saved all
films, videos, wire and tape recordings, and posters announcing his lectures,
awards, mementoes, relevant books, everything he published at various
stages, all indexes, drafting tools, typewriters, computers, furniture, file cabinets, paintings, photos, diplomas, and cartoons. He also kept an inventory
of World Resources, Human Trends and Needs, and all the World Game
records. The World Game was one of the first computer-game concepts,
whose goal was to encourage global thinking.

The output during Fuller's lifetime documented in the Chronofile is
astounding: three hundred thousand geodesic domes built around the world,
five million Dymaxion world maps, not to mention twenty-six published
books and twenty-eight patents. It is important to note that he did not believe in hiring professional public relations agents or agencies, publishing
bureaus, sales people, or promotional workers of any kind. Yet, toward the
end of his life, he did have a type of nonprofit cottage-industry operation
with many people working on the Chronofile. Ironically, this operation is
not well documented or recorded, but there are enough people who have
survived it to tell the story.[24]

Collecting and archiving for Fuller did not stop with himself, but extended
to data collection of world resources as well, which became a more ambitious project with the introduction of computer technologies: "We are going
to set up a great computer program. We are going to introduce the many
variables now known to be operative in the world around industrial economics. We will store all the basic data in the machine's memory bank;
where and how much of each class of the physical resources; where are the
people, where are the trendings and important needs of world man?"[25]

Fuller is a great example of someone who becomes more and more ambitious to document not only himself but also the world around him in the
form of a database. Later in life, he was envisioning the creation of a "Geo-
scope," which would collect all the data of "Spaceship Earth" with an elaborate computerized system. Although he did not succeed during his lifetime,

he would be pleased to see that there is a massive collective effort to document every aspect of our lives today, from our molecular and cellular structure to all of our acquired knowledge throughout history.

Documentation of an artist's life is an investment in the future of the personae that will continue to survive in the form of information. Collecting, storing, and archiving is very much connected to time, to our anxiety over the loss of time, and to the speed at which time travels. We preserve the all-important self in this age of relentless movement by creating a memory bank that testifies to our existence, our unique contribution, and the promise to be brought back to life perhaps by someone in the future who can unpack the data and place it in a space of cultural importance. How much we leave behind, how much shelf space we occupy, is how our importance is measured. Meg Cranston makes this point in a compelling way in her piece "Who's Who by Size." Edgar Allan Poe, at 633 volumes, occupies sixty-three and a half feet of shelf space, while Muhammad Ali, at a mere 15 volumes, accounts for only one and a half feet.[26] Such statistics are fast being supplanted by the number of bytes one accumulates as well as the number of "hits" on the search engine that link out to others referencing or even creating data about the person.

Fuller's Chronofile, although not without problems, is an example of a system consciously conceived without fixed categories that poses an explicit commentary on traditional modes of categorization through juxtaposition. Similarly, John Cage, who was a friend and admirer of Fuller's, in his last exhibition piece, entitled *The Museum Circle*, makes a point about categorization in cultural production and exhibition. In 1993, shortly before Cage's death, the Museum of Contemporary Art in Los Angeles realized another version of *The Museum Circle* (the first being in Munich in 1991), in which more than twenty museums participated with a large number of exhibits. *The Museum Circle* changed its order daily according to the principle of the *I Ching*. This constant change enabled new kinds of connections to emerge and cast doubt on any "truth" the works may have revealed through their former categorization.[27]

IDENTITY DATABASES

While scientists are busy discovering the structure and system of DNA and dissecting the physical body into evermore minute detail, administrators, with the blessing of politicians, create social systems of identification that are becoming evermore complex. In the United States, Social Security numbers comprise perhaps the largest social database, and most countries around

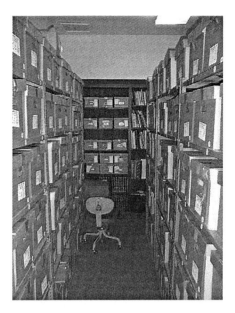

FIGURE 1.8. CHRONOFILES AT THE
R. BUCKMINSTER FULLER
ARCHIVES, SANTA BARBARA, 1997.
PHOTOGRAPH BY VICTORIA VESNA.

the world have their own systems of tracking their citizens. Although the
Social Security system was established in the 1930s by Franklin Roosevelt to
help the public withstand the devastation of the Great Depression, it has
morphed into a conglomeration that is increasingly connected to any trans-
action that has to do with money.

That this social numbering system is interconnected with various govern-
mental organizations goes without saying, but it is really difficult to identify
those connections and how they may affect our lives. Rapid technological
advances, in conjunction with the end of the Cold War and the demand for
greater bureaucratic efficiency, are promoting a seamless web of identity
tracking from cradle to grave. Now, information on almost every person in
the developed world is computerized in several hundred databases, collected, analyzed, and disseminated by governments and corporations. And
increasingly these computers are linked together and can share their cyber-
gossip. Using high-speed networks with advanced intelligence and single
identification numbers such as a Social Security number, computers can
create instant, comprehensive dossiers on millions of people without the
need for a centralized computer system. New developments in genetic and
medical research and care, advanced transportation systems, and financial
transfers have dramatically increased the quantity of detail available. A body

of national and international laws and agreements facilitates the transfer of information across state and national borders and frequently prevents local and national communities from regulating against invasions of privacy. Corporations are also quick to adapt these technologies for commercial use to target consumers, to manipulate markets, and to select, monitor, and control employees.

Perhaps the greatest technological leap in this direction is the recent development of the RFID, Radio Frequency Identification, a technology that allows an object or person to be identified at a distance using radio waves to energize and communicate with some form of tag or card. This technology is beginning to replace printed bar codes on products. RFID tags are passive and unpowered and are being used on items in warehouses and shops and on ID cards; they are also being used to track animals, and possibly humans as well. This tag goes a step beyond the chip in the body that Eduardo Kac discusses so well in his "Time Capsule" piece in this volume. Kac told me that he has problems while traveling because security checks detect the chip, which is implanted in his ankle. This may be less of a problem with the RFID, which is "noninvasive." Recently, Disney announced the availability of bracelets with RFID tags for tracking children at its theme parks, a practice many parents support for obvious reasons. Such tracking may be useful in other arenas that are perhaps not so innocent and could be embedded in objects without our knowledge or awareness.

LIBRARIES AS DATABASES OF KNOWLEDGE

> The universe (which others call Library) is composed of an indefinite, perhaps infinite, number of hexagonal galleries, with enormous ventilation shafts in the middle, encircled by low railings. From any hexagon the upper and lower stories are visible, interminably. The distribution of galleries is invariable.
>   —JORGE LUIS BORGES, *The Library of Babel*

Marcel Duchamp's dictum of concept over object in art and his eventual decision to give up painting entirely in order to become a freelance librarian at the Bibliothèque Saint Geneviève in Paris not only challenged the museum system and the idea of what can be counted as art, but it also drew attention to the intersections of information and aesthetics. The relationship between aesthetics and information continues to develop as the World Wide Web radically redefines libraries and museums, and many clues and opportunities await us in terms of becoming familiar with the directions libraries are taking with the vast digitization projects now taking place.

If we consider the invention of the printing press as the first wave of information overload, we can safely consider ourselves immersed in a second, tsunami wave. The effects of technology on human consciousness to which Marshall McLuhan pointed earlier in the twentieth century have amplified tenfold in the face of the new technologies.[28] This number may be even higher as the power of computing increases and we must begin to think about the relationship between consciousness and our organization and dissemination of data. We must also reconsider how the organization of data reflects our collective shifts in perception and our relation to information and knowledge. Knowledge production is undergoing a radical reorganization because of the huge amount of data that is systematically being digitized and made available on the Internet. This digital reorganization means that we can anticipate the relatively fast-paced demand for, and creation of, new systems and establishments. Artists are in a unique position to participate in this process as "information architects" using data as raw material.

How one moves through a physical space such as a building or a particular room is very much determined by the way an architect has conceived it. In the context of art, consider movement through Frank Gehry's Guggenheim Bilbao in Spain. The building can be understood as a sculpture, a meta-art piece in its own right. The work presented within these spaces, in other words, cannot be viewed without a strong sense of their containers. Similarly, when navigating through various software "containers" and inputting our data, we are in effect following the established parameters of information architecture. With some of the more blatant moves to create "standards," which include not only the information architecture but also our online identity and the use of agents, the idea of an overarching meta-software that is intended to be used by one and all is alarming. The visions of the *World Brain* of H. G. Wells, the *Memex* of Vannevar Bush, and the *Xanadu* of Ted Nelson are not primarily concerned with the content but rather with the shift of our attention to the way we organize and retrieve the information stored. Their work has contributed to what we know now as the World Wide Web, which acts as a window to the vast collective effort of digitization, whether organized or not.

Borges's *Library of Babel* is often summoned when describing the endlessly evolving World Wide Web and our state of information overload. The underlying history of "information overload" arrives with the introduction of the printing press and the subsequent need—the first efforts were made during the Renaissance—to organize knowledge and collections. The organization of the sudden proliferation and distribution of books into library systems happened in tandem with the categorization systems of collections that museums were establishing. Excellent examples in this respect are the curiosity inscriptions of Samuel Quiccheberg, considered the first museological treatise, and Giulio Camillo's *Memory Theater* of the 1530s. Quiccheberg's treatise offered a plan for organizing all possible natural objects and artifacts, which he accomplished by creating five classes and dividing each into ten or eleven inscriptions. This treatise allows for explorations today of the institutional origins of the museum.[29] Camillo, by contrast, created a theater that could house all knowledge, a theater that could bestow on the privileged who accessed this space actual power over all of creation. The structure took the form of an amphitheater and was composed of a viewer onstage facing seven tiers of seven rows—not of seats but drawers and cabinets containing text and objects.[30]

Current cataloguing systems generally fall into two types: those treating the item as a physical object and giving it a number or code encapsulating data about its acquisition and storage, and those that communicate the intellectual content of a work and locate it within a system of such classifications. This former type of cataloguing, which began with Denis Diderot and Jean d'Alembert's *Encyclopédie* (1751–72), codifies and systematically delineates the relationships of all branches of knowledge. The latter goes back at least as far as the Library of Alexandria (circa 100 B.C.), which was organized by the writer's discipline (for example, history or philosophy) and subdivided by literary genres.

Libraries and museums have continuously intersected and influenced each other throughout their respective histories. Museums are essentially object-oriented keepers of visual memory, much in the way that libraries are keepers of textual memory. The architectures of museums, on the one hand, determine the size and even type of collections they will accommodate, which necessarily limits their inclusiveness; rarely, for example, do museums accommodate art that involves ephemeral media. Libraries, on the other hand, accommodate the documentation of all printed matter produced by museums as well as have a close relationship to the inclusive research paradigm of academia.[31]

Digital technology is fast eroding established categories by making it possible to store all the objects traditionally separated by media or form as bits, a continuous stream of data. As such, this technology endangers the institutions that have been established to store specific types of data and indeed the way knowledge is disseminated at universities. It is becoming more and more difficult for academics to work effectively within the established departmental and specialized categories and structures of print libraries. The World Wide Web challenges the primacy of word over image by collapsing them, and, further, it functions to erode the boundaries between museums and libraries, which is true of its impact on many other institutional frames as well.

Possibly the best example of acquiring and updating encyclopedic knowledge is the Wikipedia on the Web—a free-content encyclopedia that is written collaboratively by volunteers and consists of 195 independent language editions sponsored by the nonprofit Wikimedia Foundation. Entries on traditional encyclopedic topics exist alongside those on almanac, gazetteer, and current-events topics. Wikipedia, which has become one of the most popular reference sites on the Web, is a distributed, networked system of humans interested in sharing and adding to the collective body of knowledge. It follows similar principles as the Open Source community,[32] which was foreshadowed by such visionaries in the 1940s as Vannevar Bush and H. G. Wells.

Artists have traditionally responded to archives and databases and point to issues to consider when moving toward becoming an active participant in the global information architecture. When considering the larger cultural framework, there is no longer any doubt that film was the dominant narrative of the twentieth century. As we begin the new millennium, however, we are confronted not only with a vast amount of data but also with a necessarily nonlinear system of accessing information. This has been particularly propagated by the Internet and specifically by the graphic interface to this world network of information, the World Wide Web.

With rapid technological advances in access and retrieval of information through large computer databases, libraries are changing, and thus the way we form knowledge and narrative is also changing. Even movies are available in many formats, expanding the linear narrative with DVDs and Web information on the making of, or uncut versions of, the film and segments streamed on the Web.

Moving beyond the social and knowledge spheres into the planetary aspects, space agencies such as NASA are sending satellites into space to view the earth from above. One may want to be reminded that the human race for the first time ever had this bird's-eye view of the planet only in 1969, when *Apollo* sent the famous picture back to Earth. Not only are humans engaged in gathering data about the earth and the surrounding atmospheric changes, but also, by sending unmanned satellites, robots, planes, and rockets into space, they have the ability to explore Mars, Jupiter, and beyond. I will not even try to speculate what some of the secret military missions around the world are doing in our orbit and in outer space, but surely this is the territory for warfare development that certainly trickles down to us in the various gadgets we inherit from this predatory instinct.

One by-product of weather, communication, and scientific satellites that are regularly being sent into space is the junk that is created by humans eager to explore and control the airwaves. Almost thirty thousand items of space junk—objects large enough to track with radar that were inadvertently placed in orbit or have outlived their usefulness—are floating above our planet. Payloads that go into the wrong orbit, satellites with run-down batteries, and leftover rocket boosters, all contribute to the count. This could be understood on some level as a form of pollution equivalent to any other on earth that is the product of human minds imagining themselves somehow separate—or even worse—superior in the world we inhabit. Ever since the launch of the *Apollo*, which coincided with many changes we as a planetary collective started experiencing, there has been an active movement to find out if we are indeed alone and at the center of this universe. Perhaps the most interesting project, at least conceptually, that has attempted to find an answer to this question is SETI, the Search for Extraterrestrial Intelligence, pioneered by Philip Morrison. In 1959, Morrison, who was then at Cornell University, and Giuseppe Cocconi wrote a paper proposing the potential of microwaves in interstellar communications that was published in the journal *Nature* on September 19 of that year. With "Searching for Interstellar Communications," the two physicists became the first scientists to challenge the professional community to carry out a coordinated search for extraterrestrial signals from an intelligent civilization. The Morrison-Cocconi paper laid the foundation for most of the SETI projects conducted in the past thirty-five years, and the suggestion that electromagnetic signals were the most promising means for interstellar communications became the underlying assumption of all searches, including the optical SETI searches. The assumption that any alien signal would exhibit a Doppler drift has also been incorporated into SETI projects, which check for signals at drifting frequencies. Perhaps most important was their theory that a "universal frequency" probably exists—a frequency that extraterrestrials would most likely use for their transmissions (which they suggest is 1420 megahertz). Notably, that frequency has remained to this day the most popular frequency used by SETI projects.

BEYOND THE POWERS OF TEN

> To see a world in a grain of sand
> And heaven in a wildflower
> Hold infinity in the palm of your hand
> And eternity in an hour
> —WILLIAM BLAKE, 1803

As we quickly move through molecular, biological, bodily, and social systems to the planetary and beyond, it becomes clear that at every level huge amounts of data are being discovered and generated. As artists observing this, it becomes clear that the management, storage, organization, and delivery of information overflow is the one activity in which we are all engaged. But perhaps the most interesting aspect is the obvious one—that all data

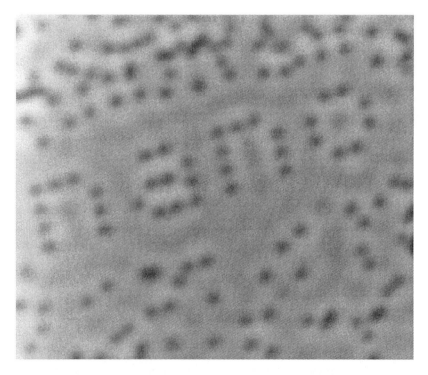

FIGURE 1.9. CARBON MONOXIDE MOLECULES MANIPULATED INTO THE WORD "NANO." IMAGINED BY VICTORIA VESNA AND CREATED AT DON EIGLER'S LAB AT IBM, ALMADEN, BY KELLY MCGRODDY, 2003.

in these various and, in many cases, disparate worlds are generated by the same computing machines. Even those who do not use computers, or who consciously refuse to, are part of this rapidly evolving data system, as we saw in the quick sweep of how easily our identities can be registered and tracked.

Nano scientists like James Gimzewski manipulate single molecules in ways that were not imaginable even a decade ago, and researchers in labs generate huge amounts of data on a daily basis that they have to manage and analyze. Indeed, creating systems for tracking and visualizing data is what much of the scientific results are dependent on, and the more advanced and innovative the research is, the more creative scientists have to be in the way they work with the large amounts of data produced daily in their laboratories.

Through our collaboration, the scientists realized that the creative output of data is many times key to discovery and that visualization in laboratories is usually formalized in ways that actually thwart progress in research. In fact, by expanding the idea of how data may be observed, together with Andrew Pelling, his Ph.D. student, Gimzewski sonified data produced by vibrations of cells. This experiment turned out to be a major step toward looking at the behavior of cells.[33]

In light of this realization about the huge amounts of data produced at every level of our existence, I will approach the broader idea of databases from the "bottom up," which is in great contrast to "top down"—the philosophy that we are more used to working with, whether on the technological, social, or political level.[34]

In this respect, it seems appropriate to end with one of the projects that I created with Gimzewski, a projection piece based on a Tibetan sand mandala—the Chakrasamvara—constructed by Tibetan monks from the Ghaden Lhopa Khangsten monastery in India. We observed the monks create the sand mandala from a few grains in the center to a structure eight feet in diameter. The mandala was not only amazing in its beauty but also was incredibly complex in its narrative. When the sand mandala was completed, we photographed it at about ten intervals with a wide-angle lens and switched the camera to the macro lens at the last level. Then one of the monks recreated the center of the mandala in Gimzewski's Pico lab, first imaged by an optical microscope and then with a Scanning Electron Microscope (SEM). Approximately one hundred of the best high-resolution photographs were chosen for the next stage of compositing. To optimize the resolution, these photos were embedded within one another.

The goal was to create one singular large image of the entire mandala all

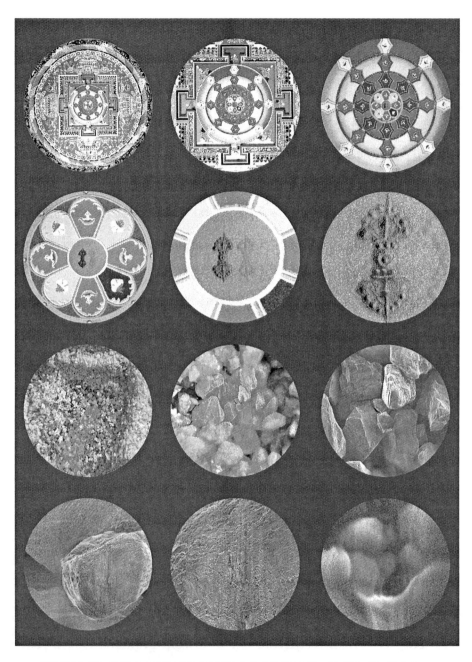

FIGURE 1.10. THREE HUNDRED THOUSAND PHOTOGRAPHS REDUCED TO TWELVE
STAGES OF THE NANOMANDALA, 2004. COURTESY OF VICTORIA VESNA.

the way down to nanoscale. After only ten photos, the image became too big for Photoshop or any other photo-manipulation software to accommodate. Next the image was divided into nine stages and at each stage the image was zoomed out by a factor of eighty-five. This number was based on the limit of Photoshop and After Effects combined. Each image file contained about ten images in stages that were photo-stitched and were to 2.7 to 3GB in size. Then each of the nine stages was transformed into a high-resolution video animation. These videos were then digitally zoomed to create a sense of continuous movement. The output was three hundred thousand individual frames, which amounted to 900GB of data. These frames were then recomposed into the fifteen-minute video of the final piece projected in the installation. To produce these images we had to use thirty-six computers that simultaneously rendered the images for two full days. Final recomposition took nine computers and several attempts to complete because the project continually crashed the system.

All of this discussion is to illustrate that at every stage, from the grain of sand to the entire complex mandala, the images contained the same amount of information in order to create a visual effect of ascending up and zooming all the way in, beyond the powers of ten. This piece is a meditation on the importance of every particle and wave, of the interconnectivity of all of us, and everything surrounding us, and on our amazing ability to take huge data sets of information and reduce them to the essential truth in the blink of an eye. The Tibetan monks who constructed the mandala told us that no one can own it, that the ownership of it is only an illusion of the mind, and so it is with all data that we collect, store, manipulate, and use in our lifetimes.

After a certain amount of time, the sand mandala is swept away by the monks and thrown into the ocean. In the case of the nanomandala, the computer and projector are shut off and only the memory in our minds remains.

NOTES

1. The effort to decipher the three billion letters of DNA that are the human genome unexpectedly became a race when the Federal Human Genome Project acquired a rival, a joint venture of the instrument maker Perkin-Elmer in Norwalk, Connecticut, and Dr. J. Craig Venter of the Institute for Genomic Research in Rockville, Maryland.

2. Marlene Cimons and P. Jacobs, "Biotech Battlefield: Profits vs. Public," *Los Angeles Times*, February 21, 1999.

3. For more information on *Eighth Day*, see http://www.ekac.org/. For more information on Joe Davis's *Audio Microscope* and *Microvenus*, see http://www.viewingspace.com/

genetics_culture/pages_genetics_culture/gc_w03/davis_audio_scope.htm. Critical Art Ensemble, *GenTerra*. Available at http://www.critical-art.net/genterra. For more information on *One Tree* and the synthetic skin culture work of Natalie Jeremijenko, see http://www.kqed.org/spark/artists-orgs/nataliejer.jsp.

4. Barbara Maria Stafford, *Body Criticism: Imaging the Unseen in Enlightenment Art and Medicine* (Cambridge, Mass.: MIT Press, 1991).

5. See http://www.nlm.nih.gov/research/visible/visible_human.html. A contract for acquisition of these pixel-based data was awarded in August 1991 to the University of Colorado at Denver. Victor M. Spitzer, Ph.D., and David G. Whitlock, M.D., Ph.D., are the principal investigators.

6. Cathy Waldby, *The Visible Human Project: Informatic Bodies and Posthuman Medicine* (London: Routledge, 2000), 12.

7. The exhibition Veered Science was curated by Marilu Knode for the Huntington Beach Art Center in California. Artists in the exhibition included Colette Gaiter, Michael Joaquin Grey, Tim Hawkinson, Laurel Katz, David Kremers, Joseph Nechvatal, David Nyzio, Alan Rath, Pauline Sanchez, Joseph Santorama, Rodney Sappington, Rachel Slowinski, Jesse Cantley, Christine Tamblyn, and Gail Wight.

8. I first intended to act as lurker/voyeur and randomly capture snippets of conversations in the chat rooms as they occurred, but then decided that names of the rooms themselves were far more seductive than the rather mundane and predictable conversations occurring within them. I was also shocked to find some nine thousand rooms at one site dedicated to sex chats.

9. Les Fox, who recently finished his studies at UCSB, had experience building with concrete and helped develop a method for bonding the prints to the concrete. The material was sponsored by the David Bermant Foundation. Harry Bowers, a photographer, professor, and director of Cactus Research and Development in New York, sponsored the large electrostatic prints.

10. For instance, Sherry and Bliss; Rods Annex; The Kinky Friends of Latex-Loving Laura; Wife-Watcher's Special; Trial-Fuck (for Beginners); Rick's American Bar; As time goes by . . . sweet, sweet bedroom of sex; The Dark Side Desert Lounge; Aimee's—Ladies Only—But guys welcome to lurk!!!; Puddles Playpen; I'm wet and need mommy . . . , etc.

11. Kenneth Fields, also known as Gustav Java and kf.oe, composed the audio that was triggered by the sensors. Jan Plass programmed the aiff file in *Director*.

12. CU-SeeME, developed at Cornell University, allows live video to be received in a small-screen format at twenty-four frames per second on a regular Mac and PC with a standard modem and telephone line.

13. The Common Gateway Interface, or CGI, is a standard for external gateway programs to interface with information servers such as HTTP servers. A plain HTML document that the Web daemon retrieves is static, which means that it exists in a constant state: a text file that does not change. A CGI program, by contrast, is executed in real time, so that it can output dynamic information. See http://hoohoo.ncsa.uiuc.edu/cgi/overview.html.

14. The project I envisioned was complex and I needed help to develop and produce it. Robert Nideffer worked with me on the interface design for the spaces I imagined, and Nathan Freitas, a musician and programmer, created all the CGI scripts and VRML spaces. Ken Fields, a Ph.D. music student at the time, composed all the sounds.

15. In 1993, I completed a three-year project called *Another Day in Paradise,* which dealt with the city of Irvine, California, one of the most elaborately planned communities in the United States. I drew from this research when designing "Home." See Victoria Vesna, "Another Day in Paradise and Virtual Concrete: Preserved Palms, Concrete, and Telepresence," *Leonardo* 31, no. 1 (1998): 13–19.

16. See http://vv.arts.ucla.edu/terminals.

17. Bodies© INCorporated was part of a large exhibition surveying historical artists' representations of bodies, entitled *Figuratively Speaking,* at the Santa Barbara Museum of Art, Santa Barbara, California, November 1996.

18. Donald Ingber, "Architecture of Life," *Scientific American,* January 1998, 48.

19. Laurence Rickles, "Mine Too," 2001. See http://www.notime.arts.ucla.edu/mining.

20. The R. Buckminster Fuller Archives, located in Stanford, California, consists of the following: The Dymaxian Index, which is a detailed cross-reference and index of twenty different sections of the Fuller archives, including his personal library, office inventory, and itinerary. The index was updated approximately every ten years during his lifetime and now comprises twenty volumes. The Chronofile begins in 1895 and is chronologically ordered; 13,500 5 × 8 cards cross-reference the Chronofile alphabetically between 1970 and 1980. The index contains more complete documentation on hundreds of Fuller's design artifacts, inventions, cartographic works, and architectural projects, including more than a thousand sketches; approximately thirty-five file drawers packed with published and unpublished manuscripts; transcripts from lectures and full working files of all of his major books; Fuller's photo and slide documentation on geodesic structures built around the globe by others; and gifts from other artists, including Isamu Noguchi, Joseph Albers, Mark Tobey, and John Cage. Media archives are kept in a separate, environmentally controlled, film vault in Hollywood. It contains approximately sixty-four thousand feet of film, fifteen hundred hours of audio, and three hundred hours of video.

21. R. Buckminster Fuller, *"Critical Path, Kiyoshi Kuromiya, Adjuvant"* (New York: St. Martin's Press, 1981), 128.

22. Fuller, *Synergistics Dictionary.* Citation from Oregon Lecture 9, July 12, 1962, 324; Fuller, *Guinea Pig B: The 56 Year Experiment* (Stanford: Critical Path Publishing, 2004).

23. Fuller, *Guinea Pig B,* 25.

24. During my research in residence at the Buckminster Fuller Institute, I met many artists, architects, and historians who were familiar with the Chronofile and tell stories of their experience with Fuller.

25. R. Buckminster Fuller, "Vision '65," Keynote Lecture, Carbondale: Southern Illinois University, October 1965.

26. Meg Cranston, "Who's Who by Size," in *In Deep Storage: Collecting, Storing, and Archiving Art,* ed. Ingrid Schaffner and Mathias Winzen (Munich: Prestel-Verlag, 1998), 106.

27. Eugene Blume, "On the Verge of Departure from Lager 1," in *In Deep Storage: Collecting, Storing, and Archiving Art,* ed. Ingrid Schaffner and Matthias Winzen (Munich: Prestel-Verlag, 1998), 263.

28. Marshall McLuhan, *The Guttenberg Galaxy* (Toronto: University of Toronto Press, 1962), 144.

29. Quiccheberg's treatise offered a plan for organizing all possible natural objects and artifacts, which he accomplished by creating five classes and dividing each into ten

or eleven inscriptions. This treatise allows for explorations today of the institutional origins of the museum.

30. See Bruce Robertson and Mark Meadows, "Microcosms: Objects of Knowledge," in *AI-Society, The Journal of Human Centered and Machine Intelligence: Database Aesthetics: Issues of Organization and Category in Online Art,* ed. Victoria Vesna (Berlin: Springer, February–March 1999).

31. University museums, a strange amalgam of qualities that do not approximate either the traditional library or museum, occupy a peculiarly marginalized position, and their role is yet to be defined. Outside both the art marketplace and scholarly research and discourse, university museums are a curious entity, a floating category.

32. Open Source is a movement in the programming community for making source code (program instructions) free and freely available to anyone interested in using or working with it. Software that is open-source is software for which the code is freely available. This means that another developer is free to modify the code according to individual needs, or to reverse-engineer a product created by the software. Language documentation created using open-source software is likely to last longer than that created using proprietary software because many programmers will be able to understand and, if necessary, reconstruct the software that makes it intelligible. Proprietary software, by contrast, is impenetrable after the developer ceases to support it. See http://www.opensource.org.

33. A. E. Pelling, S. Sehati, E. B. Gralla, J. S. Valentine, and J. K. Gimzewski, "Local Nanomechanical Motion of the Cell Wall of *Saccharomyces cerevisiae*," in *Science* (304): 1147.

34. Richard P. Feynman, "There's Plenty of Room at the Bottom," in *Science Engineering* 231 (1960): 22.

2. Database as Symbolic Form

LEV MANOVICH

The Database Logic

After the novel and subsequently, cinema privileged narrative as the key form of cultural expression of the modern age. The computer age introduces its correlate—database. Many new media objects do not tell stories; they don't have a beginning or end; in fact, they don't have any development, thematically, formally, or otherwise, that would organize their elements into a sequence. Instead, they are collections of individual items, where every item has the same significance as any other.

Why does new media favor database form over others? Can we explain its popularity by analyzing the specificity of the digital medium and of computer programming? What is the relationship between database and another form that has traditionally dominated human culture—narrative? These are the questions I will address.

Before proceeding, I need to comment on my use of the word "database." In computer science, database is defined as a structured collection of data. The data stored in a database are organized for fast search and retrieval by a computer and therefore a database is anything but a simple collection of items. Different types of databases—hierarchical, network, relational, and object-oriented—use different models to organize data. For instance, the records in hierarchical databases are organized in a treelike structure. Object-oriented databases store complex data structures, called "object," which are organized into hierarchical classes that may inherit properties from classes higher in the chain.[1] New media objects may or may not employ these highly structured database models; however, from the point of view of users' experience, a large proportion of them are databases in a more basic sense. They appear as a collection of items on which the user can perform various operations: view, navigate, and search. The user experience of such computerized collections is therefore quite distinct from reading a narrative or watching a film or navigating an architectural site. Similarly, in literary or cinematic narrative, an architectural plan and database each presents a different model of what a world is like. It is this sense of database as a cultural form of its own that I shall address here. Following art historian Erwin Panofsky's analysis of linear perspective as a "symbolic form" of the modern age, we may even call database a new symbolic form of a computer age (or, as philosopher Jean-François Lyotard called it in his famous 1979 book *Postmodern Condition,* "computerized society,"[2] a new way to structure our experience of ourselves and of the world. Indeed, if, after the death of God (Friedrich Nietzsche), the end of grand Narratives of Enlightenment (Lyotard), and the arrival of the World Wide Web (Tim Berners-Lee), the world appears to us as an endless and unstructured collection of images, texts, and other data records, it is only appropriate that we will be moved to model it as a database—but it is also appropriate that we would want to develop the poetics, aesthetics, and ethics of this database.

I will begin by documenting the dominance of database form in new media. The most obvious examples are popular multimedia encyclopedias (which are collections by their very definition), as well as other commercial CD-ROM or DVD titles, which are collections as well—of recipes, quotations, photographs, and so on.[3] The identity of a CD-ROM as a storage media is projected onto another plane, becoming a cultural form of its own. Multimedia works that have "cultural" content appear particularly to favor the database form. Consider, for instance, the "virtual museums" genre— CD-ROMs that take the user on a "tour" through a museum collection. A museum becomes a database of images representing its holdings, which can be accessed in different ways: chronologically, by country, or by artist. Although such CD-ROMs often simulate the traditional museum experience of moving from room to room in a continuous trajectory, this "narrative" method of access does not have any special status in comparison to other access methods offered by a CD-ROM. Thus the narrative becomes just one method among others of accessing data. Another example of a database form is a multimedia genre that does not have an equivalent in traditional media: CD-ROMs devoted to a single cultural figure such as a famous architect, film director, or writer. Instead of a narrative biography, we are presented with a database of images, sound recordings, video clips, and texts that can be navigated in a variety of ways.

CD-ROMs and other digital storage media (floppies, DVDs) proved to be particularly receptive to traditional genres that already had a database-like structure such as a photo album; they also inspired new database genres, like a database biography. Where the database form really flourished, however, is on the Internet. As defined by original HTML, a Web page is a sequential list of separate elements: text blocks, images, digital video clips, and links to other pages. It is always possible to add a new element to the list—all you have to do is to open a file and add a new line. As a result, most Web pages are collections of separate elements, such as texts, images, and links to other pages or sites. A home page is a collection of personal photographs. A site of a major search engine is a collection of links to other sites (along with a search function, of course). A site of a Web-based television or radio station offers a collection of video or audio programs along with the option to listen to the current broadcast—but this current program is just one choice among many other programs stored on the site. Thus the traditional broadcasting experience, which consisted solely of a real-time transmission, becomes just one element in a collection of options. Similar to the CD-ROM medium, the Web offered fertile ground to already-existing database genres (for instance, bibliography) and also inspired the creation of new ones such as the sites devoted to a person or a phenomenon (Madonna, the Civil War, new media theory), which, even if they contain original material, inevitably center around the list of links to other Web pages on the same person or phenomenon.

The open nature of the Web as medium (Web pages are computer files that can always be edited) means that the Web sites never have to be complete—and they rarely are because the sites are always growing. New links are being added to what is already there. It is as easy to add new elements to the end of a list as it is to insert them anywhere in it. All this further contributes to the antinarrative logic of the Web. If new elements are being added over time, the result is a collection, not a story. Indeed, how can one keep a coherent narrative or any other development trajectory through the material if it keeps changing?

DATA AND ALGORITHM

Not all new media objects are explicitly databases. Computer games, for instance, are experienced by their players as narratives. In a game, the player is given a well-defined task—winning the match, being first in a race, reaching the last level, or reaching the highest score. It is this task that makes the player experience the game as a narrative. Everything that happens in a game, all the characters and objects that one encounters, either take that person closer to achieving the goal or further away from it. Thus, in contrast to the CD-ROM and Web databases, which always appear arbitrary because the

user knows that additional material could have been added without modifying in any way the logic of the database, in a game, from a user's point of
view, all the elements are motivated (that is, their presence is justified).[4]

Often the narrative shell of a game ("you are the specially trained com-
mando who has just landed on a lunar base; your task is to make your way
to the headquarters occupied by the mutant base personnel . . .") masks a
simple algorithm familiar to the player: kill all the enemies on the current
level while collecting all treasures it contains; go to the next level, and so on,
until you reach the last level. Other games have different algorithms. Here
is an algorithm of the legendary game "Tetris." When a new block appears,
rotate it in such a way that it will complete the top layer of blocks on the
bottom of the screen, making this layer disappear. The similarity between
the actions expected from the player and computer algorithms is too uncanny
to be dismissed. While computer games do not follow database logic, they
appear to be ruled by another logic—that of an algorithm. They demand
that a player executes an algorithm in order to win.

An algorithm is the key to the game experience in a different sense as
well. As the player proceeds through the game, he or she gradually discovers
the rules that operate in the universe constructed by this game. The player
learns its hidden logic—in short, its algorithm. Therefore, when a game
play departs from following an algorithm, the player is still engaged with an
algorithm, although in another way; the player is discovering the algorithm
of the game itself. I mean this both metaphorically and literally. For instance,
in a first-person shooter, such as "Quake," the player may eventually notice
that under such-and-such condition the enemies will appear from the left—
that is, the player will literally reconstruct a part of the algorithm responsible for the game play. Or, in a different formulation of the legendary author
of Sims games, Will Wright, "Playing the game is a continuous loop between
the user (viewing the outcomes and inputting decisions) and the computer
(calculating outcomes and displaying them back to the user). The user is
trying to build a mental model of the computer model."[5]

What we encounter here is an example of the general principle of new
media: the projection of the ontology of a computer onto culture itself. If
in physics the world is made of atoms, and in genetics it is made of genes,
computer programming encapsulates the world according to its own logic.
The world is reduced to two kinds of software objects that are complementary to each other: data structures and algorithms. Any process or task is
reduced to an algorithm, a final sequence of simple operations that a computer can execute to accomplish a given task. And any object in the world—

be it the population of a city, or the weather over the course of a century, a chair, a human brain—is modeled as a data structure, that is, data organized in a particular way for efficient search and retrieval.[6] Examples of data structures are arrays, linked lists, and graphs. Algorithms and data structures have a symbiotic relationship. The more complex the data structure of a computer program, the simpler the algorithm needs to be, and vice versa. Together, according to a computer, data structures and algorithms are two halves of the ontology of the world.

The computerization of culture involves the projection of these two fundamental parts of computer software—and of the computer's unique ontology—onto the cultural sphere. If CD-ROMs and Web databases are cultural manifestations of one-half of this ontology—data structures—then computer games are manifestations of the second half—algorithms. Games (sports, chess, cards) are one cultural form that require algorithm-like behavior from the players; consequently, many traditional games were quickly simulated on computers. In parallel, new genres of computer games came into existence, such as a first-person shooter ("Doom" and "Quake"). Thus, as was the case with database genres, computer games both mimic already-existing games and create new game genres.

It may appear at first sight that data are passive and algorithm is active—another example of passive-active binary categories so loved by human cultures. A program reads in data, executes an algorithm, and writes out new data. We may recall that before "computer science" and "software engineering" became established names for the computer field, the field was called "data processing." This name remained in use for several decades during which computers were primarily associated with performing calculations over data. However, the passive/active distinction is not quite accurate because data do not just exist—they have to be generated. Data creators have to collect data and organize it, or create it from scratch. Texts need to be written, photographs need to be taken, video and audio need to be recorded—or they need to be digitized from already-existing media. In the 1990s, when the new role of the computer as a universal media machine became apparent, already computerized societies went into a digitizing craze. All existing books and videotapes, photographs, and audio recordings started to be fed into computers at an ever-increasing rate. Steven Spielberg created the Shoah Foundation, which videotaped and then digitized numerous interviews with Holocaust survivors; it would take one person forty years to watch all the recorded material. The editors of *Mediamatic Journal*, who devoted an entire issue to the topic of "the storage mania" (Summer 1994), wrote: "A growing number of organizations are embarking on ambitious projects. Everything is being collected: culture, asteroids, DNA patterns, credit records, telephone conversations; it doesn't matter."[7] Once digitized, the data have to be cleaned up, organized, and indexed. The computer age brought with it a new cultural algorithm: reality->media->data->database. The rise of the Web, this gigantic and always-changing data corpus, gave millions of people a new hobby or profession: data indexing. There is hardly a Web site that does not feature at least a dozen links to other sites; therefore, every site is a type of database. And, with the rise of Internet commerce, most large-scale commercial sites have become real databases, or, rather, front-ends to company databases. For instance, in the fall of 1998, Amazon.com had three million books in its database, and the maker of a leading commercial database, Oracle, had offered *Oracle 8i,* fully integrated with the Internet and featuring unlimited database size, natural-language queries, and support for all multimedia data types. Jorge Luis Borges's story about a map,[8] which was equal in size to the territory it represented, became rewritten as the story about indexes and the data they index. But now the map has become larger than the territory—sometimes much larger. Pornographic Web sites exposed the logic of the Web to its extreme by constantly reusing the same photographs from other porno Web sites. Only rare sites featured the original content. On any given date, the same few dozen images would appear on thousands of sites. Thus, the same data would give rise to more indexes than the number of data elements themselves.

DATABASE AND NARRATIVE

As a cultural form, database represents the world as a list of items, and it refuses to order this list. In contrast, a narrative creates a cause-and-effect trajectory of seemingly unordered items (events). Therefore, database and narrative are natural enemies. Competing for the same territory of human culture, each claims an exclusive right to make meaning out of the world.

In contrast to most games, most narratives do not require algorithm-like behavior from their readers. Narratives and games, however, are similar in that the user, while proceeding through them, must uncover their underlying logic—their algorithm. Just like a game player, the reader of a novel gradually reconstructs an algorithm (here I use it metaphorically) that the writer used to create the settings, the characters, and the events. From this perspective, I can rewrite my earlier equations between the two parts of the computer's ontology and its corresponding cultural forms. Data structures and algorithms drive different forms of computer culture. CD-ROMs, Web sites, and other new media objects that are organized as databases correspond to the data structure, while narratives, including computer games, correspond to the algorithms.

In computer programming, data structures and algorithms need each other; they are equally important for a program to work. What happens in a cultural sphere? Do databases and narratives have the same status in computer culture?

Some media objects explicitly follow database logic in their structure, while others do not, but behind the surface practically all of them are databases. In general, creating a work in new media can be understood as the construction of an interface to a database. In the simplest case, the interface simply provides the access to the underlying database. For instance, an image database can be represented as a page of miniature images; clicking on a miniature will retrieve the corresponding record. If a database is too large to display all of its records at once, a search engine enables the user to search for particular records. But the interface can also translate the underlying database into a very different user experience. The user may be navigating a virtual three-dimensional city composed from letters, as in Jeffrey Shaw's interactive installation *Legible City*.[9] Or, the user may be traversing a black-and-white image of a naked body, activating pieces of text, audio, and video embedded in its skin (such as Graham Harwood's CD-ROM *Rehearsal of Memory*),[10] or be playing with virtual animals that come closer or run away depending upon the user's movements (as in Scott Fisher et al. in the VR installation *Menagerie*). Although each of these works engages the user in a set of behaviors and cognitive activities that are quite distinct from going through the records of a database, all of them are databases. *Legible City* is a database of three-dimensional letters that make up the city. *Rehearsal of Memory* is a database of texts and audio and video clips that are accessed through the interface of a body. *Menagerie* is a database of virtual animals, including their shapes, movements, and behaviors.

Database becomes the center of the creative process in the computer age. Historically, the artist made a unique work within a particular medium. The interface and the work were the same—in other words, the level of interface did not exist. With new media, the content of the work and the interface becomes separate. It is therefore possible to create different interfaces to the same material. These interfaces may present different versions of the same work, as in David Blair's *WaxWeb*. They may also be radically different from each other, as in Moscow WWWArt Centre. This is one of the ways in which the principle of *variability* of new media manifests itself.

But now we can give this principle a new formulation. *The new media object consists of one or more interfaces to a database of multimedia material.* If only one interface is constructed, the result will be similar to a traditional art object. This, however, is an exception rather than the norm.

This formulation places the opposition between database and narrative in a new light, thus redefining our concept of narrative. The "user" of a narrative is traversing a database, following links between its records as established by the database's creator. An interactive narrative (which can be also called "hyper-narrative" in an analogy with hypertext) can then be understood as the sum of multiple trajectories through a database. A traditional linear narrative is one among many other possible trajectories—a particular choice made within a hyper-narrative. Just as a traditional cultural object can now be seen as a particular case of a new media object (a new media object that has only one interface), traditional linear narrative can be seen as a particular case of a hyper-narrative.

This "technical," or "material," change in the definition of narrative does not mean that an arbitrary sequence of database records is a narrative. To qualify as a narrative, a cultural object has to satisfy a number of criteria, which literary scholar Mieke Bal defines as follows: it should contain both an actor and a narrator; it also should contain three distinct levels consisting of the text, the story, and the fabula; and its "contents" should be "a series of connected events caused or experienced by actors."[11] Obviously not all cultural objects are narratives. However, in the world of new media, the word "narrative" is often used as an all-inclusive term to cover up the fact that we have not yet developed a language to describe these new strange objects. It is usually paired with another overused word: "interactive." Thus, a number of database records linked together so that more than one trajectory is possible is assumed to constitute "interactive narrative." However, just to create these trajectories is of course not sufficient. The author also has to control the semantics of the elements and the logic of their connection so that the resulting object will meet the criteria of narrative as outlined above. Another erroneous assumption frequently made is that by creating their own path (choosing the records from a database in a particular order), users construct their own unique narrative. However, if a user simply accesses different elements one after another, in a usually random order, there is no reason to assume that these elements will form a narrative at all. Indeed, why should an arbitrary sequence of database records, constructed by the user, result in "a series of connected events caused or experienced by actors"?

In summary, database and narrative do not have the same status in computer culture. In the database/narrative pair, "database" is the unmarked term.[12] Regardless of whether new media objects present themselves as linear narratives, interactive narratives, databases, or something else, underneath, on the level of material organization, they are all databases. In new media, the database supports a variety of cultural forms that range from direct translation (a database stays a database) to a form whose logic is the opposite of the logic of the material form itself—a narrative. More precisely, a database can support narrative, but there is nothing in the logic of the medium itself that would foster its generation. It is not surprising, then, that databases occupy a significant, if not the largest, territory of the new media landscape. What is more surprising is why the other end of the spectrum—narratives—still exists in new media.

THE SEMIOTICS OF DATABASE

The dynamics that exist between database and narrative are not unique in new media. The relation between the structure of a digital image and the languages of contemporary visual culture is characterized by the same dynamics. As defined by all computer software, a digital image consists of a number of separate layers, each layer containing particular visual elements. Throughout the production process, artists and designers manipulate each layer separately; they also delete layers and add new ones. Keeping each element as a separate layer allows the content and the composition of an image to be changed at any point: deleting a background, substituting one person for another, moving two people closer together, blurring an object, and so on. What would a typical image look like if the layers were merged together? The elements contained on different layers will become juxtaposed, resulting in a montage look. Montage is the default visual language of the composite organization of an image. However, just as database supports both the database form and its opposite—narrative—a composite organization of an image on the material level supports two opposing visual languages. One is modernist-MTV montage—two-dimensional juxtaposition of visual elements designed to shock because of its impossibility in reality. The other is the representation of familiar reality as seen by a photo from a film camera (or its computer simulation, in the case of 3D graphics). During the 1980s and 1990s, all image-making technologies became computer-based, thus turning all images into composites. In parallel, a renaissance of montage took place in visual culture, in print, broadcast design, and new media. This is not unexpected—after all, this is the visual language dictated by the composite organization. What needs to be explained is why photorealist images continue to occupy such a significant space in our computer-based visual culture.

It would be surprising, of course, if photorealist images suddenly disappeared completely; the history of culture does not contain such sudden breaks. Similarly, we should not expect that new media would completely substitute narrative by database. New media does not radically break with the past; rather, it distributes weight differently between the categories that hold culture together, foregrounding what was in the background and vice versa. As Fredric Jameson writes in his analysis of another shift, in this case from modernism to postmodernism: "Radical breaks between periods do not generally involve complete changes but rather the restructuration of a certain number of elements already given: features that in an earlier period or system were subordinate became dominant, and features that had been dominant again become secondary."[13]

Database narrative opposition is the case in point. To understand further how computer culture redistributes weight between the two terms of opposition in computer culture, I will bring in a semiological theory of syntagm and paradigm. According to this model, originally formulated by Ferdinand de Saussure to describe natural languages such as English, and later expanded by Roland Barthes and others to apply to other sign systems (narrative, fashion, food, and so on), the elements of a system can be related on two dimensions: syntagmatic and paradigmatic. As defined by Barthes, "The syntagm is a combination of signs, which has space as a support."[14] To use the example of natural language, the speaker produces an utterance by stringing together the elements, one after another, in a linear sequence. This is the syntagmatic dimension. Now, let's look at the paradigm. To continue with an example of a language user, each new element is chosen from a set of other related elements. For instance, all nouns form a set; all synonyms of a particular word form another set. In Saussure's original formulation, "The units which have something in common are associated in theory and thus form groups within which various relationships can be found."[15] This is the paradigmatic dimension.

The elements on a syntagmatic dimension are related *in praesentia*, while the elements on a paradigmatic dimension are related *in absentia*. For instance, in the case of a written sentence, the words that comprise it materially exist on a piece of paper, while the paradigmatic sets to which these words belong exist only in the writer's and reader's minds. Similarly, in the case of a fashion outfit, the elements that make it, such as a skirt, a blouse, and a jacket, are present in reality, while pieces of clothing that could have been present instead—a different skirt, a different blouse, a different jacket—exist only in the viewer's imagination. Thus, syntagm is explicit and paradigm is implicit; one is real and the other is imagined.

Literary and cinematic narratives work in the same way. Particular words, sentences, shots, and scenes that make up a narrative have a material existence. Other elements that form an imaginary world of an author or a particular literary or cinematic style and that could have appeared instead exist only virtually. Put differently, the database of choices from which narrative is constructed (the paradigm) is implicit, while the actual narrative (the syntagm) is explicit.

New media reverses this relationship. Database (the paradigm) is given material existence, while narrative (the syntagm) is dematerialized. Paradigm is privileged; syntagm is downplayed. Paradigm is real; syntagm is virtual. To see this, consider the new media design process. The design of any new media object begins with assembling a database of possible elements to be used. Macromedia Director calls this database "cast," Adobe Premiere calls it "project," ProTools calls it a "session," but the principle is the same. This database is the center of the design process. It typically consists of a combination of original and stock material distributed as buttons, images, video, and audio sequences, 3D objects, behaviors, and so on. Throughout the design process, new elements are added to the database, while existing elements are modified. The narrative is constructed by linking elements of this database in a particular order—designing a trajectory leading from one element to another. On the material level, a narrative is just a set of links; the elements themselves remain stored in the database. Thus, the narrative is more virtual than the database itself.[16]

The paradigm is privileged over syntagm in yet another way in interactive objects presenting the user with a number of choices at the same time—which is what typical interactive interfaces do. For instance, a screen may contain a few icons; clicking on each icon leads the user to a different screen. On the level of an individual screen, these choices form a paradigm of their own that is explicitly presented to the user. On the level of the whole object, the user is made aware that he or she is following one possible trajectory among many others. In other words, the user is selecting one trajectory from the paradigm of all trajectories that are defined.

Other types of interactive interfaces make the paradigm even more explicit by presenting the user with an explicit menu of all available choices. In such interfaces, all the categories are always available, just a mouse click away.

The complete paradigm is present before the user, its elements neatly arranged in a menu. This is another example of how new media makes explicit the psychological processes involved in cultural communication. Other examples include the already discussed shift from creation to selection, which externalizes and codifies the database of cultural elements existing in the creator's mind, as well as the very phenomena of interactive links. New media takes "interaction" literally, equating it with a strictly physical interaction between a user and a screen (by pressing a button), at the sake of psychological interaction. The psychological processes of filling-in, hypothesis forming, recall, and identification—which are required for us to comprehend any text or image at all—are erroneously equated with an objectively existing structure of interactive links.

Interactive interfaces foreground the paradigmatic dimension and often make explicit paradigmatic sets. Yet, they are still organized along the syntagmatic dimension. Although the user is making choices at each new screen, the result is a linear sequence of screens that he or she follows. This is the classical syntagmatic experience. In fact, it can be compared to constructing a sentence in a natural language. Just as a language user constructs a sentence by choosing each successive word from a paradigm of other possible words, a new media user creates a sequence of screens by clicking on this or that icon at each screen. Obviously there are many important differences between these two situations. For instance, in the case of a typical interactive interface, there is no grammar and paradigms are much smaller. Yet, the similarity of basic experience in both cases is quite interesting. In both cases, it unfolds along a syntagmatic dimension.

Why does new media insist on this language-like sequencing? My hypothesis is that it follows the dominant semiological order of the twentieth century—that of cinema. Cinema replaced all other modes of narration with a sequential narrative, an assembly line of shots that appear on the screen one at a time. For centuries, a spatialized narrative where all images appear simultaneously dominated European visual culture. Then it was delegated to "minor" cultural forms like comics and technical illustrations. "Real" culture of the twentieth century came to speak in linear chains, aligning itself with the assembly line of an industrial society and the Turing machine of a postindustrial era. New media continues this mode, giving the user information one screen at a time. At least, this is the case when it tries to become "real" culture (interactive narratives, games). When it simply functions as an interface to information, it is not ashamed to present much more information on the screen at once, whether in the form of tables, normal or pull-down menus, or lists. In particular, the experience of a user filling in an online form can be compared to precinematic spatialized narrative: in both cases, the user is following a sequence of elements that are presented simultaneously.

A DATABASE COMPLEX

To what extent is the database form intrinsic to modern storage media? For instance, a typical music CD is a collection of individual tracks grouped together. The database impulse also drives much of photography through-out its history, from William Henry Fox Talbot's *Pencil of Nature* to August Sander's monumental typology of modern German society, *Face of Our Time,* to Bernd and Hilla Becher's equally obsessive cataloging of water tow-ers. Yet, the connection between storage media and database forms is not universal. The prime exception is cinema. Here the storage media supports the narrative imagination. We may quote once again Christian Metz, who wrote in the 1970s, "Most films shot today, good or bad, original or not, 'commercial' or not, have as a common characteristic that they tell a story; in this measure they all belong to one and the same genre, which is, rather, a sort of 'super-genre' ['sur-genre']."[17] Why, then, in the case of photogra-phy storage media does technology sustain database, while in the case of cinema it gives rise to a modern narrative form par excellence? Does this have to do with the method of media access? Shall we conclude that random access media, such as computer storage formats (hard drives, removable disks, CD-ROMs), favor database, while sequential access media, such as film, favor narrative? This does not hold either. For instance, a book, this perfect random-access medium, supports database forms such as photo albums and narrative forms such as novels.

Rather than trying to correlate database and narrative forms with mod-ern media and information technologies, or deduce them from these tech-nologies, I prefer to think of them as two competing imaginations, two basic creative impulses, two essential responses to the world that have existed long before modern media. The ancient Greeks produced long narratives, such as Homer's epic poems *The Iliad* and *The Odyssey;* they also produced encyclopedias. The first fragments of a Greek encyclopedia to have survived were the work of Speusippus, a nephew of Plato. Denis Diderot wrote nov-els—and was also in charge of the monumental *Encyclopédie,* the largest publishing project of the eighteenth century. Competing to make meaning out of the world, database and narrative produce endless hybrids. It is hard to find a pure encyclopedia without any traces of a narrative in it and vice versa. For instance, until alphabetical organization became popular a few centuries ago, most encyclopedias were organized thematically, with topics covered in a particular order (typically, corresponding to the seven liberal arts). At the same time, many narratives, such as the novels of Cervantes and Jonathan Swift, and even Homer's epic poems—the founding narratives of the Western tradition—traverse an imaginary encyclopedia.

Modern media is the new battlefield for the competition between database and narrative. It is tempting to read the history of this competition in dramatic terms. First, the medium of visual recording—photography—privileges catalogs, taxonomies, and lists. While the modern novel blossoms, and academicians continued to produce historical narrative paintings all through the nineteenth century, in the realm of the new techno-image of photography, database rules. The next visual recording medium—film—privileges narrative. Almost all fictional films are narratives, with few exceptions. Magnetic tape used in video does not bring any substantial changes. The next storage media—computer-controlled digital storage devices (hard drives, removable drives, CD-ROMs, DVD-ROMs—privilege database once again. With multimedia encyclopedias, virtual museums, pornography, artists' CD-ROMs, library databases, Web indexes, and the Web itself, database is more popular than ever before.

The digital computer turns out to be the perfect medium for the database form. Like a virus, databases infect CD-ROMs and hard drives, servers, and Web sites. Can we say that database is the cultural form most characteristic of a computer? In her 1978 article "Video: The Aesthetics of Narcissism," probably the single most well-known article on video art, art historian Rosalind Krauss argues that video is not a physical medium but a psychological one. In her analysis, "Video's real medium is a psychological situation, the very terms of which are to withdraw attention from an external object—an Other—and invest it in the Self."[18] In short, video art is a support for the psychological condition of narcissism. Does new media similarly function to play out a particular psychological condition, something that can be called a database complex? In this respect, it is interesting that database imagination has accompanied computer art from its very beginning. In the 1960s, artists working with computers wrote programs to systematically explore the combinations of different visual elements. In part, they were following art-world trends like minimalism. Minimalist artists executed works of art according to preexistent plans. They also created series of images or objects by systematically varying a single parameter. When minimalist artist Sol LeWitt spoke of an artist's idea as "the machine which makes the work," it was only logical to substitute the human executing the idea by a computer.[19] At the same time, since the only way to make pictures with a computer was by writing a computer program, the logic of computer programming itself pushed computer artists in the same directions. Thus, for artist Frieder Nake, a computer was a "Universal Picture Generator," capable of producing every possible picture out of a combination of available picture elements and colors.[20] In 1967, Nake published a portfolio of twelve drawings that he obtained by successfully multiplying a square matrix by itself. Another early computer artist, Manfred Mohr, produced numerous images that recorded various transformations of a basic cube.

Even more remarkable were films by John Whitney Sr., the pioneer of computer filmmaking. His films such as *Permutations* (1967), *Arabesque* (1975), and others systematically explored the transformations of geometric forms obtained by manipulating elementary mathematical functions. Thus they substituted successive accumulation of visual effects for narrative, figuration, or even formal development. Instead they presented the viewer with databases of effects. This principle reaches its extreme in Whitney's earlier film that was made using an analog computer and was called *Catalog* (1961). In his *Expanded Cinema* (1970), critic Gene Youngblood writes about this remarkable film: "The elder Whitney actually never produced a complete, coherent movie on the analog computer because he was continually developing and refining the machine while using it for commercial work. . . . However, Whitney did assemble a visual catalog of the effects he had perfected over the years. This film, simply titled *Catalog*, was completed in 1961 and proved to be of such overwhelming beauty that many persons still prefer Whitney's analog work over his digital computer films."[21] One is tempted to read *Catalog* as one of the founding moments of new media. Now all software for media creation arrives with endless "plug-ins"—the banks of effects that, with a press of a button, generate interesting images from any input whatsoever. In parallel, much of the aesthetics of computerized visual culture is effects-driven, especially when a new techno-genre (computer animation, multimedia, Web sites) is just becoming established. For instance, countless music videos are variations of Whitney's *Catalog*. The only difference is that the effects are applied to the images of human performers. This is yet another example of how the logic of a computer— in this case, the ability of a computer to produce endless variations of elements and to act as a filter, transforming its input to yield a new output— becomes the logic of culture at large.

DATABASE CINEMA: GREENAWAY AND VERTOV

Although database form may be inherent to new media, countless attempts to create "interactive narratives" testify to our dissatisfaction with the computer in the sole role of an encyclopedia or a catalog of effects. We want new media narratives, and we want these narratives to be different from the narratives we have seen or read before. In fact, regardless of how often we repeat in public that the modernist notion of medium specificity ("every medium should develop its own unique language") is obsolete, we do expect computer narratives to showcase new aesthetic possibilities that did not exist before digital computers. In short, we want them to be new-media-specific. Given the dominance of database in computer software and the key role it plays in the computer-based design process, perhaps we can arrive at new kinds of narrative by focusing our attention on how narrative and database can work together. How can a narrative take into account the fact that its elements are organized in a database? How can our new abilities to store vast amounts of data, to automatically classify, index, link, search, and instantly retrieve it, lead to new kinds of narratives?

Peter Greenaway, one of the very few prominent film directors concerned with expanding cinema's language, complained that "the linear pursuit— one story at a time told chronologically—is the standard format of cinema." Pointing out that cinema lags behind modern literature in experimenting with narrative, he asked: "Could it not travel on the road where Joyce, Eliot, Borges and Perec have already arrived?"[22] While Greenaway is right to direct filmmakers to more innovative literary narratives, new media artists working on the database/narrative problem can learn from cinema as it is. Cinema already exists right in the intersection between database and narrative. We can think of all the material accumulated during shooting forming a database, especially since the shooting schedule usually does not follow the narrative of the film but is determined by production logistics. During editing, the editor constructs a film narrative out of this database, creating a unique trajectory through the conceptual space of all possible films that could have been constructed. From this perspective, every filmmaker engages with the database-narrative problem in every film, although only a few have done this self-consciously.

One exception is Greenaway himself. Throughout his career, he has been working on the problem of how to reconcile database and narrative forms. Many of his films progress forward by recounting a list of items, a catalog that does not have any inherent order (for example, different books in *Prospero's*

Books). Working to undermine a linear narrative, Greenaway uses different systems to order his films. He wrote about this approach: "If a numerical, alphabetic color-coding system is employed, it is done deliberately as a device, a construct, to counteract, dilute, augment or complement the all-pervading obsessive cinema interest in plot, in narrative, in the 'I am now going to tell you a story' school of film-making."[23] His favorite system is numbers. The sequence of numbers acts as a narrative shell that "convinces" the viewer that he or she is watching a narrative. In reality, the scenes that follow one another are not connected in any logical way. By using numbers, Greenaway "wraps" a minimal narrative around a database. Although Greenaway's database logic was already present in his "avant-garde" films such as *The Falls* (1980), it has also structured his "commercial" films from the beginning. *Draughtsman's Contract* (1982) is centered on twelve drawings being made by the draftsman. They do not form any order. Greenaway emphasizes this by having draftsmen work on multiple drawings simultaneously. Eventually, Greenaway's desire to take "cinema out of cinema" led to his work on a series of installations and museum exhibitions in the 1990s. No longer having to conform to the linear medium of film, the elements of a database are spatialized within a museum or even the whole city. This move can be read as the desire to create a database at its purest form: the set of elements not ordered in any way. If the elements exist in one dimension (time of a film, list on a page), they will be inevitably ordered. Therefore, the only way to create a pure database is to spatialize it, distributing the elements in space. This is exactly the path that Greenaway took. Situated in three-dimensional space that does not have an inherent narrative logic, a 1992 installation, *100 Objects to Represent the World,* in its very title proposes that the world should be understood through a catalog rather than a narrative. At the same time, Greenaway does not abandon narrative; he continues to investigate how database and narrative can work together. Having presented *100 Objects* as an installation, Greenaway next turned it into an opera set. In the opera, the narrator, Thrope, uses the objects to conduct Adam and Eve through the whole of human civilization, thus turning *100 Objects* into a sequential narrative. In another installation, *The Stairs-Munich-Projection* (1995), Greenaway put up one hundred screens throughout Munich, each screen representing one year in the history of cinema. Again, Greenaway presents us with a spatialized database—but also with a narrative. By walking from one screen to another, one follows cinema's history. The project uses Greenaway's favorite principle of organization by numbers, pushing it to the extreme: the projections on the screens contain no figuration, just numbers. The screens are numbered from

1895 to 1995, one screen for each year of cinema's history. Along with numbers, Greenaway introduces another line of development. Each projection is slightly different in color.[24] The hundred colored squares form an abstract narrative of their own that runs in parallel to the linear narrative of cinema's history. Finally, Greenaway superimposes yet a third narrative by dividing the history of cinema into five sections, each section staged in a different part of the city. The apparent triviality of the basic narrative of the project—one hundred numbers, standing for one hundred years of cinema's history— "neutralizes" the narrative, forcing the viewer to focus on the phenomenon of the projected light itself, which is the actual subject of this project.

Along with Greenaway, Dziga Vertov can be thought of as a major "database filmmaker" of the twentieth century. His film *Man with a Movie Camera* is perhaps the most important example of database imagination in modern media art. In one of the key shots (repeated few times in the film), we see an editing room with a number of shelves used to keep and organize the shot material. The shelves are marked "machines," "club," "the movement of a city," "physical exercise," "an illusionist," and so on. This is the database of the recorded material. The editor, Vertov's wife, Elizaveta Svilova, is shown working with this database—retrieving some reels, returning used reels, adding new ones.

Although I pointed out that film editing in general can be compared to creating a trajectory through a database, in the case of *Man with a Movie Camera* this comparison constitutes the very method of the film. Its subject is the filmmaker's struggle to reveal (social) structure among the multitude of observed phenomena. Its project is a brave attempt at an empirical epistemology that has only one tool: perception. The goal is to decode the world purely through the surfaces visible to the eye (of course, its natural sight enhanced by a movie camera). This is how the film's coauthor, Mikhail Kaufman, Vertov's brother and cameraman, describes it:

> An ordinary person finds himself in some sort of environment, gets lost amidst the zillions of phenomena, and observes these phenomena from a bad vantage point. He registers one phenomenon very well, registers a second and a third, but has no idea of where they may lead. . . . But the man with a movie camera is infused with the particular thought that he is actually seeing the world for other people. Do you understand? He joins these phenomena with others, from elsewhere, which may not even have been filmed by him. Like a kind of scholar he is able to gather empirical observations in one place and then in another. And that is actually the way in which the world has come to be understood.[25]

Therefore, in contrast to standard film editing, which consists of the selection and ordering of previously shot material according to a preexistent script, here the process of relating shots to one another, ordering and reordering them in order to discover the hidden order of the world, constitutes the film's method. *Man with a Movie Camera* traverses its database in a particular order to construct an argument. Records drawn from a database and arranged in a particular order become a picture of modern life—but simultaneously an argument about this life, an interpretation of what these images, which we encounter every day, every second, actually mean.[26]

Was this brave attempt successful? The overall structure of the film is quite complex, and on the first glance has little to do with a database. Just as new media objects contain a hierarchy of levels (interface/content; operating system/application; Web page/HTML code; high-level programming language/assembly language/machine language), Vertov's film consists of at least three levels. One level is the story of a cameraman filming material for the film. The second level consists of the shots of an audience watching the finished film in a movie theater. The third level is this film, which consists of footage recorded in Moscow, Kiev, and Riga and is arranged according to a progression of one day: waking up, work, leisure activities. If this third level is a text, the other two can be thought of as its metatexts.[27] Vertov goes back and forth between the three levels, shifting between the text and its metatexts—between the production of the film, its reception, and the film itself. But if we focus on the film within the film (the level of the text) and disregard the special effects used to create many of the shots, we discover an almost linear printout, so to speak, of a database: a number of shots showing machines, followed by a number of shots showing work activities, followed by different shots of leisure, and so on. The paradigm is projected onto syntagm. The result is a banal, mechanical catalog of subjects that one can expect to find in the city of the 1920s: running trams, city beach, movie theaters, factories.

Of course watching *Man with a Movie Camera* is anything but a banal experience. Even after the 1990s, during which computer-based image and video makers systematically exploited every avant-garde device, the original is still striking. What makes it striking is not its subjects and the associations Vertov tries to establish between them to impose "the communist decoding of the world," but the most amazing catalog of the film techniques contained within it. Fades and superimpositions, freeze-frames, acceleration, split screens, various types of rhythm and intercutting—what film scholar Annette Michelson called "a summation of the resources and techniques of the silent cinema."[28] And, of course, a multitude of unusual "constructivist" points of view are strung together with such density that the film can't be simply labeled avant-garde. If a "normal" avant-garde film still proposes a coherent language different from the language of mainstream cinema—a small set of techniques that are repeated—*Man with a Movie Camera* never arrives at anything like a well-defined language. Rather, it proposes an untamed and apparently endless unwinding of cinematic techniques, or, to use contemporary language, "effects."

Why in the case of Whitney's computer films and music videos are the effects just effects, while in the hands of Vertov they acquire meaning? The differences are that in Vertov's film they are motivated by a particular argument, this being that the new techniques to obtain images and manipulate them, summed up by Vertov in his term "kino-eye," can be used to decode the world. As the film progresses, "straight" footage gives way to manipulated footage. Newer techniques appear one after one, reaching a roller-coaster intensity by the film's end, a true orgy of cinematography. It is as though Vertov restages his discovery of the kino-eye for us. Along with Vertov, we gradually realize the full range of possibilities offered by the camera. Vertov's goal is to seduce us into his way of seeing and thinking, to make us share his excitement, his gradual process of discovery of film's new language. This process of discovery is film's main narrative and it is told through a catalog of discoveries being made. Thus, in the hands of Vertov, a database, this normally static and "objective" form, becomes dynamic and subjective. More important, Vertov is able to achieve something that new media designers still have to learn—how to merge database and narrative into a new form.

NOTES

This essay, which later became a chapter in my book *The Language of New Media* (Boston: MIT Press, 2001), was written in the fall of 1998. For this volume, I have made minor changes, for example, substituting a reference to CD-ROM with a reference to DVD.

   1. The definition of "database" is from Britannica Online.

   2. Jean-François Lyotard, *The Postmodern Condition: A Report on Knowledge,* trans. Geoff Bennington and Brian Massumi (Minneapolis: University of Minnesota Press, 1984), 3.

   3. As early as 1985 Grolier, Inc., issued a text-only *Academic American Encyclopedia* on CD-ROM. The first multimedia encyclopedia was *Compton's MultiMedia Encyclopedia,* published in 1989.

   4. David Bordwell and Kristin Thompson define motivation in cinema in the following way: "Because films are human constructs, we can expect that any one element in a film will have some justification for being there. This justification is the motivation for that element." Here are some examples of motivation: "When Tom jumps from the balloon

to chase a cat, we motivate his action by appealing to notions of how dogs are likely to act when cats are around." "The movement of a character across a room may motivate the moving of the camera to follow the action and keep the character within a frame." David Bordwell and Kristin Thompson, *Film Art: An Introduction,* 5th ed. (New York: McGraw-Hill, 1997), 80.

5. Chris McGowan and Jim McCullaugh, *Entertainment in the Cyber Zone* (New York: Random House, 1995), 71.

6. This is true for a procedural programming paradigm. In an object-oriented programming paradigm, represented by such computer languages as Java and C++, algorithms and data structures are modeled together as objects.

7. *Mediamatic* 8 (Summer 1994): 1860.

8. Jorge Borges, "The Library of Babel," in *Ficciones,* trans. Anthony Kerrigan (New York: Grove Press, 1962).

9. See http://artnetweb.com/guggenheim/mediascape/shaw.html.

10. Graham Harwood, *Rehearsal of Memory,* CD-ROM (London: Artec and Bookworks, 1996.)

11. Mieke Bal, *Narratology: Introduction to the Theory of Narrative* (Toronto: University of Toronto Press, 1985), 8.

12. The theory of "markedness" was first developed by linguists of the Prague School in relation to phonology, but subsequently it was applied to all levels of linguistic analysis. For example, "bitch" is the marked term and "dog" is the unmarked term. Whereas "bitch" is used only in relation to females, "dog" is applicable to both males and females.

13. Fredric Jameson, "Postmodernism and Consumer Society," in *The Anti-Aesthetic: Essays on Postmodern Culture,* ed. Hal Foster (Seattle: Bay Press, 1983), 123.

14. Roland Barthes, *The Elements of Semiology* (New York: Hill and Wang, 1968), 58.

15. Quoted in ibid., 58.

16. Since all data are stored as electronic signals, the word "material" seems no longer to be appropriate. Instead, we should talk about different degrees of virtuality.

17. Christian Metz, "The Fiction Film and Its Spectator: A Metapsychological Study," in *Apparatus,* ed. Theresa Hak Kyung Cha (New York: Tanam Press, 1980), 402.

18. Rosalind Krauss, "Video: The Aesthetics of Narcissism," in *Video Culture,* ed. John Hanhardt (Rochester, N.Y.: Visual Studies Workshop, 1987), 184.

19. Quoted in Sam Hunter and John Jacobus, *Modern Art: Painting, Sculpture, and Architecture,* 3rd ed. (New York: Harry N. Abrams, 1992), 326.

20. Frank Dietrich, "Visual Intelligence: The First Decade of Computer Art, 1965–1975," *IEEE Computer Graphics and Applications* (July 1985): 39.

21. Gene Youngblood, *Expanded Cinema* (New York: E. P. Dutton, 1970), 210.

22. Peter Greenaway, *The Stairs—Munich—Projection 2* (London: Merrell Holberton Publishers, 1995), 21.

23. Quoted in David Pascoe and Peter Greenaway, *Museums and Moving Images* (London: Reaktion Books, 1997), 9–10.

24. Pasco and Greenaway, *The Stairs—Munich—Projection 2,* 47–53.

25. Mikhail Kaufman, "An Interview," *October* 11 (Winter 1979): 65.

26. It can be said that Vertov uses the "Kuleshov effect" to give meaning to the database records by placing them in a particular order.

27. Linguistics, semiotics, and philosophy use the concept of metalanguage.

Metalanguage is the language used for the analysis of object language. Thus, a metalanguage may be thought of as a language about another language. A metatext is a text in metalanguage about a text in object language. For instance, an article in a fashion magazine is a metatext about the text of clothes. Or, an HTML file is a metatext that describes the text of a Web page.

28. Kaufman, "An Interview," 55.

3. Ocean, Database, Recut

Ocean

He looked into the water and saw that it was made up of a thousand
thousand thousand and one different currents, each one a different
colour, weaving in and out of one another like a liquid tapestry of
breathtaking complexity; and Iff explained that these were the
Streams of Story, that each coloured strand represented and contained
a single tale. Different parts of the Ocean contained different sorts of
stories, and as all the stories that had ever been told and many that
were still in the process of being invented could be found here, the
Ocean of the Streams of Story was in fact the biggest library in the
universe. And because the stories were held here in fluid form, they
retained the ability to change, to become new versions of themselves,
to join up with other stories and so become yet other stories.

—SALMAN RUSHDIE, *Haroun and the Sea of Stories*

The Story Ocean pictured by Salman Rushdie is an inspiration for interactive narrative. It combines the metaphor (by now drained of meaning) of surfing—in this case riding a single story current to take in its narrative line—with the idea of fluid dynamics. Turbulences created by the surfer's activity cause individual story streams to combine, forming new stories out of elements of the old. "It is not dead but alive," as Iff, the guide to the Ocean, expresses it.[1]

Haroun and the Sea of Stories, Rushdie's only published children's book, is an elaborate but disguised allegory. The story of the harsh dictator who has polluted the Story Ocean hints at a sullying of the luxurious Middle Eastern traditions of narrative. Central to this literature is *The Thousand and One Nights,* the thirteenth-century multivolume epic that appears again and again in our own culture—if pale, safe, and dilute—in a range from Rimsky-Korsakov to Disney, to say nothing of the thousand thousand-and-one children's illustrated Aladdins, Sinbads, and Ali Babas. It is dilute not only in the sense that the original is as erotic as *Lolita* but also because *A Thousand*

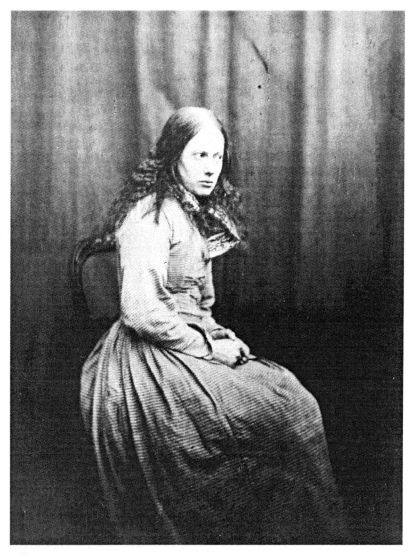

FIGURE 3.1. HUGH DIAMOND, PHOTOGRAPH OF PATIENT AT SPRINGFIELD, THE
SURREY COUNTY LUNATIC ASYLUM, 1850S. COURTESY OF THE ROYAL SOCIETY OF
MEDICINE, LONDON.

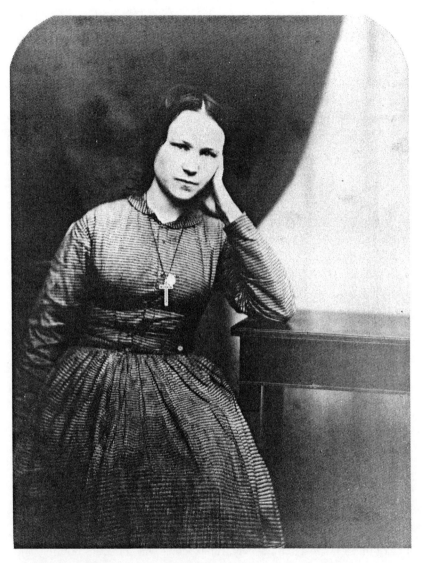

FIGURE 3.2. HUGH DIAMOND, PHOTOGRAPH OF PATIENT AT SPRINGFIELD, THE SURREY COUNTY LUNATIC ASYLUM, 1850S. COURTESY OF THE ROYAL SOCIETY OF MEDICINE, LONDON.

and One Nights is itself a multilinear ocean, or at least a great lake, of overlapping stories and stories-within-stories. Rushdie's novella is crammed with references to *The Thousand and One Nights.* The twelve-year-old title character, Haroun, for example, shares his name with the hero of many stories told by Scheherazade about Harun Al-Rashid, a wise, usually generous Caliph. One of the undercurrents of Scheherazade's storytelling is to recommend Al-Rashid's more rational style of behavior to the cruel Sultan who has sentenced her to death in retribution for his late wife's adultery. Each morning the sultan suspends her execution so that she can complete the story she has abandoned in the middle, like a Saturday afternoon serial or a daily soap opera. Scheherazade engages in close to a thousand and one nights of sexual shenanigans with the Sultan as a prelude to stories incorporating sexual encounters of all conceivable types, which she describes in fine, erotic detail. In *A Thousand and One Nights,* it is sex and allegorical narrative that together save Scheherazade from the ax; and it is patently Rushdie's dream that somehow narrative, combined with the debatable skills of the British Special Police Force, saves him from millions of Muslims charged with the duty of enacting his holy (and rewarding) murder, just as narrative (his own *Satanic Verses*) led to the Fatwah death sentence placed on him.

However, this story-current is not one that I wish to ride any further in this context. The official Fatwah on Salman Rushdie was lifted in 1998, though he will probably never be completely out of danger. And the image of an Ocean of Streams of Story is now a resonating element of our literature. In this essay I want to suggest that Rushdie's Ocean describes a shape for storytelling that is rapidly replacing the kind of narrative structure that emerged in literature in the nineteenth century, a structure greedily adopted by the cinema, which has continued to rule vast regions of media territory ever since. It is, to use an imprecise and overused terminology, a notion of "linear" structure, and my suggestion is that its replacement—Rushdie's Ocean of Stories—is a "multilinear" structure.

Film wants to be linear. In orderly procession, one frame follows another into the gate of the projector or onto the head of the VCR, forming a time line of images with a definite beginning, before which there is nothing, and a precise end, when the images stop. The very topology of film or video, a long narrow ribbon, suggests a shape for its content. To match the form of the filmstrip, the events depicted should start at one point in time and continue without break to another, always one and only one thing occurring on the screen at any given moment. Then everything should culminate and conclude in such a way that the viewer understands and accepts an ending. No loose threads. No unresolved issues. The prevention of leftovers at the end of a film naturally imposes a regime on the middle as well. Nothing can inhabit the center that cannot be adequately accounted for when the ending is reached: the ending must unravel every knot that is introduced at the beginning and progressively entangled in the middle.

But this is a story form that does not match experience. We are complex creatures, living through experiences that are not circumscribed by beginnings and endings. We perform many actions at once, some mental, some physical. We can, effortlessly, switch our attention from one thing in consciousness to another, without completely abandoning the first. And we *act* on the world. Our actions, physical and mental, disturb the objects of perception: a flick of the eyes, a turn of the head, a shove, and what we see and hear is suddenly different. So when we compress our stories to match them to the shape of a film band on which a linear progression of events is depicted, and over which we have no influence, our description both misrepresents our experience and omits crucial elements of it. And if this simplified (though often elegant) form of representation takes center stage, as it did in the twentieth century, we begin to believe that lived experience that does not conform to this structure is lacking, rather than vice versa.

These simple-minded points have been repeated ad nauseum in the last fifty years of film studies. But now, at last we have a form of audiovisual representation that is alternative and we can begin to depict the multiplicitous, complex nature of living in time. I am talking about the promise of an interactive cinema, something that has been hanging over us for decades now (not that filmmakers have not been attempting to portray the variegated textures and shapes of experience since the beginning of cinema). In the last twenty or thirty years, perhaps longer, these attempts have been outside the mainstream cinematic culture, avant-garde, independent, and often subversive (I will discuss some examples at the end of this essay). In contrast, writers have been pursuing these goals for centuries, and garnering respect for their attempts and successes. The *Thousand and One Nights* is a thirteenth-century example, as is its contemporary from the Indian subcontinent, *Kathā Sarat Sāgara,* which translates as "The Ocean of the Streams of Story."[2]

DATABASE

Lev Manovich, in an illuminating and influential series of writings in this volume and elsewhere, agrees that the narrative structures of the nineteenth and twentieth centuries are an outdated form. He proposes replacing the narrative genre with the database genre, and positing the database as a paradigm for the structure of new media works. He argues that narrative and database are polar concepts, "narrative" being the "unmarked" term of the pair, that is, the term that gets its meaning from the other.[3] His denouncement of narrative echoes a recurring theme of postmodern art practice and criticism, though it is clearly a beast that is not easily put down. I find Manovich's criterion of narrative too stringent, and I will propose that it may be more useful to look at ways that narrative can be retooled in the light of the database: that the new media open an opportunity for rethinking the notion of narrative, rather than shutting it out.

The complication inherent to these issues becomes apparent when we realize that Rushdie's *Ocean* is itself a database—a database with narratives as data. *Ocean* fulfills two basic criteria of the database: (1) it is composed of smaller elements, the story currents; and (2) it can be traversed in a multiplicity of ways. Manovich's style, and perhaps also his outlook, stands in harsh contrast to Rushdie's constructions of the imagination, but to my mind this divergence in approach is precisely what makes it useful to bring them together. Rushdie describes the Ocean of Streams of Story as "the biggest library in the universe," holding "all the stories that had ever been told . . . in fluid form."[4] For Rushdie, the Ocean is certainly a database.

If the Ocean of Streams of Stories is a database, what are its basic elements, its atoms? Rushdie writes that drinking a small cup of the ocean's liquid produces a story in the imbiber like a dream, a hallucination . . . or a first-person video game.[5] The elements of the Ocean database are stories. However, according to Manovich, a narrative is already a specific method of navigating a database, in that the shape of the path through the data endows a story with its narrative structure.[6] But now the question is more urgent: What are we navigating through so that a story is constructed? What are the elements of a story? For Manovich these elementary particles are images and sounds or linguistic granules. For him a story is constructed from textual components.[7] Narratives, however, are more than the words or images of their telling. Although we may describe the elements of a *film* as images and sounds, and the elements of a spoken or written *tale* as words, one word after another, or audiovisual elements spliced into sequences, will not yield a story. *Events,* not their *descriptions,* make a story: the story remains separate from its telling. This is why there can be different versions of the same story. Narrative structure arises from events, agents, locations, and relationships among and between them, the components of a real or imagined world described by the narrator's words or depicted by the narrator's

images. A story is a story because of what it is *about* and how that is interpreted. Connections between the events must be perceived, conceived, or
constructed, and *related*. A narrative requires a narrator to attest to connections between its components. Constituted of texts, real-world entities, and
interpretation, a narrative is more complex than a database, which is composed of nothing more than its data. Mieke Bal, a theorist referred to with
approbation by Manovich, insists on this point, expressing it as a distinction between text, story, and fabula.[8] The connections between the elements
of the fabula, or content, transform events into a story that can then be
expressed in a text. Relations between text elements are not enough.

It is one thing to arrange the data alphabetically, by size, or by color; it is
quite another to arrange it in narrative sequence. Although the complexity
of material is neither a necessary nor a sufficient condition of narrative,
the richer the database, the more discrete narrative lines may be contained
within it. In these shells we can hear the breakers of Rushdie's Ocean. This
line of critique does not have an impact on Manovich's insight that while
the dominant form of the twentieth-century *cinematic* object may be the
narrative, the new media object's form is the database. My suggestion is that
narrative and database are in different categories, so they do not fall into
the binary opposition that Manovich asserts.

For Manovich, a database represents the world as a collection of items
without imposing an order on the collection, while narrative has order—
sequence—at its center. He argues that each makes meaning in a radically
different way.

> Many new media objects do not tell stories; they don't have a beginning or an
> end; in fact, they don't have any development, thematically, formally or other-
> wise which would organize their elements into a sequence. Instead, they are
> collections of individual items, where every item has the same significance as
> any other. . . . They appear as a collections of items on which the user can per-
> form various operations: view, navigate, search. The user experience of such
> computerized collections is therefore quite distinct from reading a narrative
> or watching a film or navigating an architectural site. Similarly, literary or cin-
> ematic narrative, an architectural plan and database each present a different
> model of what a world is like.[9]

A view, a navigation, or a search always results in an order—even if it is
formless, vague, or chaotic. A database, in itself, does not *present* data: it *contains* data. The data must always be in an arrangement in order to be read.

And it must be the arrangement that gives the data its meaning. What can Manovich mean when he says that a database "presents a model of what the world is like"? How would a database have meaning?

For months after the events of 9/11, many of us living in New York found ourselves in similar conversations when we ran into friends and acquaintances we had not seen since before the events. We exchanged stories of our own experiences on that day. A number of institutions, including Exit Art and *Here Is New York,* collected and exhibited 9/11 stories and images, and one can imagine a huge collection of all these texts—spoken, written, and recorded.[10] The premise behind the Spielberg Holocaust Oral History Project, the Survivors of the Shoah Visual History Foundation, is that no single person's story can give a complete or even accurate picture of a multifaceted situation. More relevant here is the impossibility of any single person's accessing and experiencing all the data, given the quantity. However, we can attribute to these databases of stories and recordings not an unknowable entirety, but an accuracy and truth that no individual story can claim. A picture of 9/11 in New York City is contained in the database of individual texts—the truth, if not the whole truth. Perhaps it is in this wide-angle view of the *Ocean of Stories* that the meaning of a database coheres. When we access the database, we are well aware that our experience is a path through it—exactly that, *one* single path. This knowledge that we are getting a partial, though ordered, view conveys the idea of a larger meaning contained in the database as a whole, a meaning that we can never comprehend.

POINT AND CLICK

The structural model that has emerged for the World Wide Web is based on the database paradigm. More and more, we expect to find all knowledge on the Internet, in one database or another, always accessible by the point-and-click technique. And this is certainly all to the good. Information travels more freely and rapidly than it ever has before. There are problems, however. The link has become the atom of interactivity, the dot-com database the model of interactive space. The idea that there might be an expressive potential to interactivity, that we might be able to use interactivity to represent our worlds, interior and exterior, in ways not before possible, has been passed by, largely unexplored. Web sites are rarely expressive in the sense that a work of art is. The Ocean of Streams of Story remains, overall, a virtual space: "virtual" here understood in the sense of unrealized. This is true because although Rushdie's *Ocean* and Manovich's "Database" are formally related, each picture emphasizes something different. The *Ocean* is primarily an interactive space, where the swimming user affects the narrative currents and their meaning, while "Database" is a model of multilinear structure. How it is accessed, as well as its expressive potential, is secondary.

With few exceptions, making a film starts with the assembly of a database of audiovisual elements. This is the "production" phase. In the editing phase a path is cut through the database. Every film project permits alternative assemblies: even in the limiting case where a script or plan is followed to the letter, some decisions have to be made in the editing room, whether they are decisions about pacing, selection of takes, or details of sound track. The principles governing these decisions depend on the nature (or genre) of the project. Contemporary entertainment films are designed to appear seamless—as if the final film is a natural object, containing all that is necessary for it and nothing else. Decisions made in the editing room of a Hollywood film are made in support of this aesthetic, and the database on which it is grounded is hidden. However, all films do not follow this aesthetic. Television, for example, tends more and more toward self-reference and revelation of its production processes.

Manovich refers to Dziga Vertov's *Man with a Movie Camera* as an example of a film whose database origins remain manifest:[11] the organization of images does not result in an undifferentiated surface, but in contrast to standard film editing, which consists in selection and ordering of previously shot material according to a preexistent script, here the process of relating shots to each other, ordering and reordering them in order to discover the hidden order of the world, constitutes the film's method.[12]

Manovich attributes *meaning* to *Man with a Movie Camera*'s underlying database, or at least to the film's acknowledgment of it. My thesis is that the database form abounds with such expressive possibilities, largely unexplored—for example, in the very fact that a database can be a region of alternative story constructs. In describing his Ocean, Rushdie refers to this potential without himself adopting it. Works of new media make the next step, by allowing multiple pathways through a single database and permitting viewer input into, and control over, how individual paths are formed, accessed, and compounded.

Perhaps a better example of a film using the database as symbolic form is Hollis Frampton's *Zorns Lemma* (1970).[13] *Zorns Lemma* is certainly more radical in its mode of representation, made at a time when notions of representation were being subjected to fundamental challenges in all the visual arts. The central section of *Zorns Lemma* grows out of a database of images sorted alphabetically. The images are of words—street signs, shop signs, advertising signboards, graffiti—almost all filmed on the streets of New York City in the rich tradition of street photography. Frampton selects one second of each image and presents these short segments on screen one after another, sorted from A to Z. One sees an alphabetic array of words, racing by so that there is just about enough time to read each one. Then the alphabet begins again, and then again, each time with a different set of words. "Now I know my ABCs, next time won't you sing with me?" After a number of repetitions, each typographic image is replaced, one per alphabetic stanza, with an image that either has a temporal development (frying an egg, peeling an orange, painting a wall) or is cyclical (the surf on a beach, jumping rope), or is a simple record of continuing human or natural processes (men working on a building site, a fire, breaking waves). Once a typographic image has been replaced, its replacement is seen in every cycle—so that after the "X" images have been substituted with an image of a raging fire, the fire image appears after "W" and before "Y" images for each cycle— until the "W" and "Y" images are themselves replaced. Although the film appears to take form as its content, in many ways it functions as a cinematographic record, a true documentary, of the ordinary moments, the design, the "look and feel" of a specific time and place: the end of the Sixties, New York City, seen through the idiosyncratic eye of an artist. At the same time, it remains the paradigm of a film that manifests its database foundation, indeed which corrals its meaning from the database it rests on. Its cinematic architecture provides its meaning.

If Manovich's conception of database as an organizational framework is the architectural foundation of interactivity, Rushdie's Story Ocean provides a vision of movement through the completed edifice. While a particular cinematic work can instantiate one path through the database of materials, an interactive work keeps many paths open, allowing the viewer to change from one to another during the experience of the work. Thus, like *Man with a Movie Camera,* or *Zorns Lemma,* a truly interactive work draws an essential component of its meaning from its database source; but while these films refer to their underlying databases, an interactive work makes its underlying database a necessary part of the viewer's experience. In the process, the epistemology of the viewing experience changes: the viewer becomes a user.

DATA

The first step in working with a database is the collection and assembly of the data. The presentation of the database involves *sorting* and *filtering* so that some of the data is shown, some omitted. Sorting determines the sequence of presentation, while filtering gives rules for admission into the set presented. In cinema, this is the process of production and the beginning of postproduction. For the film medium, these first steps of postproduction are work-printing (making a print of the film specifically for the purpose of editing) and logging the negative; for nonlinear editing it is digitizing the video into the editing application database. In both cases, often only a portion of the material goes through this process—only favored takes are printed or digitized, resulting in a database that is a subset of the "shot material" database. Editing is selecting from the database and sequencing the selections.

For a filmmaker, database thinking is liberation—one is freed to let the material breathe. It is refreshing to concede that the finished film or videotape represents only one of many possible story-streams through an image-sound database. The question of deletion and the ugly metaphor of "cutting to the bone"—an expression that is frequently heard during the editing process—ceases to cast its shadow over the editing room. To go further: for a filmmaker the term "cutting," as "editing," loses its meaning, and "sorting," "assembling," and "mapping" become more apt metaphors for the activity of composition.

New methods of construction develop alongside new production tools and devices. In the move from the splicer to the keyboard, mouse, and stylus, motion picture editors also find themselves engaging new methods of production. The concept of editing changes as the tools change. In the next sections, I would like to look more closely at both aspects of this change: at the general side by considering the metaphors that are used to describe the activities of construction under the new technologies, and at the specific side by looking at the methods used. However, the two concepts are linked, and cannot be separated, and I will not attempt to do so. It is as if two story-strands are interwoven.

The Desktop

Before being carried further by this current, I want to step back into a more general methodological observation. A number of recent theorists have suggested that a study of the metaphors that govern a particular field of activity or subculture can yield great insights into the place of the field within the larger culture. Lakoff and Johnson's *Metaphors We Live By* is one source for this discussion, and Barbara Stafford's work on "metaphorology," a term she coined, is another.[14]

In general, metaphors apply language from a more comfortable area to a less comfortable one. I have discussed elsewhere the significance of the metaphors that surround computing—from cyberspace to virtual reality, to the desktop aggregation, including files, folders, and trashcans—to say nothing of "memory," "navigation," "saving," and "retrieving."[15] The fact that ontological categories, the bureaucratic office (or more accurately, the childhood homework environment), the manipulation of small rodents, and the language of colonialism are what we draw on to describe our most recent technologies says as much about our contemporary outlook as it does about computers. Because it could have been different: sexual or more generally biological metaphors (for example) might have driven the industry, or the language of linguistics, economics, medicine, and the like.

In the process of composition using a computer, "cut and paste" is the metaphor for a working procedure that has become central: cut-and-paste—a notion, like the files, folders, trashcans, and especially, the icon-covered work surface, that is drawn from world of early education. Adult office workers rarely cut or paste; elementary schoolchildren do it every day. Why do we want to invoke the environment and activities of childhood in speaking about something as sophisticated as the computer?

Is it because we would like it to be free of sophistication? Or referring to a time before the taint of knowledge—would we like computers to give a fresh, prelapsarian start on things? The apple metaphor: the apple that you can't eat, but it grows on the Tree of (unattainable) Knowledge. We want to invoke the mystery and great distance of the core of all knowledge contained in computers, and at the same time imply that it is as easy as childhood to obtain the forbidden fruit of mastery. Click and it is yours. Knowledge, in Genesis, comes without effort, in a single bite—similarly in the childhood land of cut-and-paste, of click and download, of save and retrieve. The digital world is a world of predigested choices, and knowledge is attained by clicking off one menu going onto the next.

There is no cutting, no pasting, and no real equivalent in adult precomputer writing. One might have rearranged large paragraphs with paper, cement, and scissors, but words and more minor changes had to be done by hand. Tolstoy's wife, so the myth goes, would stay up all night to recopy her husband's handwritten manuscripts, only to be confronted with a new set of corrections (usually of the very same pages) the following evening.

The concept of *copy* or *cut-and-paste* is built into the computer as a property of the way it stores data as patterns of adjacent numerically encoded sequences, which can be moved around as blocks, affecting a rearrangement of the whole document. So it is no accident that this technique was fundamental to the computer interface right from the beginning. Early text editors had the feature of marking the beginning and end points of a passage of text, then with a keystroke command either removing it or copying it, at which point it could be inserted into another place. The feature has hardly changed. My proposal is that cut-and-paste is basic to our operations with the computer, and that its emergence has transformed the way we work with text, with images, with sounds—in a word, with concepts.

CUT

It is of interest that the metaphor of the "cut" has remained in use as the processes of production have changed—though it has shifted in meaning with these changes in process. Cutting has been widely used as a shorthand for the process of editing film or video at least since the 1930s, and now in the most recent, highly sophisticated editing software (Apple Corporation's *Final Cut Pro*), the razor-blade icon has pride of place in the "tool panel."

But why should we consider "cutting" as metaphor, when we literally cut film in order to make an edit? The point is that the term functions as a synecdoche; the incision is a minor part of the editing process, though it is used to refer to the whole process. Cutting in filmmaking is not an end in itself. In film, cutting is a prelude to splicing, and splicing is always performed with the intention of constructing meaning. Furthermore, in video editing, no actual cutting is ever done. In "linear" editing systems, we dub the sections of a master tape to another tape, and in more recent "nonlinear" systems we select them through some kind of computer interface and watch them as the computer "finds" the images and sounds and presents them in a sequence. In these digital editing software products, data is pulled from a database and goes through a lot of processing until it is decoded into images on the screen. The arrangement is orchestrated entirely by algorithm, and the act of cutting is a distant memory, even if represented in the process by an absurd tiny scissors or razor-blade icon.

When we speak about cutting in film editing, surgery is the governing image—sharp tools, ritualistic procedures, removal and replacement of dysfunctional organs, precision and expertise, and, ultimately, healing. This is opposed to cutting in butchery, carpentry, sewing, wood carving, photography, street fighting, or food preparation. Artists often like to compare themselves to scientists. We cut film in order to put it back together, to make an improvement; we also "cut" material out, remove the unwanted, or imperfect. Thirty years ago, this metaphor led to a school of documentary filmmaking, now no longer fashionable, that conceived of editing as precisely no more than paring away the inessential pieces to leave the remaining core as the final film. The "direct cinema" or cinema verité school of filmmakers held onto that view for many years, allowing the macho cameramen to have hired hands (film editors) construct their films while retaining authorial credit for themselves.

The major question about the reconstructive concept of cutting in editing is what models, paradigms, or principles of organization are going to determine the temporal architecture of the final work? What will guide the maker as he or she pastes it together? What counts as a successful construction? When do we say "that works!"? For many years the answer to this question for the documentary filmmaker has been based on the narrow conception of narrative proposed by the classical Hollywood fiction film—the introduction of characters, meeting, conflict, progressive complications, and development, concluded with an encompassing closure at the finale.

After years of film and television viewing, most of us understand this formula too well; it almost seems "natural." Thus film editors can feel as if they are chipping away at the marble block to leave the perfect statue at the end, a filmic *David* that was trapped in the stone from the beginning. However, as styles of filmmaking have changed, the metaphor has been transformed. Highly constructed music videos and television commercials, the extensive use of digital effects and computer processes in Hollywood films, the television screen as a site of multiple information streams, and, of course, the limited interactivity of the Internet have collectively rewritten what we understand as the moving image. In this territory, the idea of cut-and-paste has become central to the entire work culture, and in the process has modified the notion of cutting as film editing. Cut-and-paste is a basic strategy in "writing" with a computer, in image making, in design work, and in composing video or music—in all constructive uses of the machine.

In the most fundamental sense, when the heart of creative activity is the action of cut-and-paste, the notion of construction becomes the notion of rearrangement. And though this is not so far removed from Descartes's conception of the imagination as the faculty that recombined elements of memory, it is something of a change in the nineteenth- and twentieth-century conception of "creativity" as the possession and employment of immeasurable, indescribable talents.

There are other effects. For one, skills seem transferable from one medium to another, since the same basic techniques are used now in writing or any other composition (music, filmmaking, image making): selecting from menus of commands and processes (the most relevant involve sorting the data according to filters and criteria of inclusion), cutting, copying, and pasting. However, the first step—collecting the material and constructing the database—becomes painfully laborious, while editing takes its place as the exercise of creativity, transformed into the site of pleasure. The idea of writing as composition recedes, to be replaced by the notion of the production of a forest of ideas, with editing as the hewing of paths through the trees. This image allows the software marketers to promote their products in terms of the sensations of strength, power, and freedom they give their users. Another result of the fading of the idea of writing as structured/structuring activity is the disappearance of the idea of *one* compositional ideal as superior to others, the modernist notion of one form as "natural" or "organic" to a particular medium. For the cinema, the dominance of narrative organization is coming to an end. Structure is what emerges in the process of massaging the underlying database to produce an output. In terms of the details of production, a quantitative arrangement type, such as alphabetic, or by age or size, is equivalent to one that links the elements in a story.

Thus I would argue that the cut-and-paste approach to writing, based on the database as a model of organization, has affected not only interactive works or works on the Internet, but that it goes much further. Certainly, the most interesting contemporary works of literature are deeply influenced by concepts of multilinearity—that ideas can be seen as producing the international phenomenon that we call "postmodern fiction," including the works of Milorad Pavic, John Barth, Graham Swift, Martin Amis, Salman Rushdie, and A. S. Byatt.

EXAMPLES

Here I want to consider three works, each from a different decade, that, though "linear" in the sense that they flow through the projector or videotape player as a single strip from beginning to end, demand a split in viewers' perceptual understanding. These are narrative pieces that refuse to tell straightforward stories in straightforward ways. In the process, they challenge the split between fiction and nonfiction, suggesting that the shape into which the conventional nonfiction film bends and distorts its material is as decidedly a fiction as any action-adventure movie.

Hollis Frampton's *(nostalgia)*

Frampton was a still photographer before he became a filmmaker, and for *(nostalgia)* (1971) he drew on a stock of his still images, most of them produced as professional commissions or self-initiated art projects.[16] The filmmaker selected twelve prints (in the process implicitly indicating the existence of a much larger database of negatives and prints) and set each one on an electric hot plate, filming it as it burned away. *(nostalgia)* is assembled so that a spoken description of each photograph anticipates its appearance on screen. In fact, the spoken description accompanies the photograph that precedes the image it applies to. At first one struggles to make the words apply to the image currently on screen but soon understands this to be fruitless. Once one realizes that the description being heard is of the upcoming image, one tries to picture it mentally, while watching the strikingly beautiful image of the current on-screen print as it darkens into the shape of the electric element beneath it, erupts into flame, and finally settles into an airy corpuscle of ash, or a black crisp of charcoal, depending on the material of the print. This split in attention draws on two different senses of time, and contrasts the process of mental imaging with the process of perception. It is apt to describe this film as weaving together two story-streams, an inner and an outer, and the viewer as watching the film with the freedom to emphasize one or the other, or to give both equal weight in consciousness.

Gary Hill's *Why Do Things Get in a Muddle? (Come on Petunia)*

Hill's videotape piece also distorts time.[17] The video artist had his performers learn to speak and move backwards, videotaped this reverse acting, and then re-recorded the tape in reverse, effectively making the action appear to be normal. The viewer understands the mechanism very quickly: one finds oneself imagining what happened in front of the camera (reverse action)

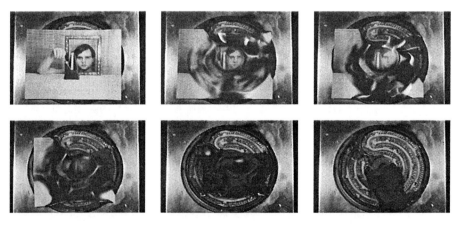

FIGURE 3.3. HOLLIS FRAMPTON, *(NOSTALGIA)*, 1971. COURTESY OF HOLLIS FRAMPTON ESTATE.

and the production process (reverting to forward action, its on-screen awk-wardness marking its reverse origin). Hill gives many clues as to how things looked and sounded when he was shooting. He often plays a few moments of the original scene, its speech an incomprehensible garble, then immedi-ately reverses it so that the voice sounds are transformed into language. As in the case of *(nostalgia)*, the viewer finds himself playing one scene in the imagination against a related scene on screen. Since the subject of the tape revolves around ideas and questions about chaos and disorder—pointing out, for example, that the production of chaos, if shown in reverse, becomes the process of arrangement, a viewer can make sense of the piece only by performing the mental act of time-reversing. One must perform a number of simultaneous acts of intellectual gymnastics to make sense of what is on screen. It is in this sense that *Why Do Things Get in a Muddle? (Come on Petunia)* (1984) is a multilinear work. At the same time, the issues raised are conceptually linked to the notion of database—for example, the notion of navigating different paths through a set of audiovisual materials, some routes yielding meaning and others not.

Dan Reeves's *Obsessive Becoming*

One of the requirements of narrative is persistence of character. There must be something that remains consistent about a character in a story—whether it is in his or her physical appearance, psychological profile, behavioral traits, or in other clues that the viewer can pick up. Without persistence of char-acter, narrative is eliminated. And we know that actors train for and work hard on the development of convincing, consistent characters. It is impor-tant that viewers recognize a character as that character reappears in a film, and when he or she changes into a werewolf or a vampire, or gets old or returns to childhood, the film has to supply a lot of indicators that it is the same person. So what happens when morphing, the process by which an image in a film is fluidly transformed into something else, is applied to images of people? Dan Reeves's experimental documentary video, *Obsessive Becoming* (1996),[18] is about how patterns of abuse within a family move from one generation to the next, and he includes an extraordinary passage where the members of his family morph into one another, one to the next, effec-tively rendering it impossible for us to separate the individual characters (the uncle, the father, the brother, the filmmaker himself), and one feels one-self as viewer in a kind of field of narrative rather than in the events of an unfolding story. This passage is the reverse side of the coin. Rather than forc-ing a split in our attention, *Obsessive Becoming* promotes unity where one

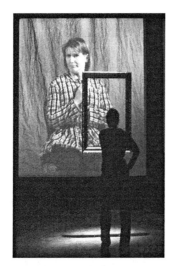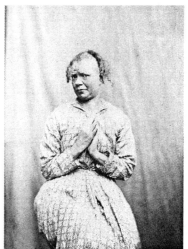

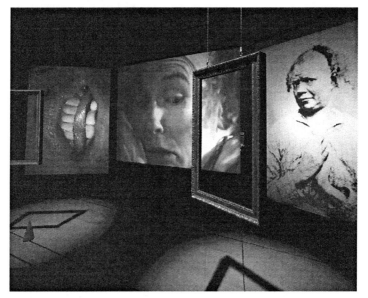

FIGURE 3.4. UPPER LEFT: GRAHAME WEINBREN, *FRAMES*, 1999.
LISA DOVE AS HUGH DIAMOND'S SUBJECT, INSTALLATION VIEW, BEALL
CENTER, IRVINE, CALIFORNIA, 2001.

FIGURE 3.5. UPPER RIGHT: HUGH DIAMOND, "INSANITY SUPERVENING
ON HABITS OF INTEMPERANCE," 1850S. COURTESY OF THE ROYAL
SOCIETY OF MEDICINE, LONDON.

FIGURE 3.6. BELOW: GRAHAME WEINBREN, *FRAMES*, 1999.
INSTALLATION VIEW, NTT INTERCOMMUNICATIONS CENTER, TOKYO.
PHOTOGRAPH BY TAKASHI OTAKA.

would expect distinction, forming new characters. Our work as viewers is to try—unsuccessfully—to separate what the filmmaker has combined. Thus, paradoxically Reeves's superlinearity promotes a version of multilinearity.

I end these short examples with a description of my own artistic contribution to these issues only because, as I always emphasize in my writing, I am primarily a practitioner and not a theorist, and my ideas are always an outgrowth of my practice. Only by producing works do I pin down the inchoate thoughts that blossom into the kinds of proposal I have made in this essay. Consequently, no piece of writing of mine is complete without a discussion of the works that stand behind and before it. In the four interactive cinema works I have completed, and the one I am currently constructing, I have attempted to use the viewer's capacity to affect the flow of images on screen as a means of indicating the sea of available material behind the screen.

Frames was produced for the 1999 Biennale of the NTT InterCommunications Center, a new media museum in Japan.[19] It is based on the first photographs made in a mental asylum, which were produced by Hugh Diamond between about 1847 and 1852.[20] I selected four Diamond images and cast four actors. In the piece, the actors transform themselves into the characters portrayed. Viewers intervene in the process by pointing through suspended empty gold picture frames at two projected images. The gold frames, which use a simple sensor technology, are a few feet in front of the projection screens. If the viewer can find the "rhythm" of the piece, he or she will succeed in bringing the character in the photograph to life, and the viewer will move from the side screen to the center screen, where he or she looks out of a window or into a mirror. Or, if there is another fully formed character produced by another viewer, the two characters might meet and interact. Another element of the piece that the viewer can find by pointing through the frames is a series of verbal descriptions of the pathologies of the patients, descriptions written by Diamond's colleague, John Connolly. Connolly saw himself and Diamond as together inventing a new diagnostic science based in photography. They saw the images of the patients as portraits without artifice, without the imposition of an artistic sensibility, given the indexical nature of photographic reproduction. Diamond and Connolly, in other words, thought of the photograph as *true* in a way that other techniques of portraiture could not be. Based on this assumption, Connolly analyzed the body position, the gestures, the facial expressions, and the bearings of the unfortunate men and women in Diamond's photographs, extracting from these features a speculative diagnosis of the patient's condition.[21]

This is, however, an odd science. The melancholic woman sits in a classical melancholy pose, hands pressed together, head downcast. The hysteric is twisted away from the camera, wrought with tension, her hands folded in an attitude of prayer. It is clear that the photographer asked his terrified patients to sit in certain ways. He *posed* his subjects to represent their condition, exactly as the fashion photographer poses models (for different, but not unrelated, ends). In my view, all photography is subject to this same ideological circularity. It is never an unbiased portrait of nature-in-the-raw. The colors are preselected by Kodak, Agfa, or Fuji, and the lens distortions (or lacks thereof) are produced by Zeiss—while the photographer crops reality to an arbitrary stoppage of the border, to say nothing of the power relations between photographer and subject, which form the underbelly of every photograph. In the Diamond/Connolly collaboration, the ideologies float, transparently close to the surface.

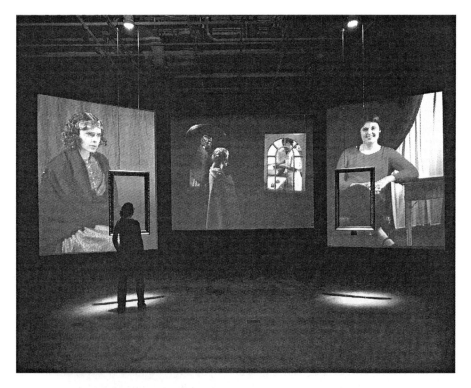

FIGURE 3.7. GRAHAME WEINBREN, *FRAMES*, 1999. INSTALLATION VIEW, BEALL CENTER, IRVINE, CALIFORNIA, 2001.

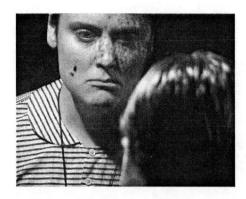

FIGURE 3.8.
GRAHAME WEINBREN.

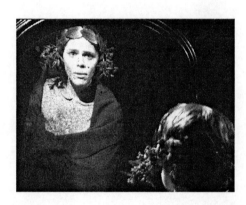

FIGURE 3.9.
CAROLYN CORBETT AS
HUGH DIAMOND'S SUBJECT.

FIGURE 3.10.
JENNIFER TIMM AS
HUGH DIAMOND'S SUBJECT.

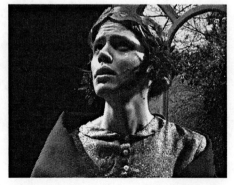

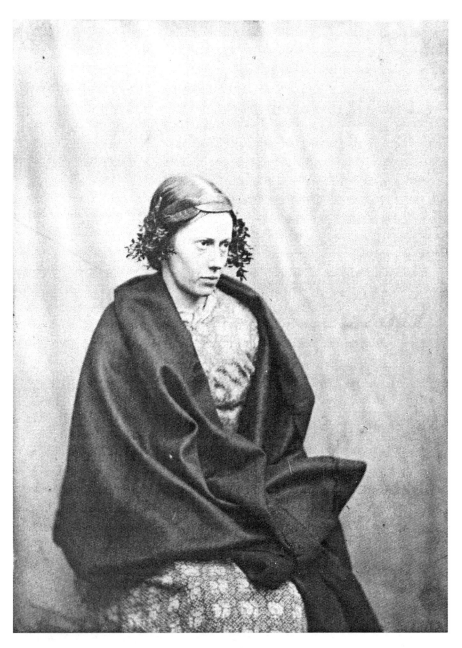

FIGURE 3.11. HUGH DIAMOND, PHOTOGRAPH OF PATIENT AT SPRINGFIELD, THE SURREY COUNTY LUNATIC ASYLUM, 1850S. COURTESY OF THE ROYAL SOCIETY OF MEDICINE, LONDON.

Frames brings together a database of images of actors in various degrees of character, with Connolly's descriptions, Diamond's photographs, and a sizable series of traveling shots up and down gloomy industrial staircases leading nowhere, and keeps it all organized by a simple set of navigational rules for moving between these elements. By this technique I hope to have raised these issues viscerally. The viewer becomes the photographer, shaping the portrait to match his or her vision of the (in his eyes) unfortunate subject, by forcing the victim to bend and twist and . . . pose for her portrait.

CHANGE

Let me end this essay by making a few tentative suggestions. First, I will try to situate or contextualize the discussion and then to make a small general proposal. Many people are engaged in these kinds of discussion, and we are all trying first to document and describe, then to understand, a shift that is taking place under our feet: a change in how we represent, communicate, conceive ourselves and others. In short, a change in what it is to be human. These are big, urgent issues. I have looked at a few instances of how image-sound streams are reorganized in time. One of the things I'd like to suggest

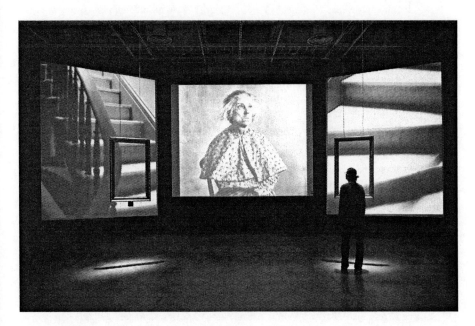

FIGURE 3.12. GRAHAME WEINBREN, *FRAMES*, 1999. INSTALLATION VIEW, BEALL CENTER, IRVINE, CALIFORNIA, 2001.

is that the idea of structure carrying meaning is now much more obvious to us than it was; it is a component of our experience of media. It is easy for us to see that the shape of narrative is something imposed on reality, something that distorts reality and produces false expectations about experience. There is no "happily ever after." To wish for such a thing is to wish for something that is neither real nor virtual, and the stories that end with a monolithic closure are lies just as the ideologies that suggest perpetual progress and natural improvements over time are false ideologies. Change is the only thing we can be sure of. We all know this now, but it was not easy to know thirty years ago. One of the evidences of these now-obvious truths is that the distinction between documentary and fiction is disappearing. A documentary, even if none of the scenes are "staged," presents a false picture if it is fitted together as a neat linear temporal object. Only when we can be made aware of the database that underlies it, and the fact that the film cuts a path of one kind or another through this database, do we begin to approach a way of representing ourselves that has some link to the way we are.

NOTES

1. Salman Rushdie, *Haroun and the Sea of Stories* (New York: Granta Books in association with Viking Penguin, 1990), 71–72.

2. *The Kathā Sarat Sāgara,* vols. 1–2, translated from the original Sanskrit by C. H. Tawney, 3rd ed. (New Delhi: Munshiram Manoharlal Publishers, 1992).

3. Manovich's position is fully developed in *The Language of New Media* (Cambridge: Mass.: MIT Press, 2002), and his articles are available on his Web site: http://www .manovich.net/texts_00.htm.

4. Rushdie, *Sea of Stories,* 71–72.

5. Ibid., 72.

6. Manovich, *The Language of New Media,* 31.

7. Ibid., 32.

8. Mieke Bal, *Narratology: Introduction to the Theory of Narrative* (Toronto: University of Toronto Press, 1997), 5–7 and 79.

9. Lev Manovich, "Database as Symbolic Form," *Millennium Film Journal* 34 (Fall 1999): 24.

10. See http://www.exitart.org/ and http://hereisnewyork.org/ (accessed September 2004).

11. Dziga Vertov, *Man with a Movie Camera* (1926, black-and-white).

12. Manovich, "Database as Symbolic Form," 42.

13. Hollis Frampton, *Zorns Lemma* (1970).

14. George Lakoff and Mark Johnson, *Metaphors We Live By* (Chicago: University of Chicago Press, 1980). Barbara Maria Stafford, *Visual Analogy: Consciousness as the Art of Connecting* (Cambridge, Mass.: MIT Press, 1999).

15. Grahame Weinbren, "The PC Is a Penguin," in *Bild Medien Kunst,* ed. Yvonne

Spielman and Gundolf Winter (Munich: Wilhelm Fink, 1999). This is printed in English even though the book title is in German.

16. Hollis Frampton, *(nostalgia)* (1971, black-and-white, sound, 36 minutes).

17. Gary Hill, *Why Do Things Get in a Muddle? (Come on Petunia)* (1984, video, color, sound, 33:09 minutes).

18. Dan Reeves, *Obsessive Becoming* (1996), video.

19. Grahame Weinbren, *Frames* (1999), interactive cinema installation (initial installation at NTT/ICC, Tokyo, 1999); catalogue published by NTT Publishing Company, Tokyo, 1999; subsequent installations at the Beall Center, Irvine, California (2001), and the Kitchen Center, New York (2003–4). See http://www.grahameweinbren.net/frames/ Frames@Kitchen_Nov2002.html.

20. This is a very early project; the invention of photography was announced in 1839.

21. Adrienne Burrows and Iwan Schumacher, *Portraits of the Insane: The Case of Dr. Diamond* (New York: Quartet Books, 1990), 137–38 and 143.

4. WAITING FOR THE WORLD TO EXPLODE: HOW DATA CONVERT INTO A NOVEL

NORMAN M. KLEIN

Our civilization has reshaped data into a form of storytelling. In the eras of the Enlightenment (1680–1820), data increasingly exemplified the scientific process. They revealed natural law. Rarely do data turn into a novel. Since 1895, it is nearly impossible to cite a narrative film (other than documentaries) dominated by laundry lists and asteroid belts of data. Soviet factography of the 1920s may be the rare exception. By 2004, however, data have been recast as a form of storytelling—in scripted spaces, in computer games, on the Internet, in mapping. This transition, this anomaly, suggests other changes, particularly the death of dramatic structure, as it has been faithfully represented on film and in literature, or at least the end of a narrative culture dominated by drama and melodrama.

Historians will remember this emergence of data story as part of a vast transformation, like continental plates cracking the earth. But at first, for many people still employed in the "developed" world or perhaps in a state of denial (speaking for myself as well), the shocks arrived rather peacefully—on computer and television screens. Data poison seemed like a date movie about catastrophe, a dark city built by alien data, a Tyrell tower that resembles a mother board, a Borgesian library turned gothic, a matrix, a bad borg fighting a good cyborg, both emotionally blank, nothing but data inside their heads. The Cold War ended. We realize now, by comparison, that the 1980s and 1990s were perversely quiet in the "West." In other words, they seemed more like an ergonomic hum compared to the noxious shock waves of steel and gas that launched industrialization after 1860.

Since 9/11, the 1990s latte pause has ended, even for the comfortable middle class, much less for the anxious artist class. Now all social classes in the United States realize that a future dominated by data systems might prove just as bloody and ironic as the twentieth century. The noisy era of data storytelling has begun. And it aches.

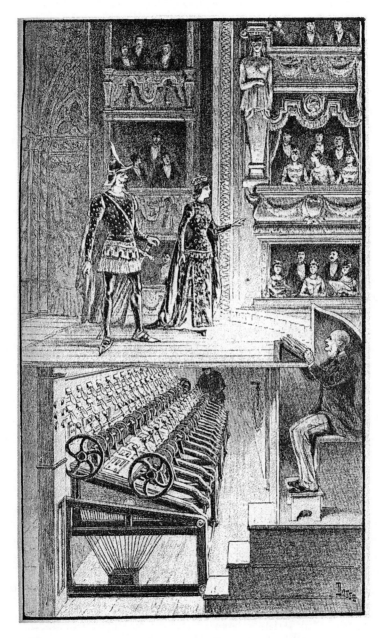

FIGURE 4.1. DATABASE OPERA FANTASY, PARIS OPERA, 1889.

The unease of data today (to reinforce terrorism, surveillance, military adventurism) brings serious challenges for the media arts. How should we adapt "data-driven" story to our tense condition as of 2007? Gloomy neo-noir will not do. The 1980s cyberpunk, neo-conceits will not take us far. No point rescripting graphic novels or further Americanizing animé. We have seen enough stories about jacking up false memories or morphing into alien data creatures. Is there a body type that Marvel Comics has missed? As an admirer of all this, but still a middle-aged adult, I am forced to wonder what must be developed next, other than gaming and hyperbolic wow. Should we try to walk arms akimbo, be cool inside a 1990s hotel? After hours at the gym, we stare blankly by the elevator, as if we were modeling underwear for a slick magazine. Or should we further datafy Christ? With great digital effects, think of how much more bleeding and scourging is possible, on the way to crucifixion (the *fictio* of the Cross). Of course, slick gore is not that different from slick graphic design. There is little point advancing our skills in data CG special-effects bloodletting. Still, the mood across America is grim. Blood as data is indeed a dark joke on us.

We probably need story forms a bit closer to home, at least home in the United States—data stories closer to our actual lives. That does not mean digitized social realism. It should drift closer to stream-of-consciousness fiction, to what Virginia Woolf called "digging caves behind characters." Most of all, a new strategy for data story points toward a new beginning for all forms of narrative, like the origins of the novel in 1740, or the historical novel in 1820, or stream of consciousness by 1910. I am reminded of Nietzsche's theory of Apollo as the sculptor who gave shape to Dionysian madness. "Story" is a sculpting of madness. But what is the madness of data in our culture?

This new direction for data/story should stand in for the severe decline of the public sector since 1970, even for the declining influence of the nation-state. Data, through media, must turn into a form of erasure, not blood-curdling realism. The photograph and the map—as data—hide as much as they reveal. In its quietude (clacking in a quiet room), data monumentalizes exclusion. It reassures us that while we may be manipulated by unseen forces, we can pretend that the global program is user-friendly. Like our daily lives today, data are diffuse and highly centralized. They even reenact human weakness. Like humans, data can forget and be corrupted. Other than that, it is an alien species.

The friendlier the data feel, the farther from control we actually are. Data remind us that we are being colonized by our own economy, outsourced and psychologically invaded. No wonder data are often represented as alien intelligence. They are the ultimate unreliable narrator. They speak any truth that fits the program.

My computer starts to beep with annoyance. A banner goes up. It demands an apology. I devote a page to praising data—as entertaining and efficient. Then, I erase and corrupt the file.

Back again.

DATA AS ABSENCE

Story is generally organized through absence. Put another way, absence is presence. That seems very much at odds with computer data. But think of the problem this way: absence is a kind of aperture. In *Bleeding Through,* I used Baudelaire as my model for aperture—Baudelairean correspondence, images that do not quite match but generate potential absence.[1] Photos should not illustrate. They should reveal the gap. Photography is a mode of erasure anyway; it camouflages while it reveals, in cinema, even in the common photograph. So one enters a world much the way James Joyce or Virginia Woolf invites us to enter.

I rummage through my archive room after the rainy season, wondering if it is slipping down my hilly backyard, like a boat barely tethered to the dock. I fill a crate with references to "absence" from some of my literary heroes.

In the short story "An Unwritten Novel," Virginia Woolf uses absence as a furtive trick, a glimpse by the writer: "Whether you did, or what you did, I don't mind; it is not the thing I want. The draper's window looped with violet—that'll do; a little cheap perhaps, a little commonplace—since one has a choice of crimes, but then so many (let me peep across again—still sleeping, or pretending to sleep)."[2] In the opening to *Mademoiselle de Maupin* (1837), Théophile Gautier describes the absence between "circumstance" and desire: "This life, although I have in appearance accepted it, is scarcely made for me, or at least is very far from resembling the existence of which I dream, and feel myself designed."[3]

I gather phrases like "the waves of lucidity . . . made scarce by the rain," in Gabriel García Márquez's *One Hundred Years of Solitude,*[4] or the ripeness of life moments from decay (as in the French for still life, *mort vivant*) in Proust's descriptions of art and fragrance in *The Guermantes Way.* Or Louis Aragon's surrealist vision of shops and workers at the arcades of Paris (*Paris Peasant,* 1926). Or Laurence Sterne attempting to make a straight line that maps his Uncle Toby's stories. Or Edgar Allan Poe designing another literary hoax.

In historical models, absence is the gap between a fact and a collective lie, whether by the historian (to make gaps fit) or a cultural moment. In architecture, absence is the space where unfinish is revealed, the *détournement*, essentially the fissure that reveals traces of old mistakes, half-completed projects, and erasures. It is the void between data and plot points.

In time lines, an absence is what cannot fit on the path. In a map, absence is what cannot be classified. In a film, absence can be what lay just outside the frame, or just before the action begins.

A ruin embraces the absence of the original act. We have only the remains of that act, what was *not* consumed by the moment.

In *Bleeding Through,* various absent spaces combine: between memory and the city, between Molly's (the principal character's) life and rumors that she killed her husband, as well as absent movie locations where crime films were shot near her house in Los Angeles, and so on. In fact, each of these blank spaces is made to support the structure. That is, each one supports the broader engineering of absences into a rhythm like a story—into apertures precisely assigned, with images that bleed through into each other, or can flash into a film, or follow rhythms set up through keywords. Thus mental paces between photos, films, and texts rhythmically operate as story.

This is a familiar strategy. Consider that absence is what the medium (in this case a computer) cannot deliver. Thus the novel is blind, as is music. Film is autistic, cannot see beyond its apparatus. And so on: each medium is magnificently endowed with absence. And that very missing touch or sight gives enormous power to the form. The visual that is not on the page acts as an occult process in literature. For example (from a text so absent that it is impossible to footnote):

> He saw a thousand men die every day of his life, but simply walked to work as quietly as he could, as if someone among the dying—in his mind's eye—might notice him, and take revenge. How this hallucination took him over no one knows, not even his wife and family, and surely no one at work. He worked a peaceful thirty years there, every day ten minutes late, then sitting very formally, with an even smile, at his desk; while inside, vividly enjoying, like Sardanapolis, how a thousand men can die at once. But now, of course, the price of his silence has struck us all very hard.[5]

Speaking with the deepest admiration, practically all my literary heroes were masters of that kind of silence, as were the great composers, perhaps even the men who wrote the New Testament. Those senses that are conspicuously absent from the medium suggest a secret place—the hidden impulse, the hidden thought. This buried place lends presence to film story, or any story.

Data are also filled with an unmistakable absence. Data cannot "conclude" a story; they cannot deliver a "suspense" ending, like a murder mystery—not in the traditional way (and I am not convinced that interactively choosing your own adventure solves this problem, even with high-resolution effects). Data are part of a process *without* an arc that requires a dramatic ending. Instead, they proceed by insinuation, by involution—toward a *beginning,* toward an *aporia* (the road without a name). That kind of journey can be extremely charming, like "a making-of" that is so massive that it does not even require a movie.

Thus, for *Bleeding Through,* we authored a story with an ending in the first tier, as an interactive visual twenty-six-minute radio "drama," but with only the skeleton of the story intact (seven chapters out of a possible thirty). Even the "dramatic" section is meant to play ironically with dramatic story (tease through absence), and still leave key plot points absent where they needed to be absent. In the rest of the DVD-ROM, the reader/user can harvest what is missing, set inside Tiers Two and Three.

Nothing is more vivid than what can *only* be imagined in the mind's eye. By the end of *Bleeding Through,* hopefully these absences (buried among 1,100 assets, 800 photos, 35 films, 250 news clippings, and more) become so charming that the reader begins to think like the author. The reader is inhabited by the potential narrative—like an author about to tell the story. One concludes *Bleeding Through* ready to begin, rather than at the third act, the final scene. That pleasure emerges out of the blindness in data. You jump through the assets, with the sense that someone (perhaps you) has destroyed the evidence. You drift with a purpose.

In data narratives, like pattern writing from the eighteenth century, digression takes you past absences on behalf of a rhythm like daily life. As Henry Fielding warned his readers in *Tom Jones,* "I think proper before we proceed any further together, to acquaint thee that I intend to digress, through this whole story as often as I see occasion."[6]

In *The Vatican to Vegas,* I write about special effects and the way we walk through scripted spaces as a mode of engineered absence. Then I point out that scripted space is occluded, to make us digress. No wonder, then, that digression is a form of Baroque storytelling. And of course, we find suddenly Baroque forms returning to our culture as well, in computer searches, games, hyperlinking, in casinos, various labyrinth forms—in database digressions as gambling, as mock adventures, as ludic pleasure.

Indeed, Fielding understood digression in much the same way, as an architectural journey through what Lev Manovich calls "navigable spaces."[7] Data are a mode of picaresque story, where clues to the unmappable are gathered on the road, clues that show us the rhythm of material culture, and mysteries left unsolved, but acutely present, like a surprise lingering after you leave. Indeed, that has a reality of its own. Very rarely does our life run like a well-tuned dramatic engine, telling its story like a drumbeat. Usually we live by digressions, surprises, misapprehensions, slippages in memory. Rarely do we act on our immediate desire. But we are filled, even melodramatic and gloomy about the remnants of acts not completed.

That slippage is ultimately how data convert into a novel. Data are made user-friendly as a scripted space that takes us on a pilgrimage filled with absences, with the ephemera that give energy to our lives—past our foibles, our mistakes, our petty grievances, our moments of shock—even occasions when we finally take charge of the problem. It is not that we are a desultory species; it is that we are too consumed by our greed, by our hunger and rages, even by our desire to redeem ourselves.

We are overwhelmed by a global culture that erodes our economic and cultural options. Increasingly, this erosion leaves a very slender place for a novel. We have trouble pausing in the old stream-of-consciousness mode, to locate "moments of being," silences. After all, very rarely do we act dramatically—on cue, as we might in a dramatic story. More often we float in fretful digressions between the deadlines of our life. And those digressions are considered the goal of good living, to be home, on holiday, "hanging out," not of nightmarish dramatic conflict.

Data then can be an honest accounting of what we fail to do, or how we hide. It is also an ideal system for "layering" techniques (for lying and hiding), where one action or object erases another. Think of layers behind facades, behind smiles, behind fears, behind kindness, behind hate. Through layers of unfinish, we locate the drama that is never seen (that is why we love to read novels; they pretend to peel away these layers). Indeed, layers are morphs (two layers merging inside the same space), or psycho-geographies (the membranes of desire and memory that affect how we navigate a space). Layers are roads reinvented backwards, through deconstruction. They are mistakes by a character you never meet that haunt a story, but never enter the plot directly.

Indeed, data are very much like Joyce's Dublin, layer upon layer traversed by Blum, a city built upon itself, like Vienna literally having a medieval city underneath it. Thus Molly, my lead character in *Bleeding Through*, is a Molly who never blooms, living inside a pattern novel, a picaresque, a stream of evidence. She was patient; that was her genius. But are we?

We wait for the world to explode. The data gather. The president gives a press conference. He recites data proving that we must act before it is too late. The data are nonsense, fiction. The layers of madness that these fictions generate require a massive sculptural performance that dominates the media for weeks. Meanwhile, the economy teeters on the brink, but never passes through, like a fever patient who never recovers, but never collapses. New economic data are released. They don't fit anyone's life that you know. Are we about to hit a wall of some kind? What are they hiding? The absence of the immediate future haunts us. Once again we wait for the world to explode. The weekend is over. The night slips into absence.

Another way to say all this? The computer changes the role of the reader, as in a scripted space. In new forms of data story, the reader imagines herself as a central character. The reader identifies with the first line not yet written, with the making of a story—much more than with the "ending," which can be contrived anyway. Or as Bertolt Brecht called it, plot points as sausage links.

Simply put, data story on the computer is a picaresque filled with aphorisms, with pieces of narrative that never "fill in the blanks." Meanwhile, the reader gets immersed in all this "atmospheric" data. Next, the reader evolves pleasantly into the author. Finally, instead of an ending, the reader imagines herself about to start writing—like the player adding a new "mod."

The aphorism announces what is absent about data. It records noise too far away to hear entirely. It is a page partially corrupted. When data absence forces you to listen, nothing is ever entirely silent.

NOTES

1. Norman M. Klein, *Bleeding Through: Layers of Los Angeles, 1920–86*, co-directed by Norman Klein, Rosemary Comella, and Andreas Kratky (Los Angeles: Labyrinth Project at the Annenberg Center, USC, and ZKM in Karlsruhe, Germany, 2003).

2. Virginia Woolf, "An Unwritten Novel," in *A Haunted House and Other Tales* (New York: Harcourt Brace Jovanovich, 1972), 13.

3. An old translation, from a downtown Los Angeles Union Rescue Mission sixty years ago, last taken out in 1978 (third paragraph of the first chapter): Théophile Gautier, *Mademoiselle de Maupin*, in *The Works of Théophile Gautier, in one volume* (Rosslyn, N.Y.: Black's Readers Service Company, n.d.), 371.

4. Gabriel García Márquez, *One Hundred Years of Solitude*, trans. Gregory Rabassa (New York: HarperCollins, 1970), 339.

5. In honor of lost data that exist without footnotes, let us imagine that the book containing this quote was left in an airplane in 1961 and almost recovered when it was used to prop up a table in a restaurant in Queens, New York.

6. Henry Fielding, *Tom Jones, The History of a Foundling*, Authoritative Edition (1749–50), trans. Sheridan Baker (New York: W. W. Norton, 1973), 28.

7. Lev Manovich, *The Language of New Media* (Cambridge: MIT Press, 2001), part 5.

5. The Database as System and Cultural Form: Anatomies of Cultural Narratives

CHRISTIANE PAUL

The term "database aesthetics" has become a catchword of the digital realm and poses interesting semantic questions that seem to outline the field of research and art relating to databases itself. What exactly do we mean by "database aesthetics"? In discourse on digital art, the term is frequently used to describe the aesthetic principles applied in imposing the logic of the database to any type of information, filtering data collections, and visualizing data. In that sense, database aesthetics often becomes a conceptual potential and cultural form—a way of revealing (visual) patterns of knowledge, beliefs, and social behavior. The term is seldom used to refer to the aesthetics of the database as structure itself, although it certainly implies that meaning and the structure of a database is inherently connected to the results produced by the filtering of the data contained in it and the nature of its visualization.

DATABASE AS SYSTEM

While a database is now commonly understood as a computerized record-keeping system, it is essentially a structured collection of data that stands in the tradition of "data containers" such as a book, a library, an archive, or Wunderkammer. Every "container" of information ultimately constitutes a dataspace and information architecture of its own, even though its characteristics are quite different from the virtual, dynamic dataspace. As Selena Sol points out in "Introduction to Databases for the Web," the "data store-houses" of the oral cultures of the past were the elders who would pass down information from generation to generation: "Apparently, and according to vast archeological data, campfires were used (like command-line middleware) by the younger members of the community to access the information stored in the minds of the elders using API's such as public *String TellUs-AboutTheTimeWhen(String s)*."[1]

What distinguishes digital databases from their analog predecessors is their inherent possibility for the retrieval and filtering of data in multiple ways. Databases can be distinguished according to different "data models"— that is, data containers and the ways in which data are stored in and retrieved from them. Among the most common data models (some of them subsets of others and sometimes used in combination) are:

- *Hierarchical Databases,* which arrange the data in hierarchies similar to a tree structure with parent/child relationships.
- *Network Databases,* which are still close to the hierarchical model but use "sets" to establish a hierarchy that allows children to have more than one parent and thus establishes many-to-many relationships.
- *Relational Databases,* the most common form, are based on the research of Dr. E. F. Codd at IBM in the late 1960s and rely on the concept of tables (so-called relations) that store all data. Contrary to hierarchical or network databases, relational ones do not require a close understanding of how exactly information within the database is structured since each table can be identified by a unique name that can be called and found by the database.
- *Client/Server Databases,* which come in various forms and allow multiple "clients" to remotely and simultaneously access and retrieve information from a database server around the clock.
- *Object-Oriented Databases,* which are designed to work well with object-oriented programming languages (such Java and C++) and make entries (objects) in the database appear as programming language objects in one or more languages.

The data container itself is not by nature beautiful, but rather seems to be characterized by non- or anti-aesthetics: it consists of tables and structures that house discrete units that in themselves carry limited meaning but have the potential for multiple relational connections. Databases, however, do not consist of only the data container. A database essentially is a system that comprises the hardware that stores the data: the software that allows for housing the data in its respective container and for retrieving, filtering, and changing it, as well as the users who add a further level in understanding the data as information.

Data models always contain a layer of mathematical algorithms and concepts. There is no digital art or new media object in the broadest sense that does not have a layer of code and algorithms, even if its physical and visual manifestation distracts from this underlying layer. Any visual, digital image—from print to video—has ultimately been produced by instructions and the software that was used to create or manipulate it. The digital medium is not by nature visual but always consists of a "back end" of algorithms and data sets that remain hidden and a visible "front end" that is experienced by the viewer/user, the latter being produced by the former. The results can range from complex visuals to very abstract communication processes. Some digital art is predominantly visual; other works are more focused on raw data and the database model. As Lev Manovich puts it, any new media object consists of one or more interfaces to a database of multimedia material, even if it does not explicitly point to its roots in a database.[2] The common understanding of "database aesthetics" seems to be more focused on the operations on the "front end"—the concept of the algorithms, its visual manifestations, and cultural implications—rather than the "back end" of the data container and its structure.

One of the inherent characteristics of digital art is the tension between the mostly linear and hierarchical structure of databases (or the Internet's territory as a multitude of servers with hierarchical directories) and instructions, on the one hand, and, on the other, the seemingly infinite possibilities for reproducing and reconfiguring the information contained within these structures. This tension between the data structure/stream and the visual form it can take is perfectly captured by the Radical Software Group's project *Carnivore* (2001–present).[3] The project is inspired by the software DCS1000 (nicknamed "Carnivore"), which is used by the FBI to perform electronic wiretaps and search for certain "suspicious" keywords via packet sniffing. While the Carnivore Server performs packet sniffing on a specific local area network and serves the resulting data stream, the "client" applications created by numerous artists interpret the data in visual ways. At the core of the *Carnivore* project are the unlimited possibilities of visualizing the server's data stream in a collaborative, "open source" way—allowing its users to create maps of the data stream that often remain detached from or obscure the original data source. Apart from illustrating the relationship between the back end of data and the visual front end, *Carnivore* also turns the client-server relationship of data into a metaphor for artistic creation.

The hidden or protected back end of any project—be it a database or code—always makes an inherently political statement about access and its control, which is perfectly captured by the implications of client-server relationships. In this context, a peer-to-peer as opposed to a client-server relationship becomes a philosophical as well as political issue. Peer to peer is the promise of liberation from the server. A project explicitly addressing the issue of server access is *life_sharing* by the Italian artists at www .0100101110101101.org, whose work generally focuses on data access, document, and archiving models as well as the political, cultural, and commercial aspects of the network. With *life_sharing* (2001), 0100101110101101 turned their Web site into public property. The project consists of the organization's hard disk, published in its entirety on the Web (although in HTML format and not by providing anybody with access to the organization's server) and thus reproducible. The philosophy of free data and information exchange is also the driving force behind the open source (and "Copyleft") movement, which promotes unrestricted redistribution and modification of source code, provided that all copies and derivatives retain the same permissions.

DATABASE AS META-NARRATIVE AND CULTURAL FORM

The aesthetics of a database are inherently relational, be it on the level of potential (the data container being its carrier) or the actual relationships established by the software component. Database aesthetics suggest the

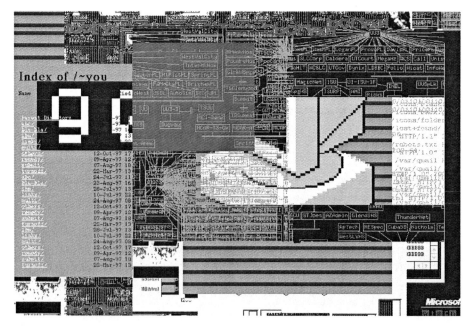

FIGURE 5.1. SCREEN SHOT FROM 0100101110101101.ORG'S LIFE_SHARING.

possibilities of tracing process—individual, cultural, communicative—in its various forms. The understanding of a database as the underlying principle and structure of any new media object delineates a broad field that includes anything from a network such as the Internet (as one gigantic database) to a particular data set.

Since the beginnings of the Internet, numerous art projects, most notably *WebStalker* and *netomat*™,[4] have questioned the conventions of exploring the Web through browsers such as Netscape and Internet Explorer, which function as portals to predesigned Web sites that are ultimately based on the page model of the printed book (or even the ancient format of the scroll). IOD's *WebStalker* single-handedly established the "medium" of alternative browsers by expanding the functionality of existing browsers in an aesthetic and creative form that revealed the Internet"s "database architecture" in a new way. In his essay "Visceral Facades: Taking Matta-Clark's Crowbar to Software,"[5] IOD's Matthew Fuller establishes a connection between the *WebStalker*'s approach to information architecture and American artist Gordon Matta-Clark's technique of literally "splitting" the existing architecture of buildings, an application of formal procedures that would result in a revelation of structural properties. Maciej Wisniewski's *netomat*™ (1999–present) abandoned the page format of traditional browsers and treats the Internet as one large database of files. Retrieving text, images, and audio in response to queries and flowing them simultaneously onto the screen without regard to the display design of the data source, *netomat*™ reveals how the ever-expanding network interprets and reinterprets cultural concepts and themes and takes visitors for a ride into the Internet's "subconscious." Both of the projects are characterized by their own distinctive "database aesthetics," which, in both cases, consist of a reconfiguration of the interface and front end through which we experience the files in the Internet's "database."

If any new media object constitutes one or more interfaces to a database of multimedia material, it ultimately always is a visualization of data, be it a "closed" database with a preconfigured, limited amount of materials or an open one that organizes real-time data flux. The visualization and "dynamic mapping" of real-time data streams has become a broad area of inquiry in digital art, and quite often several projects visualize a similar data set in distinctly different ways. Martin Wattenberg's *Map of the Market,* Nancy Paterson's *Stock Market Skirt,* Lynn Hershman's *Synthia,* and John Klima's *ecosystm,* for example, provide four radically different interfaces for understanding the stock market or financial data.[6] Each of the visualizations creates its own distinctive contextual framework for perceiving the data flux—an indication of how much "database aesthetics" depend on the algorithmic interpretation of data.

Apart from the visualizations of data sets in general, which often do not explicitly reveal the database as an underlying structure, a multitude of projects has been tracing cultural subtexts by means of arranging information in a database that then become a means of revealing meta-narratives about cultural values and conventions. As Lev Manovich puts it, "Database and narrative are natural enemies. Competing for the same territory of human culture, each claims an exclusive right to make meaning out of the world."[7] According to Manovich, the database presents the world as a list of items that it refuses to order (which is certainly true on the level of the data container), while a narrative requires a protagonist and narrator, a text and story, and cause-and-effect relationships for seemingly unordered events. This is not meant to say that database and narrative are mutually exclusive

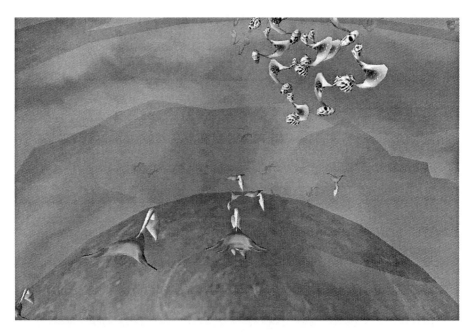

FIGURE 5.2. SCREEN SHOT FROM JOHN KLIMA, *ECOSYSTM*. *ECOSYSTM* DEPICTS GLOBAL CURRENCY DATA IN A 3D ENVIRONMENTAL SIMULATION, WHERE THE POPULATION AND BEHAVIOR OF FLOCKS OF INSECTLIKE "BIRDS" (REPRESENTING COUNTRIES' CURRENCIES) ARE DETERMINED, RESPECTIVELY, BY THE CURRENCY'S VALUE AGAINST THE DOLLAR AND ITS DAILY/YEARLY VOLATILITY.

forms. Computer games, for example, are often narratives whose constituent elements are still organized in a form of database structure. An interactive narrative or hypernarrative can be understood as "the sum of multiple
trajectories to a database."[8] While interactive and open to a reshuffling of
their constituent elements, these games and hypertexts still emphasize elements of traditional narrative over a database structure, which may support
a narrative but does not naturally lend itself to generating one. However,
databases do lend themselves to a categorization of information and narratives that can then be filtered to create meta-narratives about the construction and cultural specifics of the original material.

Art projects frequently apply the principles and logic of the database to
existing, often originally analog information—ranging from a book to movies, television series, and postcards—to reveal relationships that remain unseen in the original format. W. Bradford Paley's *TextArc* (2002),[9] for example,
treats the book—itself a data container—as a database and arranges it in
its smallest units, words, and lines that can be filtered according to various
principles. The texts processed by the project are publicly available through
the Gutenberg library. *TextArc* is a visual model that represents an entire
text on a single page. The text appears as a concentric spiral on the screen,
with each of its lines drawn in a tiny, illegible font size around the outside.
In a second spiral, each word is represented in a more readable size, and a
pool of words appearing in the middle of the spirals forms the main organizing structure. Menus allow users to turn each word contained in the pool
"on" or "off" and thus make it visible or invisible. In the central pool, words
that appear more than once are located at the average position in which
they are found in the spirals' text and frequently used words appear brighter,
standing out from the background. If users select words, thin lines appear
and connect the word to its positions in the text. A text-view window can
show every line that uses the word, and a reading function allows the text
"to read itself" by drawing a constantly moving line between the words as
they appear in sequence. Part of *TextArc*'s beauty derives from the fact that
the project creates a new form of data container and spatial model for the
book on the visual front end. The representation of a novel's entire contents
and its structural elements on a single page constitutes a radical break with
the book's traditional spatial model and a shift in focus. The narrative itself
moves to the background, while the patterns of its construction become a
focus of attention. What the project illuminates are structural patterns and
symmetries that presumably are not very obvious during the reading (and
writing) process. In *TextArc*'s reading of *Alice in Wonderland*, for example,

the word Alice holds a central position, showing an even distribution through the book (as to be expected). *TextArc* also reveals that the focus on characters seems to shift from animals in the first half of the book (caterpillar, dogs, mouse, etc.) to people in the second half (Duchess, King, Queen). A reading of Chapter 72, "The Monkey Rope," from Herman Melville's *Moby Dick,* exposes some astonishing symmetries in the constructions of the chapters. The words "harponeer" and "monkey-rope" (both of which obviously play a central role in the construction of the chapter's story) structure and frame the chapter in a distinctive and amazingly symmetrical way: the words "poison" and "peril" almost cut the chapter in half. It appears that *TextArc* illuminates the presumably unconscious level of the writing process and the construction of narrative.

A very different look at the construction of narrative, in this case visual or cultural, is provided by the works of Jennifer and Kevin McCoy, who experiment with a form of enhanced cinema that focuses on the construction of single shots and the messages they convey.[10] Using database logic as a formal strategy, their video installations *Every Shot Every Episode* (2001) and *How I Learned* (2002) carry the medium of film/video into the realm of

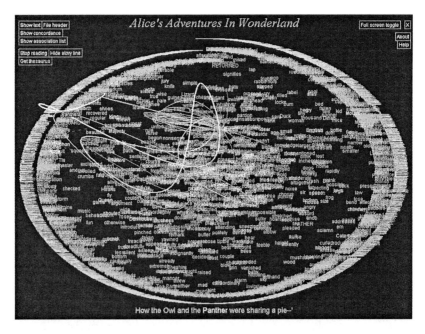

FIGURE 5.3. W. BRADFORD PALEY'S *TEXTARC* READING *ALICE IN WONDERLAND.*

digital art by fusing the inherent characteristics of the two. The works are presented as videos on CDs that are neatly stacked or arranged on the wall and can be chosen and played by the viewer in the "old-fashioned," hands-on interactive way. While the works appear to be video installations in the classical sense, they would not be possible without the digital medium's inherent possibilities for the classification and reconfiguration of existing materials in a database structure. *Every Shot Every Episode* literally consists of every shot in twenty episodes of the TV series *Starsky and Hutch,* broken down into a database of single units (such as "Every Zoom Out" or "Every Stereotype"). There is no reason to expect that this type of classification would result in the construction of an interesting new narrative in the traditional sense. What *Every Shot Every Episode* creates, however, is a record of the elemental aesthetics of familiar genres, the subtexts of stereotypes, and formulaic representation that the viewer otherwise would not necessarily perceive in this clarity. The project *How I Learned* exposes the cultural conditioning of learned behavior by structuring the Eastern-Western television series *Kung Fu* in categories such as "how I learned about blocking punches," "how I learned about exploiting workers," or "how I learned to love the land."

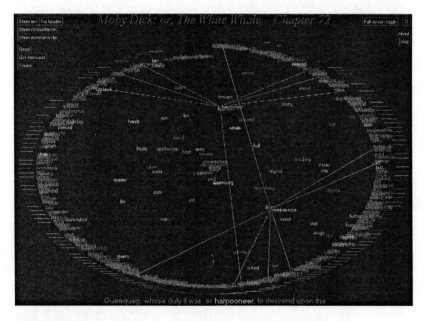

FIGURE 5.4. W. BRADFORD PALEY'S *TEXTARC* READING CHAPTER 72 OF *MOBY DICK.*

Ranging from the ridiculous to the sublime, the database categories reveal the subliminal messages carried by visual narratives. Narrative structure, with an emphasis on time, became the focus of the McCoy's *201: A Space Algorithm* (2001), an online software program that allows viewers to reedit Stanley Kubrick's science-fiction film *2001: A Space Odyssey* by selecting individual shots and compressing or expanding viewing time.[11] Users not only control the spatial components of the narrative but also its temporal construction, questioning the time-and-space paradigms of cinema.

Both *TextArc* and the McCoys' works use different ways of filtering to highlight structural elements in the construction of narrative. A broader look at cultural values and representation unfolds in the projects of George Legrady, who has consistently explored the archive and database as cultural record. His project *Pockets Full of Memories* (2001), an installation with an accompanying Web site,[12] explicitly focuses on the "mechanics" of database construction and the way in which we arrive at levels of evaluation though linguistic description. *Pockets Full of Memories* creates an "anatomy" of personal value by inviting visitors to digitally scan an object in their possession at a scanning station and answer a set of questions regarding the object, rating it according to certain attributes (old/new, soft/hard, natural/synthetic, functional/symbolic, personal/nonpersonal, useful/useless, and so on). An algorithm (the Kohonen self-organizing algorithm) classifies the scanned objects in a two-dimensional map based on similarities in their descriptions and attribute ratings. The Kohonen map generates a grid with random values for each point in the grid and all the data categories for each object. The algorithm classifies one object after the other and positions it where it finds the closest values for the respective object, so that over time all the objects are positioned in proximity to the ones with similar values. Users can review each object's data and add their own personal comments and stories. The result of the project is a growing map of relations between items that range from the merely functional to a signifier of personal value. The mapping of these objects illuminates how each object is contextualized by its surrounding data and points, to the potentiality and absurdities of classifying objects endowed with personal meaning. The project operates on the threshold between logical classification and meanings that seem to elude quantifiable values.

Legrady's interactive CD-ROM/installation *Slippery Traces* (1997) invited viewers to navigate through more than 240 linked postcards—ranging from tourist sites to personal, military, or industrial images—that were categorized according to topics such as nature, culture, technology, morality, industrial, and urban environments. Viewers first choose one of three quotes appearing on the screen, each of which embodies a different perspective—anthropological, colonialist, or media theory—and thus provides an interpretive angle for the experience of the project. Each of the postcards encountered in *Slippery Traces* contains five hot spots linked to other related images. Legrady uses postcards as a ready-made expression and trace of cultural memory, reflecting on mediated memory as it is captured in visual reproduction. Postcards are photographic memories that, as a representation of an "original," are always inscribed with an ideology, or at least a perspective. While this system may apply to any photograph, the postcard as a representation of time and place (and often, quite specifically, culture) seems to be even more inclined to transport an agenda. Because of the categorization of the material, cultural subtexts—such as colonialization, the exoticizing of the "foreign" and Other, and cultural stereotypes, for example—become a consistent visual meta-narrative. This narrative is obviously very much dependent on the database system as a whole—the interplay between the container, the algorithm, and the interpretation of the user. Database categories and the algorithms filtering them are never value-free but always are inscribed with an interpretive angle. As with most of the projects discussed here, *Slippery Traces* makes the mechanisms of its classification (its database

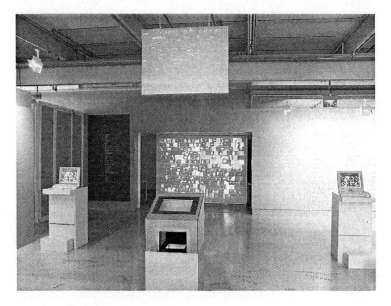

FIGURE 5.5. GEORGE LEGRADY, *POCKETS FULL OF MEMORIES*.

categories) transparent for viewers, allowing them to take a critical look at how the project itself constructs its meta-narrative.

The characteristics of the database as a collection of information that can be structured according to various criteria and result in a meta-narrative in many ways differ from the concept of the traditional narrative (in the broadest sense) as it unfolds in a book, film, or even a single visual image. While narratives can be driven by many different strategies and factors—among them character development, cause-and-effect relationships between events, spatiotemporal movement—they generally establish a sequence of events or defined relationships (for example, in an event or "scene" depicted in a photograph). Many of the projects I discuss here (*TextArc,* the McCoy projects, *Slippery Traces*) impose database logic onto traditional forms of narrative. A project that visibly juxtaposes and fuses the "narrative engines" of the database and photography/moving images is Natalie Bookchin's CD-ROM, *The Databank Of The Everyday* (1996). Bookchin's project, a conceptually infinite database of life itself in all its mundane activities, uses elements of the computer database and an image catalog and identifies the loop as a narrative engine driving both of them. The loop is not only inherently connected to the roots of cinema and moving images, which first took the form of a flip-book-like loop of images, but is also a central element of programming and algorithms, which frequently use commands such as "if/then," "while/wend," "do/until," "for/next," and "repeat/while" to create their (visual) narrative. On a more metaphorical level, the redundancy of daily activities constitutes its own ever-repeating loop. In one segment of *The Databank of the Everyday,* the screen is divided into two frames, one of them showing a looping video of a woman shaving her leg, while the other one shows code and instructions corresponding to the movement of the woman's arm. The segment thus exposes the algorithms that drive a visual representation, moving the usually hidden background of code to the visible foreground.

A very different and original approach to moving the background to the foreground unfolds in *The Secret Life of Numbers* by Golan Levin, with Martin Wattenberg, Jonathan Feinberg, Shelly Wynecoop, David Elashoff, and David Becker. The project does not take an existing "story" as its source but studies the relative popularity of every integer between zero and one million. By means of custom software, data from public search engines, and statistical techniques, the artists determined the popularity of numbers and expose their "secret life"—patterns of associations that reflect cultural interests. The mathematical tool and system that provides the basis for programming is turned into the object of analysis and reveals its own "values." As the artists put it in their statement:

> Our present relationship with numbers reveals both a highly developed tool and a highly developed user, working together to measure, create, and predict both ourselves and the world around us. But like every symbiotic couple, the tool we would like to believe is separate from us (and thus objective) is actually an intricate reflection of our thoughts, interests, and capabilities. One intriguing result of this symbiosis is that the numeric system we use to describe patterns is actually used in a patterned fashion to describe.[13]

The interactive visualization consists of two interfaces: a histogram where the popularity of numbers is indicated by the length of lines protruding from them, and a graph consisting of cells that make up a grid arranged in rows of one hundred where the more popular integers have brighter cells. A menu indicates the value of popularity for any chosen number and reveals its "associations" (such as historical dates). As to be expected, the number ten and its multiples show a higher popularity because they are driven by the base-ten numbering system. It also does not come as a surprise that, in terms of calendar years, people generally seem to be more interested in the present than in the past. Other numbers that stand out are those corresponding

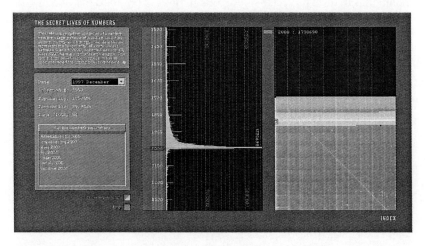

FIGURE 5.6. SCREEN SHOT FROM *THE SECRET LIFE OF NUMBERS* BY GOLAN LEVIN, MARTIN WATTENBERG, JONATHAN FEINBERG, SHELLY WYNECOOP, DAVID ELASHOFF, AND DAVID BECKER.

to important historical dates, area codes, or relating to pop-cultural phenomena such as the television show *90210.*

The fact that the data were gathered largely through Web-based statistics
also becomes a reflection of people's interest within this particular environment. It is notable that the relative "importance" of the model numbers of
products—ranging from cars and cameras to computer processors—by far
outweighs that of historical events. Applying an additional filtering mechanism, *The Secret Life of Numbers* could probably be configured into a
history of commercial products and their success. The project succeeds in
delivering what the artists refer to as a "numeric snapshot of the collective
consciousness,"[14] a revealing portrait of our interests as they manifest themselves in the descriptive systems we use.

Given the fact that database structure in the broadest sense lies at the
root of digital media, it is only natural that database aesthetics play a major
role in digital art and culture. The 1990s were a decade of major digitization, when libraries, archives, and museum collections were translated into
digital format, allowing for new forms of filtering and relational connections. However, it seems that "database aesthetics" in the broadest sense has
become emblematic of our time, extending beyond the digital realm and
transcending the traditional archives of the library and museum. The notion
of relational databases as an organizational model seems increasingly to infil-
trate culture. *Documenta XI,* for example, featured an enormous amount of
nondigital archival projects—numerous archives of photographs documenting a journey, place, condition, memories (cultural and personal); an archive
of "Insomnia Drawings" by Louise Bourgeois; Feyzdjou's boutiques, a Wunderkammer of personal history and identity; several room-size installations
that were transplants of artists' studios, archives of notes, drawings, scrap-
books; On Kawara's *One Million Years,* a database; Sanja Ivekovic's archive
Searching for My Mother, a lexical/semantic inventory of the dictionaries of
the Brothers Grimm.[15] Largely brought about by digital technologies, database aesthetics itself has become an important cultural narrative of our
time, constituting a shift toward a relational, networked approach to gathering and creating knowledge about cultural specifics.

NOTES

1. Selena Sol, "Introduction to Databases for the Web: Pt. 1." http://www.database
journal.com/sqletc/article.php/1428721.

2. Lev Manovich, *The Language of New Media* (Cambridge, Mass.: MIT Press, 2001),
227.

3. http://www.rhizome.org/carnivore.

4. IOD, *WebStalker,* http://www.backspace.org/iod. Maciej Wisniewski, *Netomat.* http://www.netomat.net.

5. http://www.backspace.org/iod/Visceral.html.

6. Martin Wattenberg, *Smart Money*'s "Map of the Market." See http://www.smart money.com/marketmap; Nancy Paterson, *Stock Market Skirt,* http://www.bccc.com/ nancy/skirt.html; Lynn Hershman, *Synthia,* http://www.lynnhershman.com/synthia; John Klima, *ecosystm,* http://www.cityarts.com/lmno/ecosystm.html.

7. Manovich, *Language of New Media,* 225.

8. Ibid., 227.

9. http://www.textarc.org.

10. http://www.mccoyspace.com.

11. http://www.mccoyspace.com/201.html.

12. http://www.pocketsfullofmemories.com.

13. Ibid., http://www.turbulence.org/Works/nums/.

14. Ibid.

15. Kassel, Germany, June 8–September 15, 2002.

6. The Database Imaginary: Memory_Archive_Database v 4.0

STEVE DIETZ

In 1968, in a report to the Rockefeller Foundation during a residency at SUNY Stony Brook, Nam June Paik argued that 97 percent of all electronic music was not recorded and that "a simple measure would solve the whole problem. An information center for unpublished electronic media should be created." At the time, this meant such a center would "provide a Xerox copy and a tape copy of musical pieces, at the request of performers, students, and organizers from all over the world."[1] Convert analog to digital, and the dream lives on, perhaps more vibrant than ever, of a universal database archive, with access to everything by anyone anywhere at any time.

But is access to information enough? As Hal Foster asked: Will such a database archive be "more than a base of data, a repository of the given?"[2] Particularly in regard to Net culture—but any dynamic activity, really—a database archive can be tantamount to "museumfication," and it is no wonder that many artists are skeptical, at best, of the mausoleumizing of the vibrant Net culture they have been creating and participating in. More to the point, the classification schema inherent in any database, to paraphrase Barnett Newman, are for art what ornithology is for birds. Many contemporary artists, however, use databases as their medium and as an aesthetic platform for their concepts, not merely as a container of metadata about them.

THE DATABASE IMAGINARY

In *Interface Culture*, Steven Johnson argues that the interface is omnipresent, a defining aspect of contemporary culture.[3] Almost unbelievably, according to Wikipedia, "Databases resembling modern versions were first developed in the 1960s."[4] Arguably, however, the database has become the "back end" of this contemporary, ubiquitous interface culture. Even when, technically speaking, a collection of data, or information, that is specially organized for rapid search and retrieval does not exist, the potential of getting-retrieving-finding what you want is omnipresent, just on the other side of the interface.

The database imaginary is only partly a reflection of the rise of the Internet and Microsoft sloganeering about "Where do you want to go today?™" It is mirrored more generally in what Simon Nora and Alain Minc described in a 1978 report to the French government as the "computerization of society."[5] Even in the art world, Leo Steinberg presciently alluded to this transformation in his classic essay, "Other Criteria":

> The flatbed picture plane makes its symbolic allusion to hard surfaces such as tabletops, studio floors, charts, bulletin boards—any receptor surface on which objects are scattered, on which data is entered, on which information may be received, printed, impressed—whether coherently or in confusion. The pictures of the last fifteen to twenty years insist on a radically new orientation, in which the painted surface is no longer the analogue of a visual experience of nature but of operational processes. . . . Yet [the flatbed] is no more than a symptom of changes which go far beyond questions of picture planes, or of painting as such. It is part of a shakeup which contaminates all purified categories. The deepening inroads of art into non-art continue to alienate the connoisseur as art defects and departs into strange territories leaving the old stand-by criteria to rule an eroding plain.[6]

Within the context of the computerization of society, many digital artists are part of this "shakeup which contaminates all purified categories," which

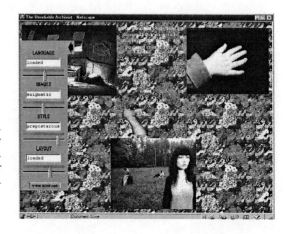

FIGURE 6.1.
SCREEN SHOT OF
THE UNRELIABLE ARCHIVIST.
COURTESY OF WALKER ART
CENTER, MINNEAPOLIS.

might be also described as the database imaginary, freeing data (content) from their metadata (classification schema). The artist, as Manuel DeLanda put it in a 1998 interview, "is that agent (human or not) that takes stratified matter-energy or sedimented cultural materials"—such as databases—"and makes them follow a line of flight, or a line of song, or of color."[7]

The Unreliable Archivist by Janet Cohen, Keith Frank, and Jon Ippolito was commissioned by the Walker Art Center in Minneapolis as both a parasitic archive of the pioneering artist Web site äda'web and a meta-commentary on the act by the Walker for archiving such a remarkable and vibrant collective project.[8] *The Unreliable Archivist,* like any good archivist, creates metadata about äda'web. In the case of Cohen et al., it just happens to be a little, shall we say, idiosyncratic. The value of a data standard like the Categories for the Description of Works of Art is its precision—at least for experts.[9] It allows the user to make minute differentiations between objects. It allows for the discovery of specific known objects from vast databases. What it is not so good at is making connections or finding things one doesn't know about. Think of the difference between searching for an eighteenth-century portrait in oil on wood [CDWA] and searching for something that has "ambiguous language," "enigmatic images," and "preposterous style" [UA].

When I first saw *The Unreliable Archivist,* I took it to be homage to the wonderful, breathtaking excesses of äda'web and those who created it. I also took it to be a parody, a tongue-in-cheek commentary on the butchery that archiving—mothballing—such a dynamic institution as äda'web could entail. I still think these conclusions are true, but my concern has changed. Rather than worrying about how unreliable the archivist is, perhaps we should map mainstream institutional collections according to these categories and values. What would happen? It is possible to imagine a future in which everything is archived—from our credit data to our memories, from world events to passionate encounters. How, then, do we create systems that allow each of us to be an unreliable archivist? To allow each of us to create the preposterous, the enigmatic? No matter how intelligent archiving agents are in the future, they will be poor substitutes if they cannot represent an individual, idiosyncratic, and imaginative point of view.

TECHNOLOGIES TO THE PEOPLE®

> It is good for the artist to insinuate himself into the open mesh of any system—not in a provocative and visible way, but mimetically, using their same mediums.
>
> —MAURIZIO CATTELAN

Daniel García Andújar's Video Collection is what I would call a prototypical net.art gesture.[10] It appropriates the developing practices of the Internet, in this case database-like streaming content as well as its series of unhelpful help-desk messages, and yokes them to cultural and societal desires—in this case database access to significant but not always easy-to-find cultural resources. While there is a clear element of *épater le bourgeois* with this work, one less predictable outcome is the economic and intellectual property issues that are raised. At least two artist and/or cultural institution representatives wrote to Andújar with questions such as "How did you do this?" (technically) and ended with more quizzical questions that, more or less, asked, "How *dare* you do this?" The issue is only partly economic. By being so opaque about his project, Andújar also highlights the tension between the ideal of transparency in Net culture and in archiving, and the fact that information is knowledge and power, whether it is about the arcana of technological capabilities such as streaming media or the arcana of classification schema.

REVERSING THE PANOPTICON

One of the cornerstones of museum culture is authoritativeness and selectivity. The pioneering example of Muntadas's *The File Room*, however, points

FIGURE 6.2.
SCREEN SHOT OF VIDEO
COLLECTION BY DANIEL
GARCÍA ANDÚJAR.
COURTESY OF
STEVE DIETZ.

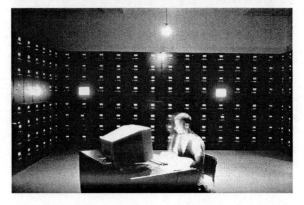

Technologies To The People Video Collection			
the use of video and television as a media of artistic expression.			
Tittle	Year	Autor	Tech.
Against Video	1973	Douglas Davis	6:33 min. Col Video
And Now This	1983	Jorge Lozano/Christa Schadt	8 min. Col Video
Animation	1975	Stuart Marshall	4 min. Col Video
Art and Technology	1975	Chris Burden	15 min. Col Video

FIGURE 6.3.
INSTALLATION VIEW,
THE FILE ROOM.
COURTESY OF
STEVE DIETZ.

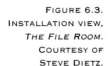

to a very different model of bidirectional information flows, multinodal information sources, collaborative filtering, multiple points of view, the transgression of geographic and discipline boundaries, and the commingling of specialist and nonspecialist.[11]

The File Room is a particularly interesting example because it is about censorship. Explicitly, it is about instances of censorship that have occurred anywhere in the world. Implicitly, however, it is about the fact that there has been no easily and publicly accessible source for this information, that subjects of censorship have often been beholden to traditional news sources to tell their stories, and, if they are told at all, they are not always the story the subject would tell. The effect of the network, allowing for distributed authorship of the censorship cases in *The File Room,* creates the possibility of an asymmetrical relationship to power and control—distributed David's fighting the centralized Goliath. Another contemporary example of this reversal of the panoptic gaze of the database is Ryan McKinley's Open Government Information Awareness project.[12] Open GIA is a response to the idea of the Total Information Awareness project, floated by the Bush administration post-9/11. And while TIA was ultimately (or temporarily, at least) shut down, it brought into focus the dark side of the database imaginary, where every shred of information is connected with every other and where total information equals total control. Through the deployment of a distributed database, however, McKinley at least imagines the possibility of a counterpanoptic gaze of the people.

DATA BODIES

> In an age in which we are increasingly aware of ourselves as databases, identified by social security numbers and genetic structures, it is imperative that artists actively participate in how data is shaped, organized and disseminated.
>
> —VICTORIA VESNA
> Introduction: *AI & Society "Database Aesthetics"*

In "Time Capsule," Eduardo Kac has taken Vesna's observation to a kind of logical extreme, self-implanting a bio-panoptic surveillance device, a microchip that contains a programmed identification number integrated with a coil and a capacitor, then hermetically sealed in biocompatible glass.[13] Scanning the implant generates a low-energy radio signal that energizes the microchip to transmit its unique and inalterable numerical code. As part of the procedure, Kac registered himself in a database set up to aid in finding lost animals, classifying himself as both animal and owner.

According to Kac, half tongue-in-cheek, half seriously, humans adapt, physically as well as emotionally, to become literal extensions of the computer, of the database interface. "It is almost as if the body has become an extension of the computer, and not the other way around."[14] "Time Capsule" literalizes this inversion of the human-computer interface, drawing attention in the process to the way our data bodies become subject to the classification and ultimately to the control of innumerable databases that are beyond our corporeal reach.

ANATOMY OF THE DATABASE

Alan Sekula, in an important essay, "The Body and the Archive," pointed out the early role of photographic archives in the normalization of the criminal surveillance system, not to mention the rise of eugenics. In terms of the origins of the photographic archive, which gave rise in many ways to our present-day surveillance society, there were two important poles:

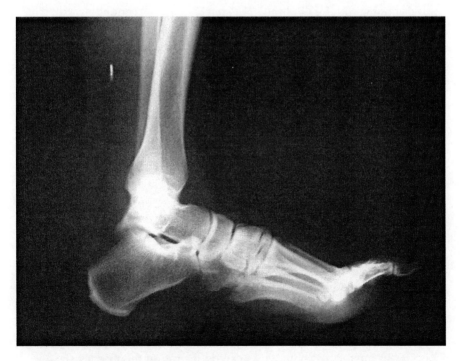

FIGURE 6.4. X-RAY OF EDUARDO KAC'S LEFT LEG MADE THE MORNING AFTER THE IMPLANT. THE MICROCHIP IS SEEN IN THE UPPER-LEFT CORNER OF THE PICTURE. COURTESY OF EDUARDO KAC.

> The Paris police official Alphonse Bertillon invented the first effective modern system of criminal identification. His was a bipartite system, positioning a "microscopic" individual record within a "macroscopic" aggregate.

and

> The English statistician and founder of eugenics, Francis Galton, invented a method of composite portraiture. . . . Through one of his several applications of composite portraiture, Galton attempted to construct a purely optical apparition of the criminal type.[15]

If the database, with its multiple fields for searching, is a direct descendant of the Bertillon cabinet, which managed to classify hundreds of thousands of subjects according to twelve measurements so that the smallest category in the system had no more than a dozen records, a descendant of Galton's composite photograph is the composite data profile.

Beginning with Lisa Jevbratt's *Stillman Projects,* and continuing with the projects *16 Sessions, 1:1,* and *SoftSub,* the artist group C5 has created a number of fascinating collaborative filtering projects that make manifest the vast and subterranean datamining efforts that big and small businesses alike are mounting to make a buck off your information—your body of data/databody.[16]

The important aspect of Galton's composite photograph was not whether someone did or did not look like it. No one did, by design. The intent was in the mean differentiation. Individuals that approached the composite profile to a certain degree were suspect. In a similar way, composite data profiles of likely buyers and likely offenders are being created and as your data profile approaches it, you will be acted on accordingly, whether it is with spam or a visit from a government authority.

SoftSub is an opt-in program—a screensaver that collects information about the file structure of a user's computer. Data are collected only if a user downloads the software and only if he or she decides to upload personal data. Here, an opposite approach to Andújar has a similar result. By foregrounding the practice of conscientious opt-in, the standard practice of hidden or murky data-gathering procedures is highlighted. It is also relevant that *SoftSub* is collecting essentially benign information. Even assuming nefarious intentions, about all C5 can do is post on the Internet the one hundred messiest desktops. C5's real interest is in trying to understand how to approach very large data sets and attempt to "understand" them, or at least create viable hypotheses about them, through a visual mapping process without having a particular target in mind and without assuming there is an objective truth or reality to be discovered. Galton and his disciples, however, attempted to assert that such visual mapping was "proof" of criminality.

DATA STORIES

There will always be a tension between the complete description of a specific individual and a generalized description of a group. Neither tells the whole story. One way to get beyond just the facts, of course, is actually to tell a story. While storytelling may seem inimical to databases, the linguistic researcher Walter Ong has determined that one of the great Western storytellers, Homer, substituted a stock set of phrases according to identifiable regular occurrences. This is not exactly the same as saying that *The Iliad* is a database-driven hypertext, but it does hint that the storytelling and information systems are not inherently incompatible.

DissemiNET, by Beth Stryker and Sawad Brooks, is a database-driven compilation of user-defined stories that is searched with a kind of fuzzy "curatorial," as they put it, that selectivity complements a dynamic visual display to create a compelling portrait of "The Disappeared" in Guatemala.[17] *DissemiNET* also has parallels to open archives such as *The File Room,* as anyone can, at least during its initial installation, upload their stories related to the topic. More than being an open resource, however, it also creates a repository for personal and social memory that "uses web technologies to give visual form to the transactions (deposits, retrievals, and loss) through which we experience memory. . . . Drawing parallels between diasporas and the dispersal of meaning over the web."[18]

DissemiNET lies somewhere between the particular instance and a composite whole, but it is particularly interesting for the way, not unlike *The*

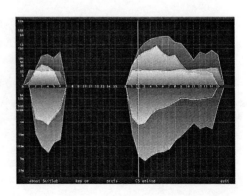

FIGURE 6.5. SCREEN SHOT OF
SOFTSUB. THIS CLIENT APPLICATION
SUMMARIZES TWENTY CHARACTERISTICS
ASSOCIATED WITH THE FILE-STRUCTURE
ORGANIZATION AND PROVIDES A REAL-
TIME VISUAL COMPARISON OF THE HARD
DRIVE AND DESKTOP CONFIGURATION.
COURTESY OF STEVE DIETZ.

Unreliable Archivist, the fuzzy algorithm creates relationships among stories—data—as a way to investigate semi-automated storytelling in relation to very large data sets.

In a slyly funny piece, *Anna Karenin Goes to Paradise,* Olia Lialina tells the story of Anna Karenin as a comedy in three acts (and an epilogue): Anna looking for love; Anna looking for train; Anna looking for paradise.[19] The way Anna "looks," naturally, is through Web searches for the words "love," "train," and "paradise." Lialina culls the results from the search engines Magellan, Yahoo! and Alta Vista into three pages of preselections, and the "reader" is invited to get lost on his or her own train of data thoughts before proceeding to the next act. An interesting and somewhat disturbing aspect of the piece is that upward of 90 percent of the links in the story now return "page not found" errors, emphasizing, perhaps, not only the ineffability of love but also the ephemerality of the Web.

Loss is an important aspect of memory, and impermanence may be the natural state of things—and not just on the Web. Noah Waldrop-Fruin's *The Impermanence Agent* is a remarkable project that starts out as the story of the death of his grandmother, but is designed to disappear.[20] As you browse the Web, the impermanence agent replaces Noah's story with snippets of text and images from your browsing, until, finally, the story is completely retold in the words of what you have been reading and looking at, with only the structure of the original story left behind.

THE ARTIST AS RELIABLE ARCHIVIST

Museums have always told stories, but there has not always been the opportunity to counter or play with them. For *Road to Victory,* a project for the Museum of Modern Art's "Museum as Muse," Fred Wilson researched

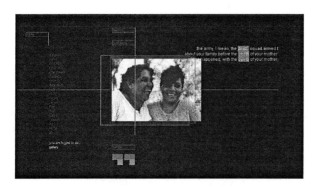

FIGURE 6.6. SCREEN SHOT OF *DISSEMINET.* COURTESY OF STEVE DIETZ.

MoMA's archives for several years and then used the Web to juxtapose different stories the museum has told over the years. In the first frame of the project, Wilson quotes A. Conger Goodyear, the first president of MoMA: "The permanent collection will not be unchangeable. It will have somewhat the same permanence a river has."[21]

For Wilson, over time MoMA had lost a certain social agenda, which it had originally intended. He wrote about the project: "These archival photographs expose the museum's use of didactic material to persuade the public of its liberal point of view as well as its aesthetic ideas."[22] Interestingly, in the very same press release that quotes Wilson, the press speaks about what the project demonstrates exactly and, presumably, unwittingly:

> Fred Wilson's online project, *Road to Victory* (1999)—titled after the Museum's 1942 exhibition that included photographs of the United States at war—explores The Museum of Modern Art's memory of itself: namely, the institution's photographic archive. Constructing narratives through juxtapositions and connections between documentary images and text borrowed from the archive, Wilson reveals much of what, though visible, is not on display: the Museum's visitors, staff, exhibition graphics, and wall texts.[23]

There is no hint that the "museum" in fact remembers the agenda that Wilson is exposing as a lacuna in institutional memory of itself. While Wilson's project is not, strictly speaking, a database, the database imaginary is of a universal database archive, with access to everything by anyone anywhere at any time, which can be used for personal, idiosyncratic, and political uses, independent and even counter to its use upon the body politic.

NOTES

Earlier versions of this essay were published in *Switch* (http://switch.sjsu.edu/~switch/nextswitch/switch_engine/front/front.php?artc=31) and presented at Fundacio "La Caixa" as part of *Imaginative Passages*, 2000 (http://www.mediatecaonline.net/passatgesimaginatius/eng/index_pre.htm) and the ISEA-sponsored *Cartographies* conference in the session "Conserving and Archiving Digital Work," October 14, 1999. It is version 4.0 of an ongoing investigation. The phrase "database imaginary" occurred in discussions with Lev Manovich and Sarah Cook concerning an upcoming exhibition on databases and art, opening at Walter Philips Gallery in Banff, August 2004, co-curated by myself, Cook, and Anthony Kiendl. See http://databaseimaginary.banff.org/index.php (accessed April 9, 2007).

    1. Nam June Paik, "Expanded Education for the Paper-Less Society" (February 1968); *Nam June Paik: Video 'n' Videology, 1959–1973*, ed. Judson Rosebush (Syracuse, N.Y.: Everson Museum of Art, 1974).

2. Hal Foster, "The Archive Without Museums," *October 77* (Summer 1996).

3. Steven Johnson, *Interface Culture: How New Technology Transforms the Way We Create and Communicate* (San Francisco: Harper, 1997).

4. Wikipedia, "Database," http://en.wikipedia.org/wiki/Database (accessed September 6, 2004).

5. Simon Nora and Alain Minc, *The Computerization of Society: A Report to the President of France* (Cambridge, Mass.: MIT Press, 1979).

6. Leo Steinberg, "Other Criteria," in *Other Criteria: Confrontations with Twentieth-Century Art* (Oxford: Oxford University Press, 1972).

7. Brett Stalbaum et al., "Interview with Manuel De Landa," *Switch* 3, no. 3 (1998). http://switch.sjsu.edu/nextswitch/switch_engine/front/front.php?artc=9.

8. *The Unreliable Archivist* and *äda'web,* along with various commentaries, are accessible from http://www.walkerart.org/gallery9/three/.

9. Categories for the Description of Works of Art is a product of the Art Information Task Force (AITF), which encouraged dialogue between art historians, art information professionals, and information providers so that together they could develop guidelines for describing works of art, architecture, groups of objects, and visual and textual surrogates. http://www.getty.edu/research/conducting_research/standards/cdwa/index.html.

10. Daniel García Andújar, *Video Collection,* http://www.irational.org/video/.

11. Antonio Muntadas, *The File Room* (1994). http://www.thefileroom.org/.

12. Ryan McKinley, *Open Government Information Awareness* (Computing Culture Group, MIT Media Lab, 2003, http://www.opengov.us/ (accessed September 6, 2004).

13. Eduardo Kac, *Time Capsule* (1997), http://www.ekac.org/timec.html.

14. Ibid.

15. Alan Sekula, "The Body and the Archive," *October* 39 (1986): 3–64.

16. For information about C5 projects, see http://www.c5corp.com/projects/index.shtml. For *A Stillman Project for the Walker Art Center,* see http://www.walkerart.org/gallery9/jevbratt/.

17. See http://www.walkerart.org/gallery9/dasc/disseminet/.

18. Ibid.

19. Olia Lialina, *Anna Karenin Goes to Paradise,* http://www.teleportacia.org/anna/.

20. Noah Wardrip-Fruin, *The Impermanence Agent,* http://www.noahwf.com/agent/index.html.

21. Fred Wilson, *Road to Victory* (1999). http://www.moma.org/exhibitions/1999/wilson/.

22. "Web Site Featuring Two Online Projects Accompanies the *Museum as Muse:* Artists Reflect at the Museum of Modern Art": See http://www.moma.org/about_moma/press/1999/muse_online_3_1_99.html (accessed September 6, 2004).

23. Ibid.

7. Recombinant Poetics and Related Database Aesthetics

BILL SEAMAN

An embodied approach to computing acknowledges the importance of the physicality of experience as it falls within the continuum that bridges the physical with the digital. To illuminate the operative nature of database aesthetics, one needs to point at a number of human processes—memory, thought, association, cataloging, categorizing, framing, contextualizing, de-contextualizing, and recontextualizing, as well as grouping. The production of boundary objects,[1] grammars of information, grammars of attention, the production of media constellations, and the exploration of principles of combinatorics[2] all become potential variables for employment in the creation of interactive works of art. Of critical importance is interface design— both physical and digital, as well as how human processes become operative through the functional nature of a relevant, robust, digitally encoded environment.

A database is derived through human activity leading to residues and/or inscriptions of experience, including such creative processes as the shooting and editing of video, the sculpting of virtual objects, the construction of sonic content, the composition of musical fragments or selections, the writing of poetic texts, the spoken recording of text, the naming of files, and the conceptual design of specific operative structures. Writing code is also a human process. Richard Hamilton and Ecke Bonk provide this perspective:

> A computer language is a notation for the unambiguous description of computer programmes. Such languages are synthetic in their vocabulary; punctuation, grammar, syntax and semantics are precisely defined in the context of a particular operating system. They suffer from an inability to cope with autonomous expression—an essential attribute of an organic language. The poetic of computers lies in the genius of individual programmers to express the beauty of their thought using such an inexorable medium.[3]

The human, the computer, code, and other mediated technology become enfolded through an ongoing flow of commingled energy processes in the service of human expression. Central to these processes is the notion of combinatorics. The mathematician Claude Berge, a member of OULIPO,[4] in *Principles of Combinatorics* provides this definition:

> We wish to offer here a definition of combinatorics, which depends on a very precise concept of "configuration." A configuration arises every time objects are distributed according to certain predetermined constraints. Cramming miscellaneous packets into a drawer is an example of a configuration. . . . The concept of configuration can be made mathematically precise by defining it as a mapping of a set of objects into a finite abstract set with a given structure; for example, a permutation of n objects is a "bijection of the set of n objects into the ordered set 1,2, . . . , n." Nevertheless, one is only interested in mappings satisfying certain constraints.[5]

The database aesthetic puts the poetic nature of composition, media configuration, sequence, media "distribution," and differing qualities of articulation *in line* (and/or in virtual time|space when we consider virtual space) with the constraint-based nature of combinatorics. Modular media-elements and/or processes are designated and/or addressed via code-enabling alternate subsections of code to become functional through a particular structural set of operative strategies that link digital potentials with multimodal physical phenomena.

Computation enables structural mappings across domains that traverse from the analog to the digital and/or become enabled as differing parts of a dynamic system. Such works always depend on physical space and human action in that these works are always embedded within a particular environment or presented via distributed space, where they are embedded within a set of interconnected physical spaces. They always depend on bodies for the activation of potential media flows, even if on the lowest level this is achieved only through observation as interaction. Particular computer-mediated mapping, operative code environments, and the dynamic coupling with physical space across differing potential domains enable media to be contextualized, recontextualized, or reconfigured in an ongoing manner. Contemporary dynamic approaches to media production provide an enhanced potentiality of relational intra-action between physical space and digital processes.

In particular, this is not a narrative strategy. It is a poetic approach to the combination and recombination of loaded poetic fields—be they imagistic, musical, textually sonic, visually textual, sculptural, environmental, or interface-related. Narrative is not central to the work. Observation of configurations of media fragments arising and changing through time-based exploration is pivotal. Thus no fixed narrative is sought—only a catalogue of shifting impressions and evocations. Interpretation is open and ongoing—an operative meaning-becoming.

Certainly one precursor/inspiration for this work (and my *Red Dice*) is Stéphane Mallarmé's "A Throw of the Dice Will Never Annul Chance."[6] This fascinating poem explores specific layout techniques as an analog structuring device.[7] Where Mallarmé's poem explored distribution across a 2D page, *The World Generator* explores the potential *open* arrangement of media-elements in a virtual volume.

Umberto Eco describes the open work: "A work of art is a complete and closed form in its uniqueness as a balanced organic whole, while at the same time constituting an open product on account of its susceptibility to countless different interpretations which do not impinge on unadulterable specificity. Hence every reception of a work of art is an interpretation and a performance of it, because in every reception the work takes on a fresh perspective for itself."[8] *The World Generator* seeks to point at the continuum that bridges the embodied physicality of sensual experience as one intermingles with both local and/or distributed digital evocations in an "open" manner.

MEMORY THEATERS AND ASSOCIATION

Two relevant precursors include the history of the memory theater as described in *The Art of Memory* by Francis Yates, in which she explores memory techniques, as well as memory-oriented physical "architectures" and devices.[9] A second important precursor is Vannevar Bush's plans for the Memex[10]—designed to facilitate the exploration of "trails and webs of association." The database in my case is used to navigate the open potentials of poetic expression, dynamic association through human process, and emergent meaning arising out of these processes.[11]

I have approached the aesthetic and operative nature of the database for more than twenty years in my artistic practice. In particular, I have focused on meta-meaning production using navigation and combinatorial strategies across a series of technological substrates. Perhaps the most complex of the works is *The World Generator / The Engine of Desire* (1996–present)—a virtual world-generating system that specifically draws on the potentials

of the database aesthetic (a collaboration with the programmer Gideon
May).[12] I will elaborate on this work as one salient example of the potential
of exploring database aesthetics.

The World Generator was a response to the question: If we think words are
particularly inadequate in reflecting the complexity of media environments
in terms of meaning generation, could we build a device that better enables
one to come to understand the nature of meaning production? Through
interaction ↤ ↦ *intra-action,* one can witness meaning as it is being formed
and changed based on individual and group involvement.

RECOMBINANT POETIC ATTRIBUTES

Specific attributes are common to all of the works that I consider to be Recombinant Poetic works. Each work contains one or more of the following:

1. A database of media-elements.
2. An operative set of interactive digital processes.
3. A particular content-based strategy toward human/computer
   interaction.
4. An interface combining both hardware and software strategies.
5. A focus on meta-meaning production.
6. A nonhierarchical poetic strategy exploring combinatorics.
7. The exploration of "fields of meaning" arising through dynamic
   interaction with diverse media-elements.
8. An open, emergent, process-based approach to meaning production.
9. The exploration of image, sonic, and textual media intrarelations.
10. Interactive engagement is sought to be empowered at a high level.
11. The artist involves media-construction as an active process in the
    work, calling forth the exploration of multiple media-element
    combinatorics and abstractions.
12. The work becomes operative through a particular structural set of
    potential relations.
13. Both the potential for constructing of multiple spatial/temporal
    structures as well as the displacement or disruption of those
    structures is embodied in the work. (Displacement illuminates
    placement.)
14. The artist defines the approach to the art content.

I have come to call this approach recombinant poetics, primarily referring
historically in my writing to this set of criteria in terms of generative virtual

worlds. I now seek to extend this definition to a larger class of generative works that will explore differing media and their concomitant qualities, although I will focus here on *The World Generator*, a virtual world-generating system. (I created the term "recombinant poetics" in 1995.)[13] The word "recombinant" is used in a metaphoric and poetic manner. In a scientific context it is defined as:

> Recombinant:
> Any new cell, individual, or molecule that is produced in the laboratory by recombinant DNA technology or that arises naturally as a result of recombination.
> Recombinant DNA technology can be defined as:
> In genetic engineering, a laboratory technique used to join deoxyribonucleic acid from different sources to produce an individual with a novel gene combination. Also known as gene splicing.[14]

The metaphor of molecular generation through recombination is central. Participants function in a unity with the media through interaction, bringing a history of media relations with them as one particular field of meaning relation.[15] By operating on the media-elements in the works, they derive or better *create* emergent meaning—intermingling their mind-set with the interpenetrating fields of the media-elements that shift in meaning in relation to constructed context and dynamic interaction. Just as in a molecule, the combination of media-elements takes on a life and new qualities through intermingling—the participant conceptually projects meaning across the entirety of the ongoing experience. Meaning is accretive and functions as an ongoing process of meaning-becoming.

A more succinct definition of the term "recombinant poetics" follows: artworks that exemplify recombinant poetics are characterized by the interaction of a participant with a computer-mediated mechanism that enables the participant to become actively engaged with aspects of experience arising from the combination and recombination of text, image, and/or music/sound elements. The functionality of these works is made operative within an authored computer-mediated generative environment. It is the technological functionality of this mechanism that enables direct engagement with digital (and/or analog) media-elements. These modular variables of text, image, and music/sound can be observed as fields of meaning experienced within a variety of constructed contexts through processes of interaction.[16] It must be noted that each of these works has been specifically authored to examine emergent meaning.

THE WORLD GENERATOR / THE ENGINE OF DESIRE

In collaboration with the programmer Gideon May, I authored a complex virtual world generator that enables users of the system to construct and navigate virtual worlds in real time by making choices from a spinning virtual interface of container wheels working in tandem with a physical interface table. These virtual container wheels house an elaborate multimedia database of media-elements and processes, including 3D objects, 2D images, poetic texts, musical loops, digital movies as well as processes relevant to different forms of media construction and abstraction. Alternately, the participant can explore a set of elaborate authored chance processes to construct worlds. Participants can also do what Erkki Huhtamo calls "World Processing," enabling them to edit and alter the virtual world in an active manner. The interactant can also attach behaviors to the media-elements and apply still and movie texture maps, as well as make the media-elements transparent. When the participant navigates through the virtual world, a "recombinant music" mix (another coinage of mine) is made, relevant to each different navigation of the environment. The piece explores emergent meaning and is different for each participant.

Here I will outline a set of salient characteristics pertinent to exploring the database aesthetic as it relates to *The World Generator:*

Set Theory

Central to database aesthetics is the notion of the arithmetic *set*. The concept of the set enables different kinds of groupings to be defined and still function as a unity. In such interactive works, meaning is always involved in a process of becoming. What strategies does the database enable in relation to the exploration of sets? The examination of a plurality of approaches to a series of media-elements is explored. A multiplicity becomes an accretive

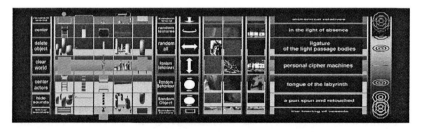

FIGURE 7.1. *THE WORLD GENERATOR / THE ENGINE OF DESIRE.* © BILL SEAMAN WITH GIDEON MAY, PROGRAMMER, 1995–PRESENT.

body of media over time and enables a dynamic investigation of recombined fragments to become a unity in an ongoing manner. This unity might arise through choice or through chance procedures. Users of the system can potentially use chance methods to define or choose a particular set from a series of potential sets.

A particular set of approaches to chance procedures was developed to enable a series of structural media construction strategies. One example, the "Random All" selection, enables the machine to choose from each of the database categories and instantly construct a virtual world using parameters that focus the range of the chance processes, derive the positioning of media-elements, draw from a set of relevant media processes and attach particular behaviors to chance derived objects.

SMOOTH AND STRIATED SPACE

The concept of both *smooth and striated space* as articulated by Gilles Deleuze and Félix Guattari in *A Thousand Plateaus* is explored in an operative manner: "No sooner do we note a simple opposition between two kinds of space than we must indicate a much more complex difference by virtue of which the successive terms of the oppositions fail to coincide entirely. And no sooner have we done that than we must remind ourselves that the two spaces in fact exist only in mixture: smooth space is constantly being translated, traversed into a striated space; striated space is constantly being reversed, returned to a smooth space."[17] By calling forth different media-elements and processes in *The World Generator,* a participant can explore both a *smooth* flowing space, defined as movement within the virtual space, as well as interact with operative fragments (sub-sets of this section) that can be recombined, recontextualized, viewed over and over again, and explored in differing ways depending on the authored functionalities of the interface system. *The World Generator* presents a series of "striated" containers to be drawn from in the service of generating a virtual world. A participant can explore alternate sets or fragments of this unity in differing orders. A structural fragment map is articulated in a relevant manner, derived via the running of the machinic code. This presents a map of all potential modular media-elements as well as prospective media processes. These become operative access points on the virtual menu system, coupling the generative nature of the virtual space, which is brought to life via specific authored code, with a dynamically explored physical interface connection. Thus, the human participant, code, hardware, environment, and related machines become intermingled through a *set* of dynamic energy exchanges.

The Exploration of Levels and Qualities of Granularity

The exploration of virtual space enables edits and abstractions that potentially are fragments of the frame itself forming the illusion of a complex 3D space. One salient characteristic particular to the database aesthetic is that differing kinds of media elements and processes can be permutated and/or interpenetrated, defining a potentially mutable media configuration that is highly visually and sonically complex.

Resonance

The question for the author of such a work is: How can the form of the work—its technological potentiality—fuse in a relevant and resonant manner with the content of the work? In *The World Generator,* I was interested in exploring a chosen set of aesthetic foci in relation to particular technological potentials. So the sets of sets accessed by the participant forms a unity out of fragments of attention—a unity that is somehow greater than the sum of its parts. We could say that resonant meaning arises out of a history of multimodal sensual experience as it is brought to bear in the current context—a context that is dynamically arising through interaction. This context is loaded with particular meaning potentialities. The dynamic structuring of media-elements forms an evocative meaning-becoming, yet it may not attempt to follow a predefined "media grammar." In fact, each participant defines his or her "use" of media in the virtual space within the range of the authored poetic/technological constraints.

The Rhizome

A growing, open "set" of experiences informing the understanding of a work arises in conjunction with the initial interactive context, through subsequent abstraction of the work as well as differing forms of recontextualization and reproduction. Deleuze and Guattari describe this concept as the "line of flight," in relation to their notion of the rhizome as developed in *A Thousand Plateaus.*[18] The concept of the rhizome is highly relevant to a discussion of shifting sets of configurations of media-elements. Although the word "rhizome" is often used, it seems relevant here to present their definition:

> Let us summarize the principal characteristics of a rhizome: unlike trees or their roots, the rhizome connects any point to any other point and its traits are not necessarily linked to traits of the same nature; it brings into play very different regimes of signs and even nonsign states. The rhizome is reducible

to neither the One or the multiple. It is not the One that becomes Two or even directly three, four, five etc. It is not a multiple derived from the one, or to which one is added ($n+1$). It is comprised not of units but of dimensions, or rather directions in motion. It has neither beginning nor end, but always a middle (milieu) from which it grows and which it overspills. It constitutes linear multiplicities with n dimensions having neither subject nor object, which can be laid out on a plane of consistency and from which the one is always subtracted ($n-1$). When a multiplicity of this kind changes dimension, it necessarily changes in nature as well, undergoes a metamorphosis. Unlike a structure, which is defined by a set of points and positions, the rhizome is made only of lines; lines of segmentarity and stratification as its dimensions and the line of flight or deterritorialization as the maximum dimension after which the multiplicity undergoes metamorphosis, changes in nature. These lines, or ligaments, should not be confused with lineages of the aborescent type, which are merely localizable linkages between points and positions. . . . Unlike the graphic arts, drawing or photography, unlike tracings, the rhizome pertains to a map that must be produced, constructed, a map that is always detachable, connectable, reversible, modifiable and has multiple entranceways and exits and its own lines of flight.[19]

Thus, *The World Generator* functions in a rhizomatic manner. Deleuze and Guattari present a number of concepts that are relevant to recombinant poetics and the database aesthetic. The concept of the machinic assemblage is pivotal.[20] They describe their concept of the mixed-semiotic "machinic statement" or "enunciation": "What we term machinic is precisely this synthesis of heterogeneities as such. Inasmuch as these heterogeneities are matters of expression, we say that their synthesis itself, their consistency or capture, forms a properly machinic 'statement' or 'enunciation.' The varying relations into which a color, sound, gesture, movement, or position enters into the same species and in different species, form so many machinic enunciations."[21] Deleuze and Guattari describe an accumulation of the various enfolded modes of the abstract machine as a "machinic assemblage."

States of Media

In terms of the concept of *lines of flight, The World Generator has* moved through a number of iterations since its inception in 1995 and is currently being re-authored for contemporary technological exploration. The importance of this approach to database aesthetics is that one version of the work being operative allows a different "perspective" into the understanding of other versions. Each version in some way informs the evocative nature of the others.

A networked version of the work has been shown internationally. This version enables participants in two parts of the world to inhabit and operate within simultaneously generated copies of the same environment, communicate via videophone, and view the alternate participant as a video avatar. As the participant moves in the alternate location, the participant's avatar also moves, positioning itself in a relevant manner in the alternate space.

A Japanese version of the work has also been authored, enabling participants to network the ICC in Tokyo with the ZKM in Germany. A third version has been authored for the Visualization Portal at UCLA, which is visible on a one-hundred-sixty-degree screen, with literally hundreds of objects/images in the environment as facilitated by an extremely powerful computer—a Silicon Graphics *Reality Monster*.

The work provides a metatext related to virtual environments as one set of media-elements for exploration. The text can be positioned in the virtual world and navigated. Central to the work is meta-meaning production as articulated through interaction with visual forms, image-based media forms, music, spoken text, movies, image-based texture maps, and media behaviors. Users actually watch and listen to meaning arise, change, and be affected in a dynamic manner as they *interact* ←→ *intra-act* with the work.

The Generator Paradigm

The notion of the ongoing participatory generation of media environments is crucial.[22] This work explores a special set of qualities relevant to operative database authorship. An enfolding of strategies enables the aesthetic and the technologically pragmatic to intermingle in the service of poetic expression. The actual physical attributes of the medium must become married to the content to produce resonant experience.

The Mutability of *Sensed* Time

Another attribute that the differing playback of media material affords is the potential to explore the mutability of sensed time. When a work is being explored as a flowing movement through virtual space, time may appear to move at different speeds. Fragmentation can promote a feeling of the elongation of time—as one observes the different media-elements and processes displayed in the menu system. Again, the flow of time falls in relation to differing qualities of navigation as well as media playback configurations.

Alternately, the exploration of ambient audio loops prompts the feeling of a meditative "suspension" of time.

RELEVANCE OF THE CUT-UP METHOD

Historically the example of the "formula" or "recipe" (or, shall we say, analog algorithm) is evident in different artists' approaches. Lewis Carroll, Leconte de Lisle, and Tristan Tzara wrote related textual formulas. In the following excerpt from *Dada manifeste sur l'amour faible et l'amour amer* (Dada manifesto on weak love and bitter love) is a translation from the French of Tzara's formula:

> To Write a Dada Poem: Take a newspaper. Take some scissors. Pick out an article which is as long as you wish your poem to be. Cut out the article. Then cut out carefully each of the words in the article and put them in a bag. Shake gently. Then take out each piece one after the other. Copy them down conscientiously in the order in which they left the bag. The poem will resemble you and you will find yourself to be an infinitely original writer with a charming sensitivity even though you will not be understood by the vulgar.[23]

One set of operative strategies in *The World Generator* is that a participant can explore computer-based randomizing processes to generate alternate audio/visual worlds. In particular, texts can be randomly spatialized to form an exciting new navigable poetic form. Another early writer exploring the cut-up, recipe method was Lewis Carroll. In the poem *Poeta Fit, non Nascitur*, Carroll lays out the following suggestion:

> First learn to be spasmodic
> A very simple rule.
> For first you write a sentence,
> And then you chop it small;
> Then mix the bits and sort them out
> Just as they chance to fall;
> The order of the phrases makes
> No difference at all.

> Then if you'd be impressive,
> Remember what I say,
> The abstract qualities begin
> With capitals always:
> The True, the Good, the Beautiful—Those are the things that pay.[24]

For each database-related work, one must define a classification system or set of systems to enable specific media-elements to become operative in a meaningful manner. Yet, chance methods are also relevant to media redistribution and meaning production. Many of my works have explored chance as a particular operative strategy. Because chance methodologies can derive media-elements from a prescribed set of choices, the chance is semirandom in nature. Marcel Duchamp's *Three Standard Stoppages* (1913–14) could be seen as a precursor for such an approach, where a single line of string was dropped deriving three different forms/trajectories that he then glued to boards. Unlike Duchamp, the trajectories that the participant derives are not stored. Often I employ in my work machine-driven chance procedures to derive new juxtapositions. This again speaks to the employment of "sets" of media-elements.

To return to our genetic metaphor, Douglas Kahn and Gregory Whitehead, in *Wireless Imagination,* point toward this metaphor in William R. Burroughs's "cut-up" work in relation to the generation of context:

> The cut-ups were derived from reworked Dada collage techniques, but Burroughs' ideas surrounding them, set forth in his novels, essays and audiotapes, elaborated a new system of recorded sound that metaphorically extended the idea of recording from a psychobiological recording at the level of the genetic code—formed the cipher of the four DNA bases—on out to the realms of political conspiracy and spiritist forces. This writing could tie together the proliferating genetic material of viruses, the syntax of language and the contagion of ideologies, the segmentations of bodies and systems.[25]

The modular fragment of media in a database is potentially alive with content, the qualities of the original recording, and the nature of the initial context. The collision/contextual formings of these contexts, derived through interaction, all facilitate what could be called "felt meaning." The constellation that this material forms and re-forms seeks to transcend the singular elements—as a molecule transcends the individual elements that make it up. Thus, the active media meaning-forces provide the participant with an evocative meaning space. Gendlin describes a "felt meaning" in terms of everyday experience: "What goes through is much more than what we 'have' (explicitly). . . . Any moment is a myriad richness, but rarely do we take the time to 'have' it. . . . Going through a simple act involves an enormous number of familiarities, learnings, senses for the situation, and understandings of life and people, as well as many specifics of the given situation."[26] As we explore material in an interactive work, meaning arises out of a subject/ object unity.[27] The participant draws on past experience and defines his or her own approach to understanding the connections between media fragments selected from the database as these fragments fall together in a context that is being constructed in an ongoing manner. Thus, meaning is always involved in a human process of becoming. Such work is always accretive in nature and open in terms of ongoing meaning production.

I am interested in exploring Wittgenstein's concept of "the meaning of the word is its use in language."[28] Where Wittgenstein was primarily interested in words, I have sought to illuminate experientially how context and meaning become related as elucidated through the active exploration of spatiotemporal media-element substitutions. One could watch meaning shift through the use of the system as potential choices were derived through interaction.

Again, *The World Generator* functions as a meta-meaning, meta-machinic assemblage.[29] The exploration of the permutation of media-elements in time/ space presents a series of meaning-forces operating on one another. In my dissertation I wrote at length about the concept of fields of meaning and I will also discuss fields of meaning in relation to *The World Generator* below.

The menu system for *The World Generator* arose out of an earlier work exploring audio/visual sentence construction: *The Exquisite Mechanism of Shivers* (1991). Could the modules that build an audio/visual sentence be modules of code that actually construct differing virtual worlds, or could they actuate a particular set of modular media processes? Thus, could we begin to build a database of modular code structures that might be explored through permutations? I am still developing this concept in my work and it has huge potential in terms of the construction of mutable computer-based tools and interface systems. *The World Generator* became one particular answer to this question.

PHYSICAL↤↦DIGITAL

Although *The World Generator* is primarily digital in nature, the notion that a selection of physical objects or behavioral processes can be dynamically linked to a database of digital media-elements and processes is essential to work that is growing out of this generator series. The computer can facilitate a linkage that is either entirely digital in nature or it can define a linkage of the digital and the analog through authored *associated* mappings across domains. Thus the metaphor of the database is made physical—suggesting that a dynamically linked, systematic coded grouping can be enabled

via code, conjoining the physical with the digital. In the inception of interactive media, we linked an analog laserdisc to a computer for interaction.
Now the potential is to associate any object or behavioral change in a physical space with linked media-elements and/or processes via new sensing and
authoring systems.[30] At this point, the physical potentials of the interface
table drive the virtual potentialities of the work.

FIELDS OF MEANING

One of the most important characteristics of the database aesthetic is the
potential of bringing different *fields of meaning* to play in the service of
meaning production. Virtual world generation opens an exciting set of operative potentials in relation to field exploration. In "Toward a Field Theory for
Post-Modern Art," Roy Ascott has outlined an approach to meaning in the
arts in terms of fields. In this text Ascott lays out the potentials of a specific
behavioral mode of psychic interplay as a particular generative methodology: "I would like to look at the attributes for a new paradigm for art, a field
theory that would replace the formalist modernist aesthetic. It takes as a
focus not form but behaviour; not an information model for sending/receiv-
ing of messages in a one-way linearity but the interrogation of probabilities
by the viewer; it looks at a system in which the art work is a matrix between
two sets of behaviours (the artist and the observer) providing for a field of
psychic interplay which can be generative of multiple meanings, where the
final responsibility for meaning lies with the viewer."[31] I earlier spoke of the
dynamic enfolding of energy processes conjoining human, machinic system,
behaviors, interface, and environment through interaction. Such a field of
interaction is central to the strategies in many of my works.

Other writers have talked about fields of meaning. Brian Massumi in *A
User's Guide to Capitalism and Schizophrenia: Deviations from Deleuze and
Guattari* makes the observation in terms of meaning production: "Meaning
is Force: This gives us a second approximation of what meaning is: more a
meeting between forces than simply the forces behind the signs. Force against
force, action upon action, the development of envelopment: meaning is an
encounter of lines of force, each of which is actually a complex of other
forces. The processes taking place actually or potentially on all sides could
be analyzed indefinitely in any direction."[32] The incorporation of differing
media-elements in a virtual volume presents a radical new space for meaning "construction" and elucidation. Gideon May and I have loaded a database with polyvalent media variables. Differing spatial configurations of
these media-elements evoke alternate understandings.

The space of *The World Generator* is often *virtually* architectonic in nature. John Frazer writes about emergent examples of virtual architecture in *An Evolutionary Architecture*. He describes another perspective on the employment of the notion of "fields":

> The idea of the field is not foreign to mainstream science, which uses the concept to explain gravitation, electromagnetism, and other phenomena that can be perceived by their effect on matter, yet cannot be explained in terms of matter. Field phenomena are exhibited in objects with holistic properties, such as a magnet or a hologram. A field is always whole. If a magnet is broken in two, each half will produce it's own magnetic field. If a hologram is shattered, each fragment will depict, not a shard of a three-dimensional image, but a complete two-dimensional image. A field is mutually tied to the material in which it is manifested. The history of the form is the history of the field. Every type of material form in the universe, from subatomic particles to the universe itself, is conjectured by [Rupert] Sheldrake to have an associated field, which guides its formation and maintains its structure.[33]

It is this dimensional holistic quality of a virtual environment that separates it from many past poetic forms. Thus the concept of "field" clearly relates to the notion of sets described above, where a series of fields (separate database variables) work together to form an emergent outcome through recombination and *interaction* ←→ *intra-action* by an engaged participant. We could say that each sense contributes to the intermingling of these fields. Thus, multimodal experience as well as the history of experience is central to the evocation of the works.

N. Katherine Hayles speaks about fields of meaning in *The Cosmic Web*. She has articulated her approach to the use of "fields" as abstracted from physics, directly relating to those suggested by Ascott:

> The field concept, as I use the term, is not identical with any single field formulation in science. For the men and women who work with the various scientific field models from day to day, they have specific meanings and applications. The term "field concept," by contrast, draws from many different models whose features are isomorphic and hence are characteristic of twentieth-century thought in general. The only way to approach a satisfactory understanding of the field concept is to examine and compare a wide range of phenomena that embody it. . . . Perhaps most essential to the field concept is the notion that things are interconnected. The most rigorous formulations of this idea are

found in modern physics. In marked contrast to the atomistic Newtonian idea of reality, in which physical objects are discrete and events capable of occurring independently of one another and the observer, a field view of reality pictures objects, events and the observer as belonging inextricably to the same field; the disposition of each, in this view, is influenced—sometimes dramatically, sometimes subtly, but in every instance—by the disposition of the others.[34]

I have been particularly interested in the way meaning arises through dynamic interaction with media-elements and processes. I see this as always involving a form of meaning summing that defines a field of fields, including the participant, the environment, the interface system, media processes and the media-elements explored through interaction. The field concept is particularly useful in talking about *The World Generator / The Engine of Desire* (1996–present).

In particular, *The World Generator* seeks to provide a place to reflect on the combinatoric and projective qualities of thought as it intermingled with matter/energy processes and experience.[35] It also seeks to provide a platform for exploring an expanded linguistic form of media authorship.

TOWARD A NEW LINGUISTICS

The World Generator begins to approach the potentials of a new linguistics. If we look at the meaning of the word "language," we can see the media-elements in the work functioning as language-vehicles. The system includes:

- Standard text, both written and spoken.
- Poetic text rendered in a 3D virtual environment.
- Images, both still and time-based, exemplifying the following section of the definition of language—any means of expressing or communicating, as gestures, signs, animal sounds, and so on.
- Music—also exemplifying any means of expressing or communicating, as gestures, signs, animal sounds.
- Computer code that exemplifies the particular words or phrases of a profession, group.

For each of these strands of "language" use, we necessarily develop our own perceptual understanding. In the techno-poetic environment of *The World Generator*, these language-vehicles can be enfolded and modify or qualify one another. We draw on our understanding of each separate "language" use within a particular context and dynamically *sum up* our perceptions to derive meaning. A particular branch of linguistics begins to approach this concept—Integrational Linguistics as defined by Roy Harris and George Wolf:[36]

> We take the term intergrationalism to allude to a recognition that what makes an utterance (or any other form of expression) language is not its conformity to the requirements of a code but its function in integrating other human activities, that integration being what makes communication between one human being and another possible. The same applies, furthermore, not only to language, but to all modes of human communication. For contrary to what is commonly assumed in orthodox linguistics, there is not a sharp dividing line separating language from other modes of communication, or linguistic behavior from non-linguistic behavior. For human beings a sign is a sign because it has an integrational function in the particular circumstance which it occurs, and when voluntarily produced by human agency its production is always a creative act on the part of one or more individuals acting in a certain situation. Whatever we recognize as a linguistic sign (by whatever criteria seems appropriate to the occasion) is always a non-linguistic sign as well. The two are never mutually exclusive. Human beings do not inhabit a communication space which is compartmentalized into language and non-language, but an integrated space where all signs are connected.[37]

It is just such an "integrated" space that *The World Generator* seeks to operationally articulate. In fact, in particular, it seeks to be a meta-meaning space, exemplifying the above notion that all signs are connected, that they are "integrated through social action" and function in unity with the participant.[38] Recombinant poetic works seek to expand such notions via the potentialities of computer-based and computer-mediated-meaning production spaces. One can project a future in which a person can seamlessly draw on vast databases and the resources of ubiquitous computing in real time to augment ongoing language/meaning production with various media-elements and processes.

SUMMARY

In *The World Generator,* the aesthetic is directly tied to what is loaded into the system (or addressable as part of the system). This includes the media variables as well as a series of operational coded structural strategies. The aesthetic is also derived through operative media processes inherent to the work as well as the interface that enables dynamic interaction. Growing out of this database work is the potential of combining digital databases with linked physical spaces. This is a central strategy to more recent sensing technologies and ubiquitous computing as well as the production of augmented reality.

The probability of the aesthetic of certain kinds of events arising through interaction is central to the work. I have defined a particular spatial media vocabulary of potential recombinance. *The World Generator* empowers the participant to disrupt and explore/redefine combinatorial strategies through direct engagement and personal interaction facilitated by the various systems. Interaction arises in a gamelike manner. In extending Wittgenstein's notion of language game described in his *Philosophical Investigations,*[39] this work provides an expanded "integrational" linguistic pattern flow game.

The operative-ness I have explored in *The World Generator* is reflected in the following concerns:

1. The potential *positioning* of variable media-elements or processes.
2. Contextualization, decontextualization, and recontextualization of media-elements.
3. Editing modules of time-based media: (a) substitution of linear time-based modules, (b) layering of sound or the calling up of alternate sound modules, and (c) automated Sorting via encoded classification (code tags).
4. Manipulating media-elements in virtual space—the participant potentially brings about: interpenetration, juxtaposition, and aesthetic alteration of media-elements through interaction with the following categories of "operative" processes: (a) poetic construction processes, (b) navigation processes, (c) processes related to authored media-behavior, (d) navigation processes, (e) editing processes, (f) abstraction processes, (g) automated generative processes, (h) processes related to distributed virtual reality, and (i) change processes of a *semirandom* nature.
5. Navigation as an operative metaphor for moving through, selecting, and/or triggering choice media-data.
6. Specificity of interaction as mode of content generation.

I have earlier (in my dissertation) coined the term *cyber-polysemic space* to refer to these differing media-conglomerate technological settings arising in a virtual environment. These spaces explore the notion of a new multi-dimensional linguistic environment as exemplified within a performative media-space populated with mutable assemblages of media-elements and processes.

A "constructed context" arises through dynamic interaction:

- as a by-product of *interactive* ↔ *intra-active* poetic-construction processes
- through navigation and temporary perspective
- through time-based viewing
- through subsequent reflection related to a remembered context
- through external conceptual framing and/or alternate versions of works

In *The World Generator,* the mutable nature of context is brought to light through some form of inter-authorship and/or *interaction* ↔ *intra-action* on the part of the "vuser" (viewer/user), or what I have more recently called "muser" (multimodal user). In particular, this work explores the dynamic nature of meaning-becoming. The interactive exploration of the database aesthetic enables a form of meta-meaning production that is central to my work.

We continue to approach meaning production when we know at best that we can only illuminate such processes by pointing (as Wittgenstein suggests). It becomes imperative to develop new technological/poetic systems to explore emergent meaning production as well as new strategies that are enabled through the potentials of the database aesthetic as exemplified in Recombinant Poetic works to better "point" at meaning production.

NOTES

1. See Susan Leigh Star and Geoffrey C. Bowker, "Sorting Things Out: Classification and Its Consequences": http://weber.ucsd.edu/~gbowker/classification/ "At this site, we present the introduction, first two chapters and concluding chapters of our book on classification systems published by MIT Press in 1999." (This reference arises out of a discussion with Sha Xin Wei on boundary objects.)

2. Claude Berge, *Principles of Combinatorics,* trans. John Sheenan (New York: Academic Press, 1971), 1–3.

3. Richard Hamilton and Ecke Bonk, "The Typosophic Texture," in *Politics/Poetics: Das Burch Zur Documenta X* (Ostfildern-Ruit: Cantz Verlag, 1997), 309.

4. See Warren F. Motte, *OULIPO: A Primer of Potential Literature* (Normal, Ill.: Dalkey Archive Press, 1998).

5. Berge, *Principles of Combinatorics,* 1–3.

6. Stéphane Mallarmé, "A Throw of the Dice Will Never Annul Chance," in *Stéphane Mallarmé: Selected Poetry and Prose,* ed. Mary Ann Caws (New York: New Directions, 1982), 103–27.

7. For an extensive guide to this genre, see Dick Higgins, *Pattern Poetry: Guide to an Unknown Literature* (Albany: State University of New York Press, 1987).

8. Umberto Eco, *The Open Work,* trans. Anna Concogni (Cambridge, Mass.: Harvard University Press, 1989), 3–4.

9. Francis A. Yates, *The Art of Memory* (Chicago: University of Chicago Press, 1966). See also Martin Gardner, *Logic Machines and Diagrams,* 2nd ed. (Chicago: University of Chicago Press, 1982).

10. See James M. Nyce and Paul Kahn, eds., *From Memex to Hypertext: Vannevar Bush and the Mind's Machine* (Boston: Academic Press, 1991); see also Michael Joyce, *Of Two Minds: Hypertext Pedagogy and Poetics* (Ann Arbor: University of Michigan Press, 1995), 22.

11. I explore these concepts in depth in "The Theatre of Interflow Architecture: An Exploration into a Poetics of Machinic Sensing, Multi-modal Searching and Thought Augmentation Approaches within Networked Architectural Spaces." See billseaman.com.

12. See Bill Seaman, "Recombinant Poetics: Emergent Meaning as Examined and Explored Within a Specific Generative Virtual Environment" (Diss., The Centre for Advanced Inquiry in Interactive Art, University of Wales, Caerleon Campus, 1999). Also available in PDF format from the Daniel Langlois Foundation and/or http://billseaman.com/.

13. Subsequent research has shown a related metaphorical use of the word "recombinant" by William Mitchell in his discussion of "recombinant architecture," in *City of Bits* (Cambridge, Mass.: MIT Press, 1995), 47; see also http://mitpress2.mit.edu/e-books/City_of_Bits/Recombinant_Architecture/index.html (chapter 4). Other artists and researchers have used the term "recombinant" in a metaphorical manner, including Arthur Kroker and Michael A. Weinstein, *Data Trash: The Theory of the Virtual Class* (New York: St. Martin's Press, 1994). Douglas Khan and Gregory Whitehead, eds., *Wireless Imagination* (Cambridge, Mass.: MIT Press, 1992), 13; Kahn also suggests poetic relations to DNA in the work of William S. Burroughs and Brion Gysin. Sergei Eisenstein, in *Film Forum: Essays in Film Theory* (trans. Jay Leyda [New York: Harcourt, Brace, 1949], 67), speaks of the "genetics" of montage methods. The Critical Art ensemble has also written about notions surrounding "recombinant" potentials (Critical Art Ensemble, "Utopian Plagiarism, Hypertextuality, and Electronic Cultural Production," in *Critical Issues in Electronic Media,* 1995, edited by Simon Penny, as found online at http://www.coe.uga.edu/reading/faculty/dreinking/Utopian_plagiarism.html). The exploration of modular, combinatoric systems can be witnessed in my artwork as early as 1981.

14. *McGraw-Hill Dictionary of Scientific and Technical Terms,* editor in chief S. Parker (Boston: Kluwer Boston, 1989), 1576.

15. See Bill Seaman and Andrea Gaugusch, "(RE)Sensing the Observer: Offering an Open Order Cybernetics," in *Technoetic Arts* 2, no. 1 (2004).

16. See chapter 1.1.6, Fields of Meaning, in Seaman, "Recombinant Poetics," 53.

17. Gilles Deleuze and Félix Guattari, *A Thousand Plateaus: Capitalism and Schizophrenia,* trans. Brian Massumi (Minneapolis: University of Minnesota Press, 1987), 474.

18. Ibid., 21.

19. Ibid.

20. Ibid., 330–31.

21. Ibid., 145.

22. In 1992, I listed the following set of potential generators. Some of these have become works exploring the database aesthetic: *Abstraction Generator, Analogy Generator, Allegory*

Generator, Artificial Intelligence Generator, Invention Generator, Nonsense Generator, Question Generator, Actor Generator, Desire Generator, History of Music Generator, Paradox Generator, Title Generator, and *Fashion Generator.*

23. Elmer Peterson, *Tristan Tzara: Dada and Surrational Theorist* (New Brunswick: Rutgers University Press, 1971), 35.

24. Lewis Carroll, *The Complete Works of Lewis Carroll* (New York: Random House, 1937), 880–81.

25. Kahn and Whitehead, *Wireless Imagination,* 13.

26. E. T. Gendlin, "Experiential Phenomenology," in *Phenomenology and the Social Sciences,* ed. Maurice Natanson (Evanston, Ill.: Northwestern University Press, 1973), 370.

27. See Seaman, Gaugusch, and Gaugusch, "(RE)Sensing the Observer."

28. Ludwig Wittgenstein, *Philosophical Investigations,* 3rd ed., trans. G. E. M. Anscomb (Englewood Cliffs, N.J.: Prentice-Hall, 1958), 20.

29. Deleuze and Guattari, *A Thousand Plateaus,* 145. I draw on this definition of machinic assemblage and use the term meta-machinic assemblage.

30. See *The Poly-Sensing Environment and Object-Based Emergent Intention Matrix: Toward an Integrated Physical/Augmented Reality Space.* On this project I collaborated with Ingrid Verbauwhede, an electrical engineer from UCLA, and Mark Hansen, from Statistics at UCLA. Two student researchers have also been working on the project: Shenglin Yang, Programmer/Researcher Electrical Engineering Department, UCLA, and Fabian Winkler, Design | Media Arts, UCLA. Initial funding for the research has come from The Academic Border Crossing Fund at UCLA and the Daniel Langlois Foundation. http://www.fondation-langlois.org.

31. Roy Ascott, "Toward a Field Theory of Post-Modernist Art," *Leonardo* 13 (1980): 51–52.

32. Brian Massumi, *A User's Guide to Capitalism and Schizophrenia: Deviations from Deleuze and Guattari* (Cambridge, Mass.: MIT Press, 1992), 11.

33. John Frazer, *An Evolutionary Architecture* (London: Architectural Association, 1995), 112.

34. N. Katherine Hayles, *The Cosmic Web: Scientific Field Models and Literary Strategies in the Twentieth Century* (Ithaca: Cornell University Press, 1984), preface II.

35. See G. M. Edelman, *Neural Darwinism* (New York: Basic Books, 1987); see also J. A. Scott Kelso, Arnold J. Mandell, and Michael F. Shlesinger, *Dynamic Patterns in Complex Systems: The Self-Organization of Brain and Behavior* (Cambridge, Mass.: MIT Press, A Bradford Book, 1988); and Esther Thelen and Linda B. Smith, eds., *A Dynamic Systems Approach to the Development of Cognition and Action* (Cambridge, Mass.: MIT Press, A Bradford Book, 1994).

36. *Integrational Linguistics: A First Reader,* ed. Roy Harris and George Wolf (New Orleans: Louisiana State University Press, 1998), 6.

37. Ibid., 1–2.

38. Ibid., 6.

39. Wittgenstein, *Philosophical Investigations,* 11.

8. THE DATABASE: AN AESTHETICS OF DIGNITY

SHARON DANIEL

SOMETHING GIVEN

The term "data" originated as the plural of the Latin word datum, meaning "something given."[1] In the world of experience, our datum is a culturally constructed social context. This context, and the socio-ideological experience of individuals in the context of contemporary Western societies, is defined by what Katherine Hayles has called the "materiality of informatics": "the material, technological, economic, and social structures that make the information age possible." Hayles's "Informatics" includes "the late capitalist mode of flexible accumulation; the hardware and software that have merged telecommunications with computer technology; and the patterns of living that emerge from and depend upon instant transmission of information and access to large data banks."[2]

Data must be interpreted in order to take on meaning and become information. A datum is a mark or trace that represents a portion of the real world. Data can be processed and transcribed into a readable language on a sustainable medium—a completed questionnaire, a taped interview, the recorded results of an experiment. Events or experiences that leave physical, virtual, or perceivable marks can be traced through data. Marks lose their status as data when they can no longer be interpreted because the code linking them to particular observations is unavailable.[3] People, and computers, find or impose patterns on data—patterns that are seen as information used to enhance knowledge, authorized as aesthetic or ethical criteria, and accepted as truth. Patterns mined from data may be structures observable through the senses (and therefore subject to aesthetic evaluation), or normative examples for behavior (subject to questions of ethics). Since actions or behavior can be said to have beauty beyond sensory appeal, aesthetics and ethics intersect. It is at this intersection that the question "How should we live?" is posed—querying methodology (how), desire (should), identity and community (we), and the conditions of existence (live). Together, ethics and aesthetics challenge the function, nature, ontology, and purpose of art. Historically, aesthetics has played a central role in the development of the ethics of the individual subject and, while the problem of "the nature of beauty" has been rendered irrelevant to some degree in postmodernist criticism, aesthetics may still be used as a tool to examine the relation between art and life. In aesthetics (and ethics), the question of beauty is linked to the question of subjectivity. Two approaches to the problem of beauty (or of morality) dominate: the objective, which asserts that beauty (or ethos) inheres in the object (or absolute) and that judgments concerning it may have objective validity, and the subjective, where the beautiful (or just) is identified or determined by the observer.

UNIFYING FUNCTIONS

Both the objective approach *and* the subjective approach presuppose the status of the object, or the work of art as a unified whole. In his 1979 essay "What Is an Author?" Michel Foucault asks, "What is this curious unity that we designate as a work?"[4] What are the limits or boundaries of a work of art? Of what is it comprised? Is it the product of an author? If so, then the question of who, or what, is an author must arise. Foucault stipulates that a "work," in the modern era, is both defined and constrained by the name of the author—the "author function." Foucault's "author function" is a system of classification where the name of the author (as opposed to "signer," "guarantor," or "writer") identifies, elevates, and frames a text. The author function has to do with ownership and transgression. The author functions as the founder of a discourse, the owner of the property of a text, and, as such, an individual subject, both privileged and psychologized, whose biography gives meaning to and takes meaning from the text.

When an individual is accepted as an author, then what, of all that the individual wrote or produced or left behind, is part of the "work"? Foucault follows this question to its logical conclusion:

> When undertaking the publication of Nietzsche's works, for example, where should one stop? Surely everything must be published, but what is "everything"? Everything that Nietzsche himself published, certainly. And what about the rough drafts for his works? Obviously. The plans for his aphorisms? Yes. The deleted passages and the notes at the bottom of the page? Yes. What if, within a workbook filled with aphorisms, one finds a reference, the notation of a meeting or of an address, or a laundry list: is it a work, or not? Why not?

and

> If an individual were not an author, could we say that what he wrote, said, left
> behind in his papers, or what has been collected of his remarks, could be called
> a "work"? When Sade was not considered an author, what was the status of his
> papers? Were they simply rolls of paper onto which he ceaselessly uncoiled his
> fantasies during his imprisonment?[5]

The author function is a "characteristic of the existence, circulation, and
functioning of certain discourses within a society." Authorship evolved as
discourses became transgressive and owners/writers/signers/identifiers of
texts could be subject to punishment. "In our culture (and doubtless in many
others), discourse was not originally a product, a thing, a kind of goods. It
was essentially an act—an act placed in the bipolar field of the sacred and
the profane, the licit and the illicit, the religious and the blasphemous. Historically, it was a gesture fraught with risks before becoming goods caught
up in a circuit of ownership."[6] To Roland Barthes, "The author is a modern
figure . . . the epitome and the culmination of capitalist ideology."[7] The individualization of the author provided a context for the objectification of the
work as both unity and commodity.

The premodernist narrator was a mediator rather than author—a shaman
whose role was performative rather than creative. The narrator's story was
an aggregate, its origin collective. The shaman/narrator performed *for* the
community narratives *belonging to* the community. Did these narratives
have the status of a work? Is, for example, *One Thousand and One Nights* a
work? Or is it a database? The author function unifies a "text" or a body of
work so that the relation between a group of texts is fixed. The storyteller
draws on and contributes to an evolving database—searching, selecting,
elaborating, contributing. There is no fixed relation, no unity, no single
author—only stories that continuously unfold to reveal increasingly complex topologies. These fluid configurations, the fleeting figures and patterns
they reveal, are the concern of ethics and aesthetics in the context of the
materiality of informatics—not "What constitutes a work?" or, "Who is to
be identified and accepted as an author?" The insistence on the unity of a
work is as problematic as the notion of the author's individuality, or the
idea of the uniqueness of the subject.[8] Authorial individuality and authority is already "de-centered" by the fragmentation of the social world, by
the relativity and relationality of the worldviews of any of its actors. The

problem of representation in art, literature, and politics is analogous to the "propositions of relativity and quantum physics, that can make no statements about nature that are independent of the framework of the investigation."[9]

UNCERTAINTY FIELDS

Quantum physics is, to quote Nicholas Mosley in *Hopeful Monsters,* "the study of things that cannot exist using methods that are admitted not to refer to what they talk about."[10] Quantum physics locates the interaction of or exchange between two separate physical systems, for example, two bodies, to a "field" that extends from one to the other. In physics, a "field" is a region under some influence, such as gravitation. A system, like a body, consists of components, which are organized to facilitate the flow of information, matter, or energy. A system may be open or closed, (homeo)static or dynamic. "At arbitrary boundaries, a collection of interrelated components may be declared a system and may further be abstracted to be declared a component of a larger system. An open system can be influenced by events outside the declared boundaries of a system. A closed system is self-contained: outside events can have no influence upon the system. Dynamic systems have components and/or flows that change over time."[11] Physicist Werner Heisenberg posited the simultaneous absence and presence of matter where every object can be understood both as a localized point (finite, bounded, specific) and as a variably distributed wave function (spreading infinitely).[12] Heisenberg's uncertainty principle is taken to mean that on an elementary level, the physical universe does not exist in a deterministic form, but rather as a collection of probabilities, or potentials. The Principle of Uncertainty states that at the quantum scale, both the location and the velocity of a particle cannot be known simultaneously because the act of observation (performed through electromagnetic instruments) itself introduces energy into the system of particles observed, thereby influencing them so that their behavior cannot be known independently of the observer. This unknown quality led to the debates about how deep uncertainty goes. Is uncertainty fundamentally a part of how nature works? In other words, are the behaviors of the particles themselves uncaused and unknown to them before they move?[13]

Outside the contexts of physics and computer science, "field" is defined as "a complex of forces that serve as causative agents in human behavior" and a system is understood as "a complex of methods or rules governing behavior."[14] Uncertainty is an inevitable part of the assertion of knowledge.

Everything said is said to an observer; knowledge of reality is dependent upon the perceptions of the observer. Observation or measurement affects the state of the object being observed—that is, objective measurement or observation from outside a system is not possible, and the act of observing makes the observer part of the system under study. The observer, whose observation is initiated in order to produce a representation of the system observed, is progressively incorporated into the system. The authority of representation, as such, is compromised. Uncertainty is thus implicated in the disappearance of the author/observer. His disappearance, or death, is produced and reproduced in a variety of narratives that originate in diverse discourses from semiotics to cybernetics. Cybernetics and computational biology (or Artificial Life research) offer models for rethinking representation and authorship in the epistemology of autopoiesis, and emergent systems called cellular automata.[15] These models move beyond the interpretation of "uncertainty" as the collapse of the separation between subject and object—the death of the author—and posit multiple differentiations, and proliferating perspectives—*emergent dialogism.*

DIALOGISM

Autopoetic systems, as articulated by second-order Cybernetitians Humberto Maturana and Francisco Varela, incorporate the observer as part of the system. Through recursive interactions with its own linguistic states, an autopoetic system may always linguistically interact with its own states as if with representations of its interactions. An autopoetic system is self-reflexive, self-organizing, self-making. Such systems are "informationally closed," responding to environmental stimuli based on their own, internal self-organization.[16] An autopoetic system envelops the observer/subject within its field. What is seen by the subject is seen through the filter of the system—from inside the system's perspective. In an autopoetic system, system and subject, perception and representation, are collapsed, elided—there is no exterior. Subjectivity is system-dependent and systemic. There is no representation external to the experience of the system itself. As in Bakhtin's dialogic, polyphonic, multivocal model for narrative, in an autopoetic system there is "first, not one entity or consciousness absorbing others into itself as objects but a whole formed by the interaction of many entities or consciousnesses none of which entirely becomes an object for the other, and . . . second, an avoidance of objectification—non-participating third parties are not represented in any way—only participating voices speak within and through their own intersubjective experience."[17]

EMERGENCE

In *Cellular Automata Machines: A New Environment for Modeling,* Thomaso Toffoli and Norman Margolus maintain that cellular automata "are the computer scientist's counterpart to the physicist's concept of "field."[18] Cellular automata are self-evolving or emergent; cellular automata are systems that extend in space and evolve in time according to local laws. The automata is a field or frame, usually represented as a two- or three-dimensional grid of cells or pixels. Each cell or pixel may "behave" independently at each "step" in time based on a table of rules and a given initial condition. The table of rules is a set of definitions for the behavior of each pixel or cell in relation to the state of each neighboring pixel or cell. Given any initial condition, a global state emerges from the local interactions of discrete entities in an iterative and evolving system.

Where subject and system collapse in autopoetic epistemology (causing perception and representation, which are dependent upon the organizing principle of the system, to be played out in self-reflexive reiteration) in emergent systems like cellular automata, subjectivity is socialized and the system functions as a "community." The subject position posited by the cellular automata model is relational and associative—both distributed and discrete. A global perspective and a multitude of particularized, local perspectives exist in simultaneous interdependence. In cellular automata, the contradiction between individual autonomy and community collapses. Cellular automata embody an oscillating, productive tension between the individual and the social—there is no observer, only interdependent agents or actors.

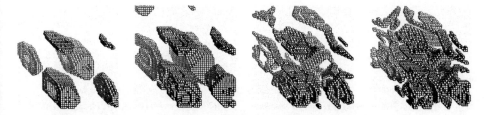

FIGURE 8.1. FOUR TIME STEPS IN THE EVOLUTION OF A CELLULAR AUTOMATA VISUALIZED WITH TRESVITA V3.2 SOFTWARE CREATED BY ALEXANDER MIECZYSLAW KASPRZYK. TRESVITA IS SHAREWARE, AVAILABLE AT HTTP://ALIFE.CCP14.AC.UK/ MACSOFT2/WWW/TRESVITADOCS.HTML. FOR THIS EXAMPLE THE RULE-SET WAS SEQUENTIAL AND REQUIRED FOUR MINIMUM, FIVE MAXIMUM NEIGHBORS FOR SURVIVAL AND FIVE MIN/MAX FOR GROWTH. SEED DENSITY WAS SEVEN IN A 30 x 30 x 30 GRID.

The problem of the role of the observer in physics and cybernetics is parallel to the problem of authorship and representation in art. As the relation of observer and observed is redefined so that it may be possible to "reexamine the privileges of the subject" and the function of the author as suggested by Foucault, ". . . In short, it is a matter of depriving the subject (or its substitute) of its role as originator, and of analyzing the subject as a variable and complex function of a [system or] discourse."[19]

Collaborative Systems

Foucault's reexamination of the privileges of the subject interrogates the conditions of possibility and the rules under which "something like a subject" might appear and function in discourses/systems/texts. Here he poses a challenge:

> I seem to call for a form of culture in which fiction would not be limited by the figure of the author. It would be pure romanticism, however, to imagine a culture in which the fictive would operate in an absolutely free state, in which fiction would be put at the disposal of everyone and would develop without passing through something like a necessary or constraining figure. . . . The author has played the role of the regulator of the fictive, a role quite characteristic of our era of industrial and bourgeois society, of individualism and private property, still, given the historical modifications that are taking place it does not seem necessary that the author function remain in constant form, complexity, and even in existence. I think that, as our society changes, at the very moment when it is in the process of changing, the author function will disappear, and in such a manner that fiction and its polysemous texts will once again function according to another mode, but still with a system of constraint—one which will no longer be the author, but which will have to be determined or, perhaps experienced.[20]

The historical modifications and social changes that Foucault anticipates are manifest in the "materiality of informatics." We must try to reimagine the pervasive systems and interfaces of "informatics," which have become the unacknowledged tools of the everyday as a datum, "something given" on which to build a space for polysemous texts and Bahktinian polyphonies— a space that will allow a plentitude of voices; a space for collective self-representation; a space where nonparticipating third persons are not represented in any way.[21]

This free space, "in which fiction would be put at the disposal of everyone and would develop without passing through something like a necessary or constraining figure," is embodied (made possible) in "collaborative systems."[22] I use the phrase "collaborative systems" to describe public art produced in collaboration with local and online communities and structured on the model of the spatially and temporally distributed dynamics of cellular automata. Collaborative systems are both social and technological: As Stephen Willats notes: "Any social organization can be thought of as a complex, evolving system insofar as it generates behavior that is unpredictable, non-linear, and capable of producing multiple outcomes."[23] Social systems, like cellular automata, are rule-based emergent systems. In social systems, however, as in collaborative systems, the initial condition of the system (the state or condition of the field or world at the first step of evolution) is contingent upon tangible, global conditions that are in flux, and its rule table (directions for the behavior and interaction of its "cells") is, itself, emergent. Therefore, the rule-base of a collaborative system is dynamic and self-reflexive. A collaborative system may frame human participants, artificially intelligent agents, computer algorithms, and computer or community networks in the location of the individual "cells" within a field. Each "cell," entity, or human participant has agency—playing a role in the "inter-authorship" of the system in response to the conditions of the field.[24]

A collaborative system generates a material condition for the disappearance of the author function and fulfills Foucault's prediction regarding a "system of constraint—one which will no longer be the author, but which will have to be determined or, perhaps experienced." A collaborative system makes no reference to "originality," authenticity, or psychologizing identification with an author. Collaborative systems focus instead on how a discourse can circulate, who can productively appropriate a discourse, "what are the places in it where there is room for possible subjects? and, who can assume these various subject functions?"[25] In collaborative systems, the author function is supplanted by a "subject function," where "subject" is a variable: a quantity that can assume any of a set of values. This variable "subject-function" speaks with many voices. In a collaborative system, public-information spaces and communications technologies are exploited in order to establish a framework (designed in dialogue with a community), in which collaborating participants can build databases of texts, sounds, and images from their own world of reference or experience and structure and interpret that data themselves. Through this collaborative process, the individual private subject consciously engages a sociopolitical network, the sociopolitical merges into the private/personal, and the subject emerges as a politicized participant in an intersubjective network.

The Bahktin circle, which combined the study of philosophy, social theory, and criticism with collective literary production, is both a precursor and an influence on collaborative systems.[26] The circle frames a field of discourse, and patterns of thought emerge through collective articulation. For Mikhail Bahktin, meaning is derived from dialogue, which is grounded in a social context. He adheres to the idea that social and aesthetic forms are produced under particular circumstances. These provide a resource for an analysis of everyday life. There is no place for the heroic author or actor in Bahktin's analysis. Rather, he seeks out the voices of those excluded from "history"—voices "that reveal the details of everyday life—in order to decode the social world."[27] Bahktin's theory of dialogism assumes that no individual ever writes, or authors, alone. "Writing" (imaging, speaking) is the result of our interactions with the world. "The Author is . . . the ideological figure by which one marks the manner in which we fear the proliferation of meaning."[28] To write and construct *new knowledge and meaning,* the subject must be a variable—we must engage in a dialogic process where "the words and images of one individual are examined and primarily understood in relationship to the words and images of others."[29] This interaction requires an infrastructure like that of a database.

DATABASE AESTHETICS

A database is relational and nonhierarchical. It is a structure that persists while its content evolves and is displaced. The structure of the database comprises an initial condition for the evolution of a system. Evolution and displacement are fundamental to the dialogic process. Through this process all the possible meanings of stories, statements, images, and words interact, and possibly conflict, to affect and change their future meanings. Collaborative systems are dialogic spaces in which the acts of writing, imaging, storytelling, and political statement are a collective production, a process rooted in social interaction and dialogue that produces a narrative without authorial consistency. This notion of a multivocal, but authorless, narrative necessitates a radical rethinking of aesthetics, suggesting the possibility of an aesthetics of "Database."

"Aesthetics" has traditionally meant "a theory or conception of beauty."[30] A "conception" of the "beauty" of a database is not located in the viewer's interpretation of a static form but in the dynamics of how a user inflects the database through interaction with its field or frame. A database incorporates contradiction; it is simultaneously recombinant and indexical, precise and scalable, immersive and emergent, homogeneous and heterogeneous. It is a field of coherence and contradiction. The aesthetic dimensions of the database arise when an agent traverses this field of unresolved contradictions. The database is comprised of nested subfields, which are activated, and given ontological status by the agent's trajectory through its field. Continuously emergent ontological states resolve as new subfields from each interaction and are integrated into the field, changing and transforming the content and structure of that field and constituting not an "art object," but a continuously evolving and fluid system. These are the conditions of possibility of "database aesthetics."

An argument for the "conditions of possibility" of database aesthetics can be grounded in the analysis of systems found in the world. The following four "found" systems provide external evidence of and extended context for an aesthetics of the database.[31] Each example is an archive, artifact, or instance of a specific, social, economic, political, and/or cultural response to a materially and historically contingent, phenomenological field. The Paris catacombs, Sainte-Chapelle, the insect collection of Anne and Jacques Kerchache, and the city of Venice itself are material/experiential manifestations of the impulse to order, classify, name, and systematize relations of meaning within specific social, cultural, and political contexts. Each in turn is evidence of a particular process or perspective. The Paris catacombs were created through a process of displacement, fragmentation, reorganization, and redistribution that transferred the locus of identity from the individual body to its discrete parts and place of origin. The stained-glass windows of Sainte-Chapelle are a kaleidoscopic database of instructions embedded in a narrative designed to be traversed on multiple levels of temporal scale. Their overall pattern reveals, through shifts in time and light, subfields of social and moral particularity. There can be no one-to-one map of Venice because no absolute or fixed representation of its features is possible. Every feature of the city has been named and renamed from a continuously shifting and overlapping multiplicity of perspectives. Every map of Venice is larger than its territory. The Kerchache collection is a crystallization of formulations of power—in its aestheticization of "nature" (a reification of relations of difference and similarity), and in its rational capitalist method—acquisition, accumulation, classification, and display. Each is an example of a unique system of representation, method, or perspective by which a social system organizes (organized) data in response to evolving phenomenological processes within a socioeconomic, political, moral/religious, or scientific field.

FOUND SYSTEM: THE PARIS CATACOMBS

The Paris catacombs constitute a massive database of the dead, embodied in an immersive environment. After a long, winding descent, narrow stone corridors suddenly transform into stacks and rows of human skulls and femurs ten feet in depth and rising eight, lining what appears to be an infinitely receding passageway. Shock registers in sudden breathlessness. Immersion here means immersion in a monumental volume of loss and decay. However, after this first bodily response, the response-type that is the locus of traditional aesthetics, one's perception shifts to the obsessive, repetitive, endless, stacking, ordering, patterning, and cataloging of human remains. These remains are organized and categorized; identified in groups by their location of origin in once consecrated graves. The algorithm used to construct the catacomb: exhume skeletons, reduce individual skeletons to skull and femur, remove fragments to catacomb, situate in subfield identified with graveyard of origin. Identity and location have been displaced by a general categorization of fragments that constitutes a field. Each particular body as organic whole is lost—its history and context subsumed in subfields. In this example, database aesthetics works through displacement that resolves into a pattern, which constitutes an immersive, phenomenal space. The Paris catacombs were once a dynamic system that has ceased to evolve. They are a reflection of a specific historical/material circumstance and a complex of

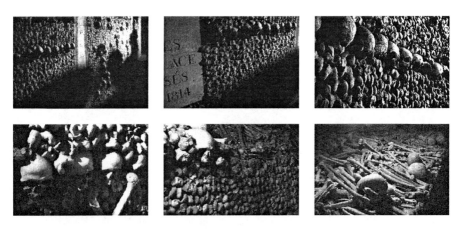

FIGURE 8.2. DETAILS OF PARIS CATACOMBS, WHERE SEVEN MILLION PARISIANS' SKELETONS, LONG SINCE DISINTERRED FROM THE CHURCHYARD GRAVES WHERE THEIR SURVIVORS BURIED THEM, ARE NEATLY STACKED AND ALIGNED TO FORM THE WALLS OF NEARLY ONE KILOMETER OF WALKING PASSAGE. PHOTOGRAPH BY SHARON DANIEL.

political and socioeconomic priorities: state over individual, progress over history, place over person.

FOUND SYSTEM: SAINTE-CHAPELLE

The chapel as a whole is an information system with a nested or "whole-to-part" structural organization.[32] This structure was designed to regulate temporal and social experience. The walls of the upper chapel are formed by fifteen stained-glass windows, which comprise the data-field of the chapel (Figure 8.3). Each window is divided into subfields, or self-contained

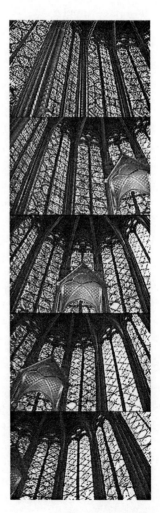

FIGURE 8.3. SEQUENCED DETAIL OF THE CHAPEL AND CANOPY AT SAINTE-CHAPELLE. PHOTOGRAPH BY SHARON DANIEL.

individual panels. No two panels are alike. This idiosyncratic differentiation
is mediated by the ordering frame of the chapel's architecture, which produces the appearance of a coherent pattern. The aesthetic experience is one
of oscillation between the impact of the architectural frame, or field, and
the stimulus of the visual and narrative figuration, descriptions, and instructions in the individual panels of the windows, or nested subfields.

Each panel or group of panels has a narrative structure meant to didac-
tically prescribe a moral code and outline a spiritual practice. Together, the
panels function as an immersive rule table. Parishioners are meant to emu-
late the characters depicted in the stories and structure their social interactions accordingly.

The experience of the chapel for a parishioner was time based; the illu-
mination of the chapel's narrative database is subject to the cycles of night
and day, and to the longer units of yearly seasonal change. The chapel is
therefore a clock that temporally orders the live of its members as well as a
social and moral handbook that regulates their behavior.

FOUND SYSTEM: VENICE

The database for the "conditions of possibility" of the city of Venice is a field
defined by excess and necessity, decadence, and survival. Here water, architecture, commerce, and tourism comprise a system that is both emergent
and immersive: a physical and historical "collaborative system." The lagoon
and canals frame the complex fields and subfields of the city, while, simultaneously, the city frames their tidal flow. Venice is a body floating, suspended
in its own fluids. Water contains and fills, encompasses and embodies it.

The vector that traverses the field of Venice is the loss of perspective.
Venice is a manifestation in experience of the condition of schizophrenia.
As Fredric Jameson notes: "When the links of the signifying chain snap,
then we have schizophrenia in the form of a rubble of distinct and unrelated
signifiers."[33] There is no way to get one's bearings regarding the relation of
past to present and present to future, name to place—language. If, as a tourist, one wanders in the city, then any street, campo, canal, or fondamente is
the way (or means) and the end. The experience is immersive. There is no
distance, no possibility of objectivity. No matter how many maps of the city
one has, it is impossible not to get lost. Every small alleyway, canal, campo,
fondamente, has several names—or rather, each may be individually named
and all the names may represent the same physical point but from different
frames of reference or perspective locations. It is possible to consult many
maps of Venice of varying degrees of scale, detail, and resolution, overlaying

map upon map. Maps representing different and multiple perspectives leave one always in some sense lost—as no one map or combination of maps coincides with one's own immediate subjective and physical location. "With the breakdown of the signifying chain, therefore, the schizophrenic is reduced to an experience of pure material signifiers, or, in other words, a series of pure and unrelated presents in time" (ibid.). To "lose one's way" in the city would be oxymoronic—it is the condition of being in Venice, as such. After all, where is one attempting to go? One is constrained by the boundaries of the "world" or system, which both frame an empty space and reconstitute a new field.

In this context, the movement of an individual is linked to the movements, constraints, and containments of light, sound, and water within the system of canals and fondamenta. This interdependency functions like a four-dimensional mesh where the displacement of one node or intersection necessarily distorts the surface of the whole, collapsing and expanding the individual interstices accordingly. The construction of Venice was an expression of power—the desire to dominate nature for the sake of commerce and control. Composed of incompatible elements, the flickering insubstantiality of its fluid markers, names and traces, Venice teeters on the brink of submission—power giving way to impossibility.

FOUND SYSTEM: NATURE DEMIURGE

Most exemplary of the connection between classification and the dominance of nature is the exhibition Nature Demiurge. Insects from the collection of Anne and Jacques Kerchache were displayed at the Foundation Cartier pour l'art contemporain like a collection of precious jewels.[34] Identical, velvet-lined vitrines embedded in the walls at eye level circumscribed the gallery in a single, luminous line. Each elegant case contained a number of specimens from a particular species of insect. The specimens in each case were nearly identical. Upon close inspection, subtle variations in pattern or color could be detected. The exhibition constituted a database of continuous differentiation—a play of difference along a spectra of metonymically arranged data. The focus of the exhibition as a whole was the demiurge: the pattern of patterning, the designing of design. Through a strategy of iteration, the collection of individual cases displayed the inescapable interweaving of the homogeneous and the heterogeneous.

In incremental steps, the variety of pattern within the strict parameters of a "world" or species was expressed. The range of difference was so small that field and subfield were nearly coextensive. Nested within each subfield, the metonymy operates at the level of individual specimens—for example, the iteration of difference in pattern across the individual wings of one butterfly. In one example, a species of butterfly whose wing pattern includes large and intricate "eyespots" (Figures 8.4 and 8.5), the pattern formed a recognizable image that appeared to employ the representational devices of mathematical perspective and chiaroscuro. Each eyespot was comprised of a two-dimensional border encircling a form that appeared to be rendered in three dimensions. On each of the wing segments, the "rendered" form was similar in "style" but was unique in size and shape. This was true of each of the six specimens. Of the examples of this species exhibited, no two "rendered" forms were identical, although their location, scale, and "style" were similar. The "style" of the rendering was equivalent to a hatched and shaded, volumetric and perspectival, charcoal drawing. The volumes thus "rendered" were complex, organic topologies resembling droplets of water. These fascinating and intricate designs in some sense suggest conscious perception and subsequent description—intentional representation of a type attributed to an author. Together they formed a subfield that illustrated the complexity of the rule-base of the system.

A database is a picture, an image of a system of meaning organized from a social perspective. While each of the preceding "found" database examples emerged from a particular civic or religious institution's perspective, the collection of Anne and Jacques Kerchache illuminates larger, more encompassing perspectives—those of the Enlightenment and scientific rationality. Here the dominance of man over nature is expressed through accumulation, classification, and aestheticization. The collection incorporates the aesthetics of the database, as an organized representation of an emergent field of differentiation, but simultaneously reveals an ethics of dominance—as a paean to the demiurge, author, collector. The act or process of collection is a narrative of mastery and a master narrative; the impulse, scientific and/or aesthetic, is a product of power and privilege. The collector functions as author, one who possesses, names, and classifies. The collection is identified with the collector and this identification imposes a unity on the contents of the collection.

NATURE?

A collection is produced through processes of selection and differentiation—sorting, classifying, rejecting anomalies—making patterns. Recognizing the patterns is aesthetic. Appreciating the connections is aesthetic. Manipulating the patterns is an expression of power. In the project *Nature?* artist Marta de Menezes imposes her aesthetic will on the development of eyespot patterns in the wings of butterflies. The following is a description of the work posted by Ars Electronica during its exhibition at the festival 2000 "Next Sex":

> *Nature?* involves the interference with the developmental program of butter-flies in order to generate live butterflies with wing patterns never seen in nature. Although the patterns are artificially determined, they are made of normal live cells—examples of something simultaneously entirely natural, but not de-signed by nature. In *Nature?* the artist only modified the pattern of one wing of *Bicyclus* and *Heliconius* butterflies. Through this asymmetry the similarities and differences between the unmanipulated and manipulated, between the natural and the novel natural are emphasized. The changes are not at the genetic level, and the germ line is left untouched. This form of art has a life span—the life span of a butterfly. It is a form of art that literally lives and dies. It is simultaneously art and life. Art and Biology.[35]

For what are apparently purely aesthetic reasons, Menezes performed micro-surgical interventions on the cellular level that alter the pattern and color of "eyespots" on only one of two wings of a butterfly.[36] These are nongenetic manipulations that do not cause changes in behavior or longevity. Menezes has exploited two methods of changing the pattern of a wing without inter-vening genetically. The first method involves transplanting small parts of the fabric from one area of a wing to another. The second operates at the cellu-lar level: Menezes corrodes cells with a small needle, thus affecting commu-nication between the cells. Her goal, as articulated in a paper she presented at a conference titled *The Aesthetics of Care?*[37] is to use biology as a new mate-rial and medium for a very traditional type of art practice. Like so much paint, the cell structure of a living thing is manipulated for a purely visual effect that can be evaluated only within the criteria of an ethics and aesthet-ics of dominance. *Nature?* has been spoofed by the *Artistic License* project, whose trademark bears the imprint "because it is art." Hubris Inc. is also the umbrella for ego.com (whose logo include the phrase "it's all about me™"). *Artistic License* is a division of Hubris Inc., which "proudly sponsors artists who work with emerging technologies to create high profile safe spaces where the public can come to appreciate [and accept] potentially threaten-ing technologies."[38] The parody project *butterfly technology* (the online proj-ect description refers directly to Menezes with a now-broken hypertext link) proposes the use of DNA modeling to produce butterflies for corporate office parks whose wing patterns are manipulated to display corporate logos.

Nature? is an extreme example of the practice of the aesthetic of dominance, one that may be offensive or reprehensible. I use it as an example to trouble the question of the author in the context of database aesthetics and to discuss the potential for the aesthetics of database to become entangled with an aesthetics of dominance. If the database is seen as formal, as opposed to social, it can certainly be seen as a field for the play of dominance. For example, from a purely formal or structural perspective, Menezes might see the cell structure she manipulates simply as a database that might be traversed and reconfigured for her own aesthetic pleasure, or as a means to participate in a narrative about the relation between art and science.

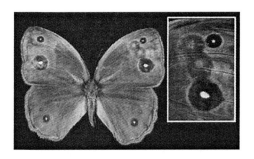

FIGURE 8.4.
HTTP://WWW.LELIEUUNIQUE
.COM/SAISON/0203/2/
MARTADEMENEZES.HTML.

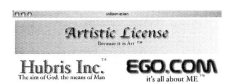

FIGURE 8.5. SCREEN SHOT
OF OPENING PAGE OF
"ARTISTIC LICENSE."
HTTP://ONLINE.SFSU.EDU/
~ART511_I/PUBLIC_HTML/
JAMESMASTER/JAMESPROJECT1F/
PAGES/ABOUT.HTML.

There are master narratives implicit in the origin of each of the found systems that I have used as examples of the conditions of possibility of database aesthetics—complex and coextensive contradictions. A database can represent the operative or dominant cultural perspective of given society—mapping and visualizing its rule table and recording the patterns that result. Naming, classifying, and categorizing have been acts of domination and ownership since the Bible. Recognition of difference (and similarity), rationalization, and discrimination are an integral part of Western culture. Taxonomies, entomological or otherwise, impose order according to presumed natural relationships. Anthropological taxonomies of race, class, gender, origin, culture, and difference-on-down-the-line are instruments of political and social othering that secure the metacategories of us and them. Sorting, classifying, rejecting anomalies, making patterns—these are protective mechanisms, methods of observation that affirm the assumptions of the observer.

By acknowledging the role of ideology and desire in the process of ethnographic observation and cultural representation, Clifford and Marcus's collection, Writing Culture, showed us that "evidence" can be taken as discourse, and, specifically, that the ethnographer engages in "rhetoric and other weapons of persuasion—metaphor and metonymy, tropes, and so on."[39] Classification, description, and categorization are central to the formulation of knowledge—"the troubled, experimental knowledge of a self in jeopardy among others."[40] But, along with Nicholas Mosley, we may ask: "Might there not be an anthropology in which the observer is seen as part of what he observes: in which his observing is taken into account as affecting what he observes? . . . Might there not be some anthropology to do with change? If we stand back from the part of ourselves that is part of what we see . . . might there not be freedom for change?"[41] Database aesthetics can provide a free space, a field for dynamic interaction. But this field, unfortunately, may be framed and the data may be organized around existing narratives of cultural domination and patterns of objectification.

SOCIAL AESTHETICS

To avoid making and reproducing patterns of aestheticization or objectification in the field of the database, the aesthetics of the database must be practiced or applied in conjunction with a commitment to cultural democracy and linked to an "aesthetics of dignity."[42] My argument here, in part, is that the aesthetic dimensions and processes of the database, a "pragmatic" approach to praxis (asking "What can art do?" in reference to social/political realities), and a recognition of the value of voices that do not belong to authors, taken together, may serve as a point of departure for "social aesthetics" to emerge.

The quilts of Gee's Bend displayed in an exhibition at the Whitney Museum of American Art in New York in 2002 present an interesting example. These quilts were created by a group of women who live in the isolated, African American hamlet of Gee's Bend, Alabama. Like many American quilters, the women transformed a necessity into a work of art—but their innovative, minimalist approach to design is unique. "The compositions of these quilts contrast dramatically with the ordered regularity associated with Euro-American quilt making. The sixty quilts in the exhibition, created by forty-two women spanning four generations, provide a fascinating look at the work of twentieth-century artists who have lived and worked in solitude."[43] Gee's Bend is located in southwest Alabama, about thirty miles southwest of Selma, on a sliver of land five miles long and eight miles wide, a virtual island surrounded by a bend in the Alabama River. Bounded by the river on three sides, the community of about seven hundred, descendants of slaves on the former Pettway plantation, has always been an isolated enclave. Geographically cut off from the world, the women in the community created quilts from whatever materials were available, in patterns of their own design. The programs of the New Deal in the 1930s and 1940s helped the families survive, modernize, and, finally, take ownership of the property they had cultivated for generations, though the community continued to have little contact with the outside world. Until the late 1960s, there was not even a paved road. During the civil rights movement, the Freedom Quilting Bee, a quilt-making cooperative that employed the women of Gee's Bend, brought the quilters' work to eastern department stores and they gained widespread recognition.

But marketing the quilts meant reproducing identical examples of the same quilt, which was inconsistent with the process and approach of the women in Gee's Bend.[44] Their process was often collaborative, social, transformative—a process of voices emerging through conversation, improvisation, and dialogue.

"One time me and I think it was about five of us started to quilting from one house to another. Quilt one or two for one person, go to the next house, do the same thing. Way back yonder. From house to house, quilting quilts. . . . I didn't start young. I just tried to survive. You learn to do things from other people. You see them do it, you learn. If you ain't you don't want to learn. I can't piece by no pattern. . . . I get some blocks sometimes other peoples put together, give them to me, and I put them blocks in my quilts. I put somebody's blocks, my cousin Edna, and an old lady Annie, lived up there, put them in, put some variety in."[45]

Historically, quilting has provided generations of women with an outlet to express their creativity, their convictions, and their skill. The quilts of Gee's Bend are the result of an unusual degree of cultural continuity and collaboration. Here one can see evidence of the development of a visual language across three and sometimes four generations of women in the same family, or works that bear witness to visual conversations among community quilting groups and lineages. "These women learn from one another but strive to be themselves. The quilts are both the signatures of individuals and banners of a community":[46]

"After I was married, my mother-in-law, Jennie, taught me how to . . . just follow my imagination. I had not made that sort of stuff, 'cause I thought they was ugly, but when my mother-in-law learned me how to make them beautiful, I didn't want to make nothing else. I watched her tear up old dress tails and make a quilt any kind of way she wanted to. . . . Jennie Pettway told me, 'You don't have to worry yourself trying to make . . . any of those things you got to follow a pattern for. Just take what you know and do what you want to.' And that's what I did, and I do it yet, and it's a good way, too. It was when my mother-in-law told me I didn't have to follow nobody's ideas that I learnt myself to follow my head." Arlonzia Pettway—"acknowledging her mother-in-law, Jennie Pettway as an artistically liberating influence"[47]

Closely linked to family well-being, a sense of identity for the individual quilters, and the cultural continuity of their community, a Gee's Bend quilt represents a focus on such everyday concerns as salvaging discarded fabric, recycling old clothing, and finding ways to keep the families warm and comfortable. For these women the process of quilting is about communication and connection, which fills both emotional and material needs. "I got good ideas from my mother-in-law, Henrietta. Me and her sewed together. When I had children I had to do better. Made quilts out of old dress tails, shirt tails, that's the way I did so the children would be covered up."—Allie Pettway[48]

In his Foreword to the complete catalogue, *Gee's Bend: The Women and Their Quilts*, Peter Marzio, director of the Museum of Fine Arts in Houston, describes the quilts as "works of art that just happen to be made for utilitarian purposes." His position is problematic. I am disturbed by his modernist reading of the quilts, his comparison to Willem de Kooning and Jackson Pollock, his statement that the quilts "look brilliant in an exhibition gallery," and his assertion that the art museum functions as an "honest broker of beauty."[49] Of course, the quilts are works of art and they do look brilliant in the blank white space of an exhibition gallery. But they do not need to be authorized by major mainstream arts institutions largely curated by white men to function as works of art, and they should not be confused with modernist avant-garde painting in a de-contextualizing formalist analysis—looks-like-is-like[50]—especially as their most important function as works of art is exactly the function they serve in the community they came from. As one of the women explained, a quilt "represents safekeeping, it represents beauty, and you could say it represents family history."[51] While the designs appeal to a sophisticated modernist/minimalist sensibility, the aesthetic

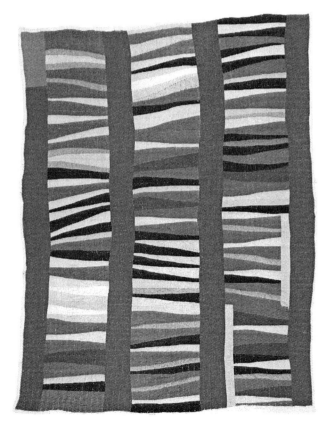

FIGURE 8.6.
JESSIE T. PETTWAY
(BORN 1929),
BARS AND STRING-
PIECE COLUMNS,
1950S. COTTON,
95 X 76 INCHES.
PHOTOGRAPH BY
STEVE PITKIN/
PITKIN STUDIOS.
COURTESY OF
TINWOOD VENTURES,
ATLANTA.

employed in the creation of these quilts was born entirely from the social world and material environment of the women who made them.[52] They are the result of a historically evolving communal practice that has produced a social aesthetic. The quilters of Gee's Bend already speak with force and power as artists in their own social world. Their speech isn't dependent upon having an audience at the Whitney and the Corcoran. The traveling exhibition is a gift to the "us" of mainstream culture—allowing us to hear and see and providing us with a social model of individualism in consonance with community. We must not make the mistake of aligning the aesthetics of the quilts with the aesthetics of rupture employed by the modernist avant-garde merely because there is, on the surface, a formal similarity. We devalue the quilts and their makers if we do not value them in terms of social aesthetics.

Social aesthetics are "style-less." Style, which is an attribute of the personal,

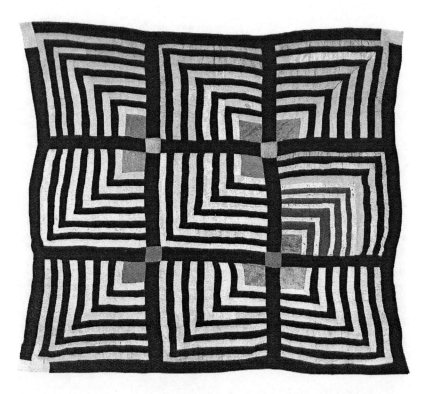

FIGURE 8.7. SUE WILLIE SELTZER (BORN 1922), *HOUSETOP*, CA. 1955. COTTON AND SYNTHETIC BLENDS, 80 X 76 INCHES. PHOTOGRAPH BY STEVE PITKIN/PITKIN STUDIOS, COURTESY OF TINWOOD VENTURES, ATLANTA.

is secondary to cooperation and intervention. Social aesthetics does not operate on the plane of uniqueness but rather in the realm of community and in terms of audiences to be addressed. Notions of value are derived from the social world of the participating community and focused on transformative process, not product. I would like to appropriate this notion of social aesthetics, first articulated by William Olander and Craig Owens in the catalogue for the exhibition "Art and Social Change, U.S.A." in 1986, and expand it to address public art that critically engages the "materiality of informatics" by employing information and communication technologies.[53]

AESTHETICS OF DIGNITY

Hayles's "Informatics" is an infrastructure that is of, by, and for the technologically enfranchised socioeconomic/political elite, but no one in reach of

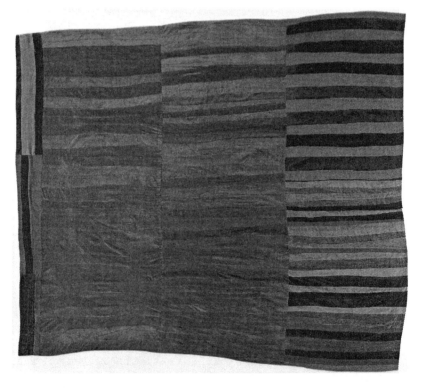

FIGURE 8.8. ANNIE MAE YOUNG (BORN 1928), *STRIPS*, CA. 1975. CORDUROY, 95 x 105 INCHES. PHOTOGRAPH BY STEVE PITKIN/PITKIN STUDIOS. COURTESY OF TINWOOD VENTURES, ATLANTA.

globalized capitalism, however far outside the infrastructure, is exempt. Informatics provides an environment in which there is "continuing pressure to substitute information for direct experience with material conditions."[54] Certainly, wherever the interpretation of available data is privileged over embodied experience and the consumer is the only acknowledged citizen, the material conditions of the technologically and economically disenfranchised may be ignored, their social role devalued, and their rights systematically erased.

Because political and economic power are increasingly dependent upon access to and presence within the global information culture, the voices of the "underserved" are becoming less and less audible. This dangerous trend could be reversed if communities of interest across the socioeconomic spectrum had access to information technologies and the ability to represent themselves, and their positions, in information space. Any adequate statement on the modern condition requires a plentitude of voices speaking directly from a multitude of contexts about their own socio-ideological situations. This might be achieved through a radical appropriation of informatics as a means to the ends of cultural democracy. As Catherine Stimpson points out in her introduction to Jane Kramer's "Who's Art Is It?" an essay about John Ahearn's controversial public art commission in the South Bronx, it is difficult to "do cultural democracy." "Doing Cultural Democracy demands . . . the incessant recognition of the moral, cognitive and cultural lives of others." In this dialogic imaginary everyone would have:

1. A right to public speech.
2. A right to pride in one's historical and cultural traditions.
3. The responsibility to engage in exchanging and mixing narratives—
   (departing from one's own perspective to engage that of others).
4. The courage to allow diversity, "no matter how blasphemous,
   painful, corrupt, bigoted, and stupid."
5. The burden of engaging in the nearly impossible struggle to locate
   the point at which pain, bigotry, and stupidity become intolerable
   and to whom.
6. The responsibility to develop a common political language that has
   "no shared moral, religious or artistic system . . . but binds together
   by binding to cultural diversity."[55]

To "do cultural democracy" now, in the context of the materiality of informatics, means:

- Distributing control over the processes of the database—the accumulation and interpretation of information, the naming and classification of data, for the collective construction of a new social semiotics.
- Building and/or annexing social and technological infrastructures that can enable communities to become the co-designers and creators of programs and systems that facilitate their own reclamation, reintegration, and sustainability.

By "doing cultural democracy," we can fill the space left empty by the death of the author—not to rejuvenate or even democratize the author function, but to assert the place of the participant as a subject. The participant's statement is subjectifying and empowering but, simultaneously, an anonymous act. It does not make reference to "originality." It does not encourage psychologizing identification or suture. The participant's statement is a self-articulation that unfolds in a polyphony of speaking subjects. The name-of-the-author is erased. Thus, "all discourses, whatever their status, form, value, and whatever the treatment to which they will be subjected, [will] then develop in the anonymity of a murmur." Foucault quotes Samuel Beckett, "'What does it matter who is speaking?' someone said, 'What does it matter who is speaking?'" to establish this "indifference" as a matter of ethics regarding the death of the author.[56]

One of the "themes" of the death of the author, for Foucault, is "writing's" relationship with death, or, rather, writing as an effort to elude death. He offers the example of the *Arabian Nights*. "The theme and the pretext of Arabian narratives—such as *The Thousand and One Nights*—was also the eluding of death: one spoke, telling stories into the early morning, in order to forestall death, to postpone the day of reckoning that would silence the narrator. Scheherazade's narrative is an effort, renewed each night, to keep death outside the circle of life."[57] Scheherazade was not an author—she spoke in order to sustain her life and save the lives of others. Her storytelling was a political act. *The Thousand and One Nights* has no single author, only "compilers" of editions and versions—it is a database, a frame tale, stories within a story. The frame tale is a conceit for the organization of a set of smaller narratives, popular tales, which have also been collectively authored, evolving over time and giving voice to many anonymous narrators. Many of Scheherazade's tales are also frame tales—nested subfields in the field of a narrative database. The figure of Scheherazade is that of a performer or participant who traverses this field, spinning and weaving a single story out of many. Her storytelling produces a nonauthorial, collective subject whose life/lives are saved through this process of subjectification.

The Medea Project: Theater for Incarcerated Women is a contemporary *Arabian Nights*.[58] The project is a collective effort to save lives by soliciting and telling stories. Rhodessa Jones, founder and artistic director, uses "self-exploration" techniques with an ensemble of professional actresses and incarcerated women to develop and stage performances derived from the prisoners' own stories. The texts of Medea Project performances are derived from the real-life experiences of the women performing on the stage. During the Medea Project workshop process, the inmates, like Scheherazade, are given nightly writing assignments. They are asked to analyze a key element of a myth Jones has chosen for the performance in relationship to their [own] lives.[59] For Jones, mythology provides a point of departure for exploring the "cultural narratives and the social rituals that directly contribute to women's incarceration."[60] The women read their narratives aloud to the group each day. "The ensemble uses the prisoners' language, their stories, songs, prayers and lies, to shape a script.... Storytelling can be a con game, a trick used against one's foes. It can also be the beginning of a different drama—a way to imagine, if not live out, a new life."[61]

The Medea Project uses theater to encourage each woman to examine her participation in her own incarceration and explore a wide range of cultural issues and attitudes that perpetuate incarceration and recidivism, including fear of others, drugs, prostitution, poverty, and single parenthood. "Jones works with women in jail, not prison. San Francisco County Jail serves as a temporary holding cell for women who are awaiting trial and cannot post bail or for inmates who are serving sentences shorter than twelve months. This means that the Medea Project works with a highly transitory population. In the three- to four-month period that the Medea Project is working on a production, the entire cast can change several times over. In fact, the cast is never finalized until the day of the performance."[62] By the end of the workshop process, any participant can incorporate and embody any of the multiple voices that are ultimately heard in the performance. This is significant in terms of the role of the participant subject—the story is not restricted or linked in any fixed way to one writer/performer but is truly collective. "Medea Project public performances transcend the realm of ordinary aesthetic production.... These performances, in which inmates' autobiographical narratives are staged for both audience members and law enforcement officials, are acts of juridical and political testimony. In this setting the women become the morally and legally recognized source of (self) narration and re-symbolization, and in so doing they create the conditions under which a claim to dignity is possible. It is this claim to dignity . . . that enables these women to challenge principles of distributive justice"—and to save their own lives.[63]

The Medea Project is just one example of a paradigm shift in art practice from the aesthetics of object defined by the author function to an activist "aesthetics of dignity" that employs both database aesthetics and social aesthetics. This new paradigm is defined by the participant-subject (who is subjectified through individual and collective storytelling) and the context-provider (who establishes a framework in which the "participant-subject" may emerge and make a "statement" or "articulation" in concert with other participant-subjects—thus producing collective statements out of individual, nonauthorial voices).[64] This can be accomplished through participatory theater like the Medea Project and John Malpede's LAPD (Los Angeles Poverty Department) and in public-information space through the design of collaborative tools and community networks. Together these tools and networks form collaborative systems through which the context-provider (artist, software designer, activist, organizer) assists communities in collecting their stories, solicits their opinions on politics and social justice, and builds the online archives and interfaces required to make these data available across social, cultural, and economic boundaries.

My own art practice involves the development of collaborative tools and community networks. This has taken basically two forms: I have engaged in custom software development, building tools like *Palabras_* [http://palabrastranquilas.ucsc.edu] that facilitate collective self-representation among technologically disenfranchised communities, and I have established ongoing project collaborations that empower participants from specific marginalized groups to represent their own experiences in information space such as *Public Secrets* and *Need_X_Change.*[65] Each of these projects engages the philosophy of an "aesthetics of dignity" by combining database aesthetics with social aesthetics.

*Palabras_* is both a set of tools, designed to facilitate collective self-representation and promote social inclusion, and an expanding network of ongoing collaborations with nonprofit organizations that serve socially marginalized and technologically disenfranchised communities. The *Palabras_* Web site provides access to an archive of more than two thousand video clips created in Buenos Aires, Argentina; Kiel, Germany; San Francisco and San Jose, California; and Darfur, Sudan. The *Palabras_* workshops, tools, and online browser adopt the folksonomic (folk + Taxonomy) or social classification

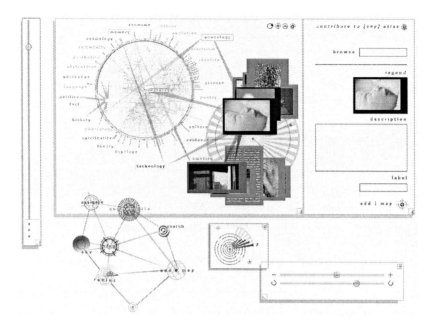

FIGURE 8.9. *PALABRAS_* CLIP AND SEQUENCE BROWSER INTERFACE.

method to give participants the opportunity to then interpret and classify their own data. This method also simultaneously generates a map of semantic associations between the self-representations created by participant communities across languages and cultures.

*Palabras_* moves beyond the model of "personal computing" and "virtual" community. Unlike other media-sharing Web sites that use folksonomies, like Flickr and YouTube, *Palabras_* employs tagging in the context of place-based workshops designed to allow communities that may not normally have access to the Internet to use media and information technologies to represent themselves and their own circumstances. *Palabras_* also adopts the tactics of Do-It-Yourself technology to provide low-cost and context-appropriate media-acquisition tools.

At each *Palabras_* site, inexpensive, disposable digital video cameras ("hacked" or transformed into reusable cameras) are distributed. These cameras allow participants to document and represent their own experience in their own way. In *Palabras_* workshops, participants "tag," organize, and share their videos online using *Palabras_* Web tools (clip browser, tagger, and editor). The Web application is designed to facilitate the discovery of connections between participants' personal stories, at each site and across cultures, by allowing participants to label or "tag" their video content with a shared vocabulary that is both originated by and familiar to them. This form of social classification allows multiple interpretations and associations to emerge among participants' video clips. The Web application also provides simple tag search, editing, and sequencing tools participants can use to create video sequences using their own clips and those created by members of their community.

The *Palabras_* public browser interface allows a global and international audience online to see the ways in which place-based communities describe their own social contexts. Visitors to the site may also add tags to clips and sequences in the archive through the public browser. Therefore, what is shared among and between participant communities, and interpreted by both visitors and participants, is visualized in the tag cloud and can be seen in the videos as an improvised map of correspondences across cultures.

Mapping is intersubjective communication: the visualization or representation of data and information. The term "map" applies both to a clear representation, one capable of communicating intersubjectively, and the act of analysis required to create such a representation. A map has no single author. To map is to locate, to assign a correspondence. A map fulfills the functions of both record and statement—it is a history of the subject's, or mapmaker's, relation to that which is mapped and an act of communication with others who will interpret and use it. To map is to locate—but position is always "relative to . . ." associative and perspectival. Intersubjective communication occurs when the meaning of data or information is accessible to, or established for, two or more subjects. In intersubjective communication, values and truths are inseparably intertwined. Interpretations and representations are produced dialogically—in cooperation with a "text" or data set. None of the participants is assumed to be a *subject presumed to know*—an unquestionable *authority*—so objective knowledge is displaced by shared subjectivity. To map social and cultural experience accurately requires infrastructures and interfaces that facilitate intersubjective communication, favor dialogue over monologue, and allow representations and interpretations to emerge and evolve—an infrastructure like the database.

Building databases that dialogically map the intersubjective experience of social "others" is a practical and intellectual endeavor that challenges the historical separation between technological development in digital media art and political activism. This work requires sustained interaction with nonprofit organizations that serve marginalized and disenfranchised communities.

For several years I have worked in various ways with the HIV Education and Prevention Program of Alameda County (HEPPAC) in an effort to engage injection drug users in a process of self-representation. The first phase of this collaboration involved training the organization's staff and clients to use disposable cameras and author Web sites populated with their own images. This work resulted in the Web site *Need_X_Change* (now archived). *Need_X_Change* was intended to generate a social and technological interface—a work of technology-assisted community-based public art that would help the staff and clients of Casa Segura/HEPPAC attain social and political "voice" through self-articulation and participation in the global information culture. During the second phase of my work with HEPPAC, I recorded many hours of conversation with injection drug users who use the needle exchange. These recordings form the basis of an online audio archive entitled "Blood Sugar."

During roughly the same period of time, I have also worked with the nonprofit, human rights organization Justice Now and twenty women incarcerated at the Central California Women's Facility (CCWF) in Chowchilla, California, the largest female correctional facility in the United States. Access to prisoners and prisons by the media or human rights investigators is virtually nonexistent. Several states, including California, have enacted media bans, making it illegal for the media to conduct face-to-face interviews with prisoners that are not controlled and censored by prison officials. For the past four years I have intentionally circumvented the California Prison media ban, gaining access to incarcerated women by posing as a legal advocate. The conversations recorded during these visits comprise the audio database of *Public Secrets* [http://www.vectorsjournal.org/index.php?page=8|2&projectId=57]. Where *Public Secrets* reveals the secret injustices of the criminal justice system and the Prison Industrial Complex, *Blood Sugar* examines the social and political construction of poverty, alienation, addiction, and insanity in American society through the eyes of those who live it.

My collaborations with HEPPAC and Justice Now are motivated by our collective desire to create a context in which the voices of marginalized and disenfranchised persons, their stories and their perspectives, can be heard in the public domain. Our objectives are:

- To enhance awareness of the relation between poverty, addiction, and HIV transmission and the social and political implications of the "war on drugs," including the disproportionate incarceration and subsequent political disenfranchisement of impoverished people of color, and the inherent injustice of current sentencing laws like California's "three strikes."

- To empower the participants to represent themselves in the media and, thus, to participate in and shape the public discourse around the social conditions and material circumstances they face on a daily basis.

For both of these groups, injection drug users living outside the norms of society in the shadow of the criminal justice system and women trapped inside the prison system, our recorded conversations are a means of critical resistance. The following is just one short example from one of the transcripts of a recording made at HEPPAC by Tanya, a woman who had just been released after nine months in county jail for possession of five dollars' worth of heroin.

> I've tried methadone—I've been on methadone many, many times—off and on, off and on—methadone is, I don't know, I feel like it's just the government's Band-Aid for a gaping wound. It's just to pacify us and to push us away and they know where we are going to be today and they know where we're going to be tomorrow morning and I, I don't know what the cure is—it's just an ongoing struggle and I don't know who's going to win, you know—and me— I know how heroin is, I'm going to lose every time. I'm either going to be in the hospital or I am going to be in jail. Sometimes it takes years and sometimes it takes a month, you know? It just—it just—and I don't know personally, how to stop—I am a pretty strong person, but I don't know how to beat this thing—and it's because the drug is so powerful it really takes over your whole—it's not recreational where my body feels high and I'm having fun and I'm laughing and I'll recuperate tomorrow and go to work on Monday—Sunday rolls into Monday, you know, and it's a drug used where you can deal with your life not to add to your life—like you drink alcohol at a party—heroin is not like that, heroin you get up with and you eat it like breakfast and then you eat it like lunch and it puts you to bed at night—and any comfortable feeling that you're gonna have, any level of comfort that it's going to give you—that's how bad it's going to make you feel when you don't have it.

Through the voices of participants like Tanya, *Blood Sugar*'s audio database challenges us to the question, "What is the social and political status of the addicted? Is the addict fully human, diseased, or possessed by an 'other inside,' or wholly 'other' and thus rendered ideologically appropriate to her status as less than human?" Because they must fear encounters with regimes of enforcement, participants like Tanya are afraid to be seen—but they do want to be heard. Theirs are the most important voices in the discourse around addiction, public health, poverty, and belonging in America. Through *Blood Sugar*, which in this respect follows the example of the Medea Project, a community of homeless, injection drug users "become the source of self-narration and re-symbolization, and in so doing they create the conditions under which a claim to dignity is possible."[66]

*Palabras_*, *Public Secrets*, and *Need_X_Change/Blood Sugar* are examples of collaborative systems designed to enable participants in their own social context and to produce new forms of understanding between specifically defined communities. I introduce the example of *Need_X_Change/Blood Sugar* in particular in order open a discussion of just some of the ethical questions and contradictions that can arise in attempts to embrace the aesthetics of dignity.

PRACTICAL ETHICS

Needle-exchange programs are a controversial, but proven, method of reducing needle-related HIV risk behaviors among injection drug users. Although critics claim that Casa Segura's needle exchange attracts drug dealers and users, encourages drug use, and increases incidences of dealing and other related crimes in the Fruitvale neighborhood, where it is located, statistics show that this is not the case. Asked why people become injection drug users, Rand Corporation sociologist Ricky Bluthenthal answers, "For most folks it's a pretty tortured path, and it certainly isn't based on the fact that you have a program that's taking used syringes from current users and replacing them with clean ones. I'd be interested to meet the person who said they started using because there was a needle exchange program in their neighborhood."[67] Needle-exchange programs are part of a therapeutic strategy called "harm reduction." Harm reduction is a type of practical ethics: a process of de-escalating moral conflicts to the point of nonviolent resolution, reducing potential for harm, and educating as required so that each participant in a given circumstance can effectively see the other's point of view. Practical ethics is central to cultural democracy. I share the philosophy behind "harm reduction" therapy, which is based on a recognition of the value and dignity of all individuals, their experiences, and their perspectives. I began the work of *Need_X_Change/Blood Sugar* by asking, "What do you think—what is your experience?" of those who are rarely, or never, asked. Participants in the first phase of the project told their own stories in their own words, using their own images, texts, and sounds. I worked one-on-one with participants to teach them basic computer literacy and Web publishing. Most of the participants had never used a computer and, though they said they had "heard about" the Internet, they had certainly never been online before. They were subject to the force of the materiality of informatics without having the opportunity to touch or test it—it was a kind of glass ceiling, a pervasive ghost. Imagine every instance of "http://www . . ." on a sign or set of instructions as a statement in a vaguely foreign language.[68]

ONE EXAMPLE: A——

In this context I work at the margins of mainstream society with individuals who operate according to exigencies far removed from the comfort zones of middle-class America. This work is akin to ethnography in the sense that participants are encouraged to tell their own stories without mediation. But I make no pretense to objective evaluation, and I have no intention of leaving my subjects in the "pristine" state of "nature." This work is activist, and is meant to change the material and social conditions of those with whom I work, not to preserve them as they are. My goals are to avoid representation (a primary agent of domination) and not to attempt to speak for others, but to allow them to speak for themselves. This work provides an alternative context for self-articulation and collective speech to an extremely marginalized community.

In 2000, I started attending the Tuesday night needle exchange in Fruitvale every week. It took nearly a year of weekly contact to develop a working relationship with A——, a forty-two-year-old heroin addict. A—— is a substance abuser with mental illness, commonly referred to as "dual diagnosis," meaning someone with one diagnosis of mental illness and a second diagnosis of substance abuse disorder. As Lonny Shavelson explains in *Hooked,* his excellent book on failures and challenges of the drug rehabilitation system, the trademark of dual diagnosis clients like A—— is "disorder." A—— lost her social service insurance and Medi-Cal because she failed to keep required appointments. Insisting that a dually diagnosed client like A—— keep a complex sequence of appointments, on time, to have an opportunity to get access to treatment, is "like ordering swimming students to float on their first day of class—they are likely to drown—making further instruction difficult."[69] Without Medi-Cal, A—— is unable to afford her prescribed mental health medications or methadone. Without free methadone doses, she resorts to prostitution to support her drug dependency. She is an easy target for police given her prison record, her history as an addict and prostitute, her mental health problems, and her homelessness. Our work is often interrupted while she is incarcerated for one reason or another.

In order to work with A—— and others in similar circumstances, I tried to help her engage the institutional infrastructures that might address her immediate, material needs. I felt I had to try to help her save her own life. I stipended her with grant funds and helped her reconstruct her social service network by offering her transportation, attending appointments with her, speaking on her behalf in court, and coordinating her work on the project in order to facilitate appointments with mental health and case workers at Casa Segura. During this period, A—— wrote, designed, and published approximately fifteen Web pages. The project she defined for herself was threefold: first, to make a political statement about the nature of addiction and in support of harm-reduction therapy; second, to relate the story of her life; and third, to keep an online journal as part of her attempt to stabilize her mental health.

INFRASTRUCTURES

Building a collaborative relationship in this context requires developing social, institutional, and technological infrastructure. A—— and several other participants published a number of Web pages after learning to use a standard WYSIWYG HTML application and image editor. This required considerable effort for A——, given the extremity of her circumstances. Many of Casa Segura's clients were not able to make the sustained commitment required to benefit from this type of training. Most continuously live on the edge of desperation, like A——, in need of housing and food as well as methadone treatment or clean needles, and some, like J——, then a seventy-three-year-old heroin addict (now deceased), were relatively stable and committed but not necessarily capable of learning how to use complex, proprietary software. I used existing technology (for example, free Weblog interfaces provided by blogger.com) and some simple form templates built on the ZOPE open-source content-management system (<http://zope.org>) to keep some participants active who could not follow through with training. But others, like J——, for example, first had to learn how to use a keyboard. Clearly, special intuitive and nonprescriptive tools are needed to help this type of user community have a voice in information culture. The principal question is this: How to design interfaces that will solicit direct and meaningful responses from inexperienced users without overdetermining the results. This problem is simultaneously technical, aesthetic, and political. I am convinced that some sort of frame is necessary to identify a field of potential—an open space allowing and provoking meaningful responses from participants who are so unaccustomed to having their perspectives valued or even queried. I am concerned, however, that the technological interfaces and the power relations implicit in the social and institutional context may combine to repress or prescribe, to enforce normative values, and impose master narratives. (For example, participants are called "clients" by Casa Segura staff, which represents a particular type of institutional relationship. Many of these "clients" have difficulty accepting the possibility of collaboration and self-articulation and strive to give "appropriate" responses instead of direct or honest ones. I see these individuals as "participating subjects" and try to get them to see me as just another participating subject.)

Building social and technological infrastructures for cultural democracy is a complex challenge. *Need_X_Change* provides a kind of case study that embodies some of the complexities, questions, conflicts, and contradictions inherent in this challenge. I would like to address only two of these in closing: first, to pose the question of context or appropriate technology, and, finally, to return to the problem of aesthetics.

THE QUESTION CONCERNING TECHNOLOGY

Is the Internet "appropriate technology" with which to enable this community? As noted above, *Need_X_Change* was designed to empower participants by helping them to achieve social and political citizenship through self-representation within the global information culture—to engage and annex "informatics" for a new collective participant-subject. Self-articulation is only one step in attaining "citizenship." Many of the clients of Casa Segura live on the street, have no form of official identification because they have no fixed address, and thus have no access to basic civic and social services. They are invisible in the context of the "materiality of informatics." This absence in the virtual world has serious implications in the physical world. The complex struggle over civil liberties and social rights in electronically mediated information space is materially different from the one on the street.

Access isn't everything. There are ethical issues to resolve. The political assumptions embedded in the design of digital tools reinforce the boundaries between the technologically and economically enfranchised and disenfranchised. I hate the idea of training homeless, dually diagnosed, needle-exchange participants to use proprietary programs like Microsoft Word in which the spell-checker resolutely insists on changing "underserved" to "undeserved. This is an example of the political subtext of digital design.

THE NATURE OF BEAUTY

A context provider committed to an activist aesthetic of dignity must ask after Foucault: How can a discourse circulate—who can productively appropriate it?—"what are the places in it where there is room for possible subjects?" and "Who can assume these various subject functions?" It does, in this sense, "matter who is speaking."[70]

In what you have just read, I have traversed a field of data and activated a set of associations: the death of the author and the role of the observer; the aesthetics of the database; parallels among complex social and collaborative systems; social aesthetics in the context of the materiality of informatics; the emergence of the collective-narrating-participant-subject; and the philosophy of an activist aesthetics of dignity. I hope these associations emerge as a new ontology of aesthetics that will change and transform the structure of that field.

Now I want to return to the question: What aesthetic criteria can be used to evaluate systems and infrastructures (like the Medea Project, *Need_X_Change,* and *Subtract the Sky*) that support cultural democracy? Are the criteria of an aesthetics of dignity "saving lives" in some form? In other words, "Is it art or is it social work?" I would like to quote Rhodessa Jones here, who has been known to say that "great art should also be great social work."[71]

NOTES

1. *American Heritage Electronic Dictionary,* 3rd ed. (Houghton Mifflin, 1993).

2. Katherine N. Hayles, "The Materiality of Informatics," in *Configurations. A Journal of Literature, Science, and Technology,* ed. Wilda C. Anderson, James J. Bono, and Kenneth J. Knoespel (Baltimore: Johns Hopkins University Press and the Society for Literature and Science, 1993), 149.

3. Wikipedia: the free encyclopedia, online at *http://www.wikipedia.org/wiki/;* the article on "data" is paraphrased and developed in this paragraph.

4. Michel Foucault, "What Is an Author?" in *The Foucault Reader,* ed. Paul Rabinow (New York: Pantheon Books, 1984), 103.

5. Ibid., 103–4.

6. Ibid., 108.

7. Roland Barthes, "The Death of the Author," in *Image/Music/Text,* ed. and trans. Steven Heath (New York: Hill and Wang, 1977), 142–43.

8. Foucault, "What Is an Author?" 104.

9. Stanley Aronowitz, "Literature as Social Knowledge: Mikhail Bakhtin and the Reemergence of the Human Science," in *Dead Artists, Live Theories, and Other Cultural Problems* (New York: Routledge, 1994), 161.

10. Nicholas Mosley, *Hopeful Monsters* (Elmwood Park, Ill.: Dalkey Archive Press, 1990), 249.

11. Wikipedia: the free encyclopedia, online at *http://www.wikipedia.org/wiki/.*

12. Werner Heisenberg was part of the Copenhagen school of quantum physics and discoverer of the "Principle of Uncertainty," the "hidden variable" hypothesis, which claims that some hidden variable remains to be discovered that will ultimately explain away Heisenberg's dilemma.

13. I refer to the "hidden variable" hypothesis, which claims that some hidden variable remains to be discovered that will ultimately explain away Heisenberg's dilemma, or around the belief that there is no hidden variable awaiting discovery but that uncertainty is fundamentally a part of how nature works. In other words, the behaviors of the particles themselves are uncaused and unknown to them before they move.

14. *Merriam-Webster OnLine* (Springfield, Mass.: Merriam-Webster, 2003), http://www.m-w.com.

15. Artificial Life is the study of artificial systems that exhibit behavior characteristic of natural living systems: self-organization, adaptation, evolution, coevolution. This includes biological and chemical experiments, computer simulations, and purely theoretical endeavors. Processes occurring on molecular, social, and evolutionary scales are subject to investigation. In the field of computer science, Artificial Life researchers model evolutionary and emergent behavior using genetic algorithms within graphical environments. For more information on Artificial Life research, see Steven Levy, *Artificial Life* (New York: Random House, 1994). *Exploring Emergence,* an "active essay" by Mitchel Resnick and Brian Silverman of the Epistemology and Learning Group at MIT's Media Laboratory at http://lcs.www.media.mit.edu/groups/el/projects/emergence/index.html, presents examples of emergent behavior and cellular automata models.

16. Katherine N. Hayles, "Making the Cut," in *Observing Complexity: Systems Theory and Postmodernity,* ed. William Rasch and Cary Wolfe (Minneapolis: University of Minnesota Press, 2000), 153, 158. For a general reference, see Humberto R. Maturana and Francisco J. Varela, *The Tree of Knowledge: The Biological Roots of Human Understanding* (Boston: New Science Library, 1987).

17. This interpretation of Bahktin's dialogic narrative relies on a general discussion of Bahktin in George Landow, "Hypertext and Critical Theory," in *Hypertext* (Baltimore: Johns Hopkins University Press, 1992).

18. Thomaso Toffoli and Norman Margolus, *Cellular Automata Machines: A New Environment for Modeling,* 5th ed. (Cambridge, Mass.: MIT Press, 1991), 5.

19. Foucault, "What Is an Author?" 118.

20. Ibid., 119.

21. Aronowitz, "Literature as Social Knowledge," 156.

22. Foucault, "What Is an Author?" 119.

23. Stephen Willats, *Concerning Our Present Way of Living* (London: Whitechapel Art Gallery and Westerham Press, 1979), 1.

24. My thanks to artist Bill Seaman for this term.

25. Foucault, "What Is an Author?" 120.

26. For more information, see http://www.geocities.com/CollegePark/Campus/8297/bakhtin.html and http://www.utm.edu/research/iep/b/bakhtin.htm.

27. Aronowitz, "Literature as Social Knowledge," 140–41.

28. Foucault, "What Is an Author?" 119.

29. Allan Jeong, quote from "Theoretical Frameworks for Learning with Group Discussion & Collaboration." This online text (no longer available) provided a summary of

social constructionism as a theoretical framework that informs much of the research and the practice of collaborative learning, including an explanation of Bahktin's dialogic process: "The theory of dialogism assumes that no individual ever writes alone because writing is the result of our interactions with the world. To write and construct *new knowledge and meaning*, we must engage in a dialogic process where words of an individual are examined and primarily understood in relationship to the words of others. Fundamental to the dialogic process is that all possible meanings of words interact, and *possibly conflict* to affect and change future meanings of words. Socializing the writing context contributes to this dialogic process by bringing voice to thought."

30. *Merriam-Webster OnLine* (Springfield, Mass.: Merriam-Webster, 2003), http://www.m-w.com.

31. I refer here to the type of aesthetic object made famous by the French painter and conceptual artist Marcel Duchamp, which he named "found object." Found objects are anything found in the world, often considered unauthored, and definitely not created by the artist who uses such objects, and simply designated as works of art by the artist. My term "found systems" follows in this same tradition.

32. Sainte-Chapelle was commissioned by Saint Louis (Louis IX) in 1242 to be a royal chapel and a shrine for the relics of Christ's Passion, including the Crown of Thorns. More than 6,400 square feet of stained glass occupy the walls of the upper chapel. To justify his claim to the royal throne, Saint Louis used Sainte-Chapelle and the holy relics as prominent symbols of his authority. This is most evident in the content and placement of several of the stained-glass windows. The windows are arranged starting from Genesis in the northwest corner of the chapel, and all but one lancet depicts a biblical story. Genesis, Exodus, Numbers, Joshua, Judges, Isaiah and the Jesse Tree, the Childhood of Christ (Saint John), The Passion, Saint John the Baptist, Daniel, Ezekiel, Jeremiah and Tobias, Judith and Job, Esther, Kings, and the final lancet depicts the history of the Relics of the Passion. At the west end a rose window depicts the Apocalypse. The unusual thing about the windows is that the placement of the book of Numbers is directly over the King's stall (and out of sequence with the books of the Old Testament). Every scene from Numbers depicts the coronation of a prophet or king. The story of the relics demonstrates St. Louis's right to the throne in that by allowing Louis to have custody of "the complete set," the pope indirectly was blessing his authority.

33. See Fredric Jameson, *Postmodernism, or, The Cultural Logic of Late Capitalism* (Durham: Duke University Press, 1991), following explanatory quote can be found online at http://xroads.virginia.edu/~DRBR/JAMESON/jameson.html#return13. "When that relationship breaks down, *when the links of the signifying chain snap, then we have schizophrenia in the form of a rubble of distinct and unrelated signifiers.* The connection between this kind of linguistic malfunction and the psyche of the schizophrenic may then be grasped by way of a twofold proposition: first, that personal identity is itself the effect of a certain temporal unification of past and future with one's present; and, second, that such active temporal unification is itself a function of language, or better still of the sentence, as it moves along its hermeneutic circle through time. If we are unable to unify the past, present, and future of the sentence, then we are similarly unable to unify the past, present, and future of our own biographical experience or psychic life. With the breakdown of the signifying chain, therefore, the schizophrenic is reduced to an experience of pure material signifiers, or, in other words, a series of pure and unrelated presents in time."

34. Nature Demiurge (Foundation Cartier pour l'art contemporain, June–July 1998). Composed of sixty-nine boxes, Jacques Kerchache's insect collection is part of a tradition that dates back to the Renaissance, when, "spurred on by the great voyagers and navigators, collectors created curio rooms in which fauna, flora, minerals, fossils, skulls, shells, and insects were classified and arranged." Claude Lévi-Strauss rightly observed: "A bird, a beetle, a butterfly invite the same rapt contemplation that we reserve for a Tintoretto or a Rembrandt." In Jacques Kerchache, *The Hand of Nature: Butterflies, Beetles, and Dragonflies* (London: Thames and Hudson, 2001).

35. Description of project *Nature?* on Ars Electronica Web site at http://www.aec .at/festival2000.

36. See "Ein Kunstwerk, das lebt und stirbt!" an e-mail interview with Marta de Menezes by Simon Hadler at http://www.kultur.orf.at/000904-4098/4085txt_story.html.

37. Marta de Menezes, "The Laboratory as an Art Studio," presented in August 2002 at a symposium, "The Aesthetics of Care? The artistic, social, and scientific implications of the use of biological/medical technologies for artistic purposes." The papers, with titles such as "The Workhouse Zoo Bioethics Quiz," "Recombinant Aesthetics," "Cute Robots / Ugly Human Parts," and "Test Tube Gods and Microscopic Monsters" may be read in the proceedings of the symposium, sponsored by Symbiotic A: The Art and Science Collaborative Research Laboratory and the Institute of Advanced Studies, University of Western Australia. Menezes's butterfly-wing paper is on page 53 of the PDF document linked here. http://www.tca.uwa.edu.au/publication/THE_AESTHETICS_OF_ CARE.pdf.

38. See http://online.sfsu.edu/~art511_i/public_html/jamesmaster/jamesprojectif/ pages/about.html.

39. Aronowitz, "Literature as Social Knowledge," 142.

40. *Writing Culture: The Poetics and Politics of Ethnography,* ed. James Clifford and George Marcus (Berkeley and Los Angeles: University of California Press, 1986), jacket flap.

41. Nicholas Mosley, *Hopeful Monsters* (Elmwood Park, Ill.: Dalkey Archive Press, 1990), 293.

42. Sara Warner, "Mythic Proportions: The Medea Project Theater for Incarcerated Women and the Art of Creative Survival" (Ph.D. diss., Rutgers University, 2003). Abstract from chap. 4, "Creative Survival: An Activist Aesthetic of Dignity."

43. http://www.whitney.org/information/press/102.html.

44. "The Quilts of Gee's Bend" at the Corcoran Gallery of Art Web site, http://www .corcoran.org/exhibitions/Exhib_current.asp?Exhib_ID=69.

45. Sue Willie Seltzer, quoted by John Beardsley, from "Arrival: Quilts and Community," in *Gee's Bend: The Women and Their Quilts,* ed. William Arnett (Atlanta: Tinwood Books, 2002), 441.

46. Peter Marzio, Foreword to *Gee's Bend: The Women and Their Quilts,* ed. William Arnett (Atlanta: Tinwood Books, 2002), 9.

47. Arlonzia Pettway, quoted by John Beardsley, in "Arrival: Quilts and Community," 249.

48. Allie Pettway, quoted by John Beardsley, in "Arrival: Quilts and Community," 272.

49. Peter Marzio, Foreword to *Gee's Bend,* 9.

50. The same mistake made by the Museum of Modern Art's 1984 *Primitivism* show. For more on this topic, see James Clifford, "Histories of the Tribal and the Modern," in

Primitivism and Twentieth-Century Art: A Documentary History, ed. Jack Flam with Miriam Deutch (Berkeley and Los Angeles: University of California Press, 2003).

51. The Quilts of Gee's Bend at the Corcoran Gallery of Art Web site, http://www.corcoran.org/exhibitions/Exhib_current.asp?Exhib_ID=69.

52. There is, no doubt, a connection here to modernism's appropriation of traditional African artifacts. While the quilters are not likely to be overly influenced by modernist aesthetics, their audience is.

53. William Olander, "Social Aesthetics," in *Art and Social Change, U.S.A.* (Oberlin, Ohio: Allen Memorial Art Museum, Oberlin College, 1983).

54. N. Katherine Hayles, "The Materiality of Informatics," 150.

55. Catherine R. Stimpson, in *Introduction to Jane Kramer, Who's Art Is It?* (Durham: Duke University Press, 1994), 31.

56. Foucault, "What Is an Author?" 119, 101. "Beckett nicely formulates the theme with which I would like to begin: 'What does it matter who is speaking,' someone said, 'what does it matter who is speaking.' In this indifference appears one of the fundamental ethical principles of contemporary writing (écriture). I say 'ethical' because this indifference is not really a trait characterizing the manner in which one speaks and writes, but rather a kind of immanent rule, taken up over something completed, but dominating it as a practice."

57. Ibid., 102.

58. General information about the Medea Project was gleaned from the project Web site at http://www.culturalodyssey.org/ and from exposure to several videotapes, particularly Larry Andrews's documentary of the Medea Project workshop process.

59. Sara Warner, "'Do You Know What Bitch Is Backwards?' Mythic Revision and Ritual Reversal in the Medea Project: Theatre for Incarcerated Women," *Dialectical Anthropology* 26, no. 2, Special Edition on Mythology (Summer 2001) (Dordrecht: Kluwer Academic Publishers: www.kluweronline.com. The essay is online at http://complit.rutgers.edu/swarner/html/publications.html), 167.

60. Warner, *Mythic Proportions*, 1.

61. Rena Fraden and Angela Davis, *Imagining Medea: Rhodessa Jones and Theater for Incarcerated Women* (Chapel Hill: University of North Carolina Press, 2001), 48.

62. Warner, "Do You Know What Bitch Is Backwards?" 162.

63. Warner, *Mythic Proportions*, 2.

64. Sharon Daniel, "Systems and Subjects: Redefining Public Art," ed. Victoria Vesna, Margot Lovejoy, and Christiane Paul (Minneapolis: University of Minnesota Press, forthcoming).

65. *Need_X_Change* is a collaboration with the staff and "clients" of the HIV Education and Prevention Project of Alameda County and Casa Segura, the "safe-house." The project has been supported by the Creative Work Fund of the Columbia Foundation and the University of California Institute for Research in the Arts. http://needxchange.org is a work in progress.

66. Warner, *Mythic Proportions*, 2.

67. Bluthenthal was quoted in an article by Kyra Platoni in the *East Bay Express* in the spring of 2000 (Emeryville, Calif.), http://www.eastbayexpress.com.

68. Because Casa Segura provides needle exchange, it is politically embattled and continuously attacked by its district city council representative and others interested in

the "economic development," or gentrification, of the Fruitvale neighborhood of Oakland, where it is located. There can be no better example of this fact than the arson perpetrated against the safe house on New Year's Eve in 2000. This horrible act of violence, thought by many to have been sanctioned, if not solicited, by the district city council representative, demonstrates how serious the problem is. After the fire, Casa Segura struggled for years to find a new home in the neighborhood. During this time the *Need_X_Change* project computer lab was located in administrative offices ten miles from the exchange site, where most participating clients lived. It was extremely difficult for participants to make and keep appointments at this site and eventually, first the lab and then the office itself were closed. The project was suspended for several years due to these circumstances. In 2005, Casa moved into new, permanent facilities and the project was restarted in the form described here. We had come to the conclusion that the technical training piece of the original proposal was not entirely viable for most of Casa Segura's "client" population and was much too ambitious in the institutional context of HEPPAC. We decided to shift the entire focus of the project toward getting the voices of the clients, their stories, and their perspectives into public media space by creating a series of audio-recorded conversations that could be disseminated online and via radio. Needle exchanges are still held weekly in tents in a cul-de-sac under Highway 880 in Fruitvale, near the old safe house building, which has never been repaired.

69. Lonny Shavelson, *Hooked: Five Addicts Challenge Our Misguided Drug Rehab System* (New York: New Press, 2001), 52.

70. Foucault, "What Is an Author?" 119, 101.

71. Quote from video documentation shot by Sara Warner of the Medea Project performance, "Can We Get There by Candlelight?" http://complit.rutgers.edu/swarner/movies/mp.mov.

9. NETWORK AESTHETICS

WARREN SACK

USER-FRIENDLY, COMMONSENSICAL INTERFACE DESIGN

> In order for an interface to work, the person has to have some idea
> about what the computer expects and can handle, and the computer
> has to incorporate some information about what the person's goals
> and behaviors are likely to be. These two phenomena—a person's
> "mental model" of the computer and the computer's "understanding"
> of the person—are just as much a part of the interface as its physical
> and sensory manifestations. . . . Faced with this nightmare, our seminar
> at Atari abandoned the topic and we turned our attention to more
> manageable concepts, such as the value of multi-sensory representations
> in the interface.
>
> —BRENDA LAUREL, *Computers as Theatre*

Brenda Laurel unearths a potentially mountainous obstacle for interface
designers. Most interface designers want to create something that is user
friendly. Some of these designers have taken the approach of graphically
sophisticated, direct-manipulation interfaces that are intuitive to use.[1] In
contrast, artificial intelligence (AI) researchers often insist that the interface
per se is not that important for the goal of user-friendly software. If the computer's "understanding" of the person is a deep and profound understanding,
then the computer can anticipate or sensitively perceive what a given person
wants and fulfill those wants with minimal interaction with the user. This
has been called the "intelligent agents' approach to interface design."[2]

Note, however, that both the agents and the graphical interface approaches
require some notion of what might be called *common sense,* or common-
sense knowledge. The AI researchers assume that the common sense can be
coded into a computer program so that the computer can "know" what the
person knows. The graphical interface designer assumes that an intuitive
interface is one that does not require a user to read a thick manual before
the user can use it. In other words, the interface should be designed so that

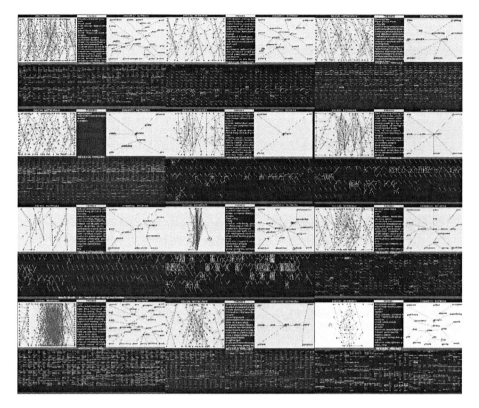

FIGURE 9.1. A MATRIX OF CONVERSATION MAPS: A VISUALIZATION OF NETWORK
AESTHETICS (SEE SACK, "WHAT DOES A VERY LARGE-SCALE CONVERSATION LOOK
LIKE?" 2002).

the user does not have to rely on some specialized knowledge, but rather
can rely on their own common sense to use the interface.

Many AI researchers have believed that this common sense can be coded
as a computer program. Graphical interface designers do not necessarily
think that the common sense can be coded, but they must at least rely on
their own intuitions about what is commonsensical in order to determine
if an interface design is in practice easy to use without specialized, non-
common-sense knowledge. But what is common sense? Marvin Minsky,
one of the founders of AI, said in an interview:

Q. How do you define common sense?

A. Common sense is knowing maybe 30 or 50 million things about the world and having them represented so that when something happens, you can make analogies with others. If you have common sense, you don't classify the things literally; you store them by what they are useful for or what they remind us of. For instance, I can see that suitcase (over there in a corner) as something to stand on to change a lightbulb as opposed to something to carry things in.[3]

Minsky's definition of common sense can be discussed using a linguistic terminology. Given a term like "suitcase," it should be possible to associate it with actions like "carry" and "stand." That is, those who possess common sense should be able to employ "suitcase" as the indirect object of the verbs "stand" and "carry." Expressed in this terminology, however, it becomes clear that there is a set of cultural dependencies implicit in Minsky's definition. What parts of common sense are missing in the knowledge of a non-English speaker who doesn't know the word "suitcase"? Probably nothing is missing for speakers of a language that have some equivalent to "suitcase" (for example, "une valise" in French). But more important, what is different, missing, or added for those whose language or culture contains nothing like a suitcase?

Some have suggested that it might be possible to divide common sense into two kinds: a culturally dependent common-sense knowledge and a culturally independent sort of knowledge:

I have suggested that people analyze the world, sort it into categories, and impose structure on it, in order to avoid being overwhelmed by its richness. I have implied that this procedure is not deliberate: the widely held notion of "common sense" suggests that people believe that their theory of the way the world works is a natural reflection of the way the world does work. If we look at the sources of categories, we find that some are natural in origin, but the majority are social. Research suggests that a number of basic "cognitive categories" do arise in individuals naturally, being a product of the way we are constructed biologically. These include basic colour categories, such as black and white, red and green; certain geometrical figures, such as circle, triangle, and rectangle; notions of movement, such as up, down, forward, backward; logical relationships, such as oppositeness, identity, and causation. But the majority of our ideas are not natural. . . . What counts as an instance of a category is subject to negotiation and revision. Can a lion count as a pet? Yes, the magistrates say, provided it is locked up securely. Clearly the idea of "pet" cannot be derived from any list of actual animals; it is not a natural feature of certain animals but a property of the culture's system of attitudes toward animals.[4]

Such a culturally dependent/culturally independent division of common sense—like the one offered by Roger Fowler in the quote above—might be a workable means with which interface and/or AI designers approach their work. Such an approach, however, would still require different designs for different cultures if the software was supposed to operate in a domain that did not occupy a "basic" category of knowledge. Conversation, for instance, is a culturally dependent domain if only because topics of conversation are rarely if ever entirely culturally independent. Very large-scale conversation is an even more eclectic domain because, as it is practiced on the Internet, participants can come from a wide diversity of cultural backgrounds, and so what is or is not commonsensical cannot be enumerated beforehand.

Instead, what is necessary is a design perspective that allows one to see how, for instance, over the course of a long-term conversation, common sense is produced, reproduced, extended, and changed by a group of potentially culturally diverse participants. The political philosopher Antonio Gramsci gives us just such a picture of common sense:

> Every social stratum has its own "common sense" and its own "good sense," which are basically the most widespread conception of life and of men. Every philosophical current leaves behind a sedimentation of "common sense": this is the document of its historical effectiveness. Common sense is not something rigid and immobile, but is continually transforming itself, enriching itself with scientific ideas and with philosophical opinions which have entered ordinary life. . . . Common sense creates the folklore of the future, that is as a relatively rigid phase of popular knowledge at a given place and time.[5]

From this perspective, common sense is accumulated and transformed through the process and productions of science, philosophy, and other powerful conversations, discourses, and practices. This perspective has been useful for understanding the workings of older media (newspapers, television, film) and could, potentially, be of use to understand and design new forms of media like those of the Internet.[6]

This exercise is probably easier said than done. Not just interface designers, but many other kinds of artists and designers have consciously or unconsciously relied on some notion of "culturally independent" common sense to make aesthetic decisions. To ferret out this dependency in software design and find a workable alternative for thinking about the aesthetics of Internet interface design, this essay will first explore how common sense has been discussed and used in software, specifically artificial intelligence design.

It is shown, historically, that the connections between aesthetic decisions and terms central to AI work—especially goals and common sense—are long-standing concerns. It is thus necessary to get some historical and philo-sophical perspective on discussions of common sense and aesthetics in order to propose true alternatives. The primary goal of this essay is the formula-tion of an approach to the design of interfaces for Internet-based software that can show the production of common sense (especially the common sense of conversation) and who is responsible for its production. Rather than depending upon an a priori defined notion of common sense, a work-able approach to the aesthetics for Internet design must take into account the fact that common sense is being produced and changed through the conversation itself. After looking at the history of AI, common sense, and aesthetics, an alternative approach is outlined.

Artificial Intelligence and Aesthetics

Artificial intelligence is an area of research and design of "intelligent" com-puter hardware and software. The term "artificial intelligence" was coined for a conference at Dartmouth College held in the summer of 1956.[7] The Dartmouth conference brought together the majority of researchers who are today considered the founders of the field including John McCarthy, Marvin Minsky, Herbert Simon, Alan Newell, and others. While AI has pri-marily been a concern of computer scientists, its multidisciplinary mem-bership (including also mathematicians, philosophers, engineers, and social scientists) was evident even at the time of the Dartmouth conference. AI did not have a name before the Dartmouth conference yet it nevertheless par-ticipates in older intellectual and design traditions, which have investigated mechanical and symbolic systems and human cognition and perception for centuries. Consequently, as an area of design concerned with cognition and perception, AI can be understood as the latest manifestation of certain views of aesthetics that have their roots in older philosophical, scientific, and artistic projects.

The purpose of the following sections is to give a short history of AI that highlights its relations with a Kantian view of aesthetics. Its purpose is *not* to give a comprehensive overview of AI (see Shapiro for one such overview).[8] Instead, this chapter's focus is the intersection of AI and aesthetics. Thus it supplements, but does not largely overlap, two different histories that have been repeatedly told about (1) AI and science and (2) AI and art. A history of AI concerned with its scientific roots would emphasize its relations to the development of calculating machines, logic, and mathematics.[9] An art history of AI would, by contrast, detail its similarities and differences with ancient and modern myths, literatures, and depictions of robots, cyborgs, and artificially (re)created humans like Frankenstein's monster.[10] For expository purposes, these other histories (of AI, art, and science) are mostly left to the side so that a single, streamlined story, focusing on AI and aesthetics, can be told. At the end of these sections, the "streamlining" is questioned by examining some of AI's relationships to other (non-Kantian) aesthetics. This "unstreamlining" makes it possible to propose a set of alternatives to a common-sense-based aesthetics to interface design.

Early AI

Throughout its almost fifty-year history, AI has never been a discipline without internal differences. Nevertheless, until about the mid-1980s it was possible to say that a large majority of AI researchers were concerned with the elaboration of a *rationalistic* understanding of cognition and perception.[11] Within the rationalistic tradition, human identity and the thinking, calculating mind tend to become conflated. AI's rationalistic bent can be understood by examining it as a reaction against behaviorism, the approach that dominated the social sciences for most the first half of the twentieth century in the United States, and an outgrowth of cybernetics, an interdisciplinary effort born during World War II to study social, biological, and electromechanical systems as systems of control and information.[12]

Behaviorism and AI

Behaviorists' preference for studying external, empirically observable behaviors rather than, for example, a method of introspection or the analysis of verbal reports of others' thinking, effectively divided psychology (and other social sciences) from closely related disciplines like psychoanalysis that were founded on the postulation of internal, mental structures and events. As computers became more common, the behaviorists' hegemonic position in American social science began to wane. Behaviorists were unwilling to postulate the existence of intentions, purposes, and complicated internal, mental mechanisms. Yet, during and after World War II, as computers were built to do more and more complicated tasks, not only computer engineers but also the popular press began to call computers "electronic brains" and their internal parts and functions were given anthropomorphic names (computer "memory" as opposed to, for instance, the synonymous term, the "store" of the computer). Concomitantly, some social scientists began to take seriously the analogy between the workings of a computer and the workings of the human mind.[13] This set of social scientists went on to found AI and cognitive science as a whole, the area of science that includes AI and a variety of other "computationally inspired" approaches to cognition in linguistics, anthropology, psychology, and neurophysiology.[14]

Cybernetics and AI

At the same time—during and immediately after World War II—the science of cybernetics gained prominence. Cybernetics differs from most work done within the confines of a strict behaviorism in at least two ways: (1) whereas behaviorists postulated linear relationships between an external stimulus and an organism's response, cybernetics introduced the idea of recursive (circular) relations between perception or sensation and action known as positive and negative feedback circuits; and (2) while behaviorists avoided labeling any behavior "goal-directed" (because it would imply the postulation of internal representations), cyberneticians (re)introduced teleology into scientific descriptions of behavior.[15]

Subsequently, the earliest work in AI elaborated on the cyberneticians' usage of "goal-directed behavior" and de-emphasized external contexts and empirically observable stimuli—the preoccupation of the behaviorists. Consequently, AI immediately began to diverge from cybernetics as a result of AI's neglect of an analysis of feedback from the environment. Some contemporary work addresses this early neglect, but early work in AI—the work of Newell, Simon, and Shaw on the General Problem Solver (GPS)—explored feedback only insofar as the "external world" could be internalized in the computer.[16] To work, GPS required that a full and accurate model of the "state of the world" (insofar as one can even talk of a "world" of logic or cryptarithmetic, two of the domains in which GPS solved problems) be encoded and then updated after any action was taken, for instance, after a step was added to the proof of a theorem. This assumption that perception was always accurate and that all of the significant details of the world could be modeled and followed was incorporated into most AI programs for decades and resulted in what became known to the AI community as the "frame problem"—the problem of deciding what parts of the internal model to update when a change is made to the model or the external world.[17] Not surprisingly, AI robots built around strict internal/external divisions sometimes exhibited extremely erratic behavior when the robots' sensors were even slightly inaccurate in the measurement of the external world.

AI as a Kantian Endeavor

Early AI's antibehaviorist, inward turn to focus on internal representations (like "goals") led to what can be understood as the reinvention of philosophical rationalism's problems and "solutions." Or, since AI has routinely been concerned with the difficulties and sometimes the limits of rationality (expressed, for example, in Herbert Simon's notion of "bounded rationality"),[18] its "reinventions" more specifically resemble not rationalism per se, but philosophical responses to rationalism like Immanuel Kant's *Critiques*. Indeed, the rationalistic approach to perception and cognition pursued by a large majority of AI researchers until the mid-1980s can be explained in Kantian terms.

The following explanation of AI using Kantian terms relies on a well-known reading of Kant formulated by the philosopher Gilles Deleuze.[19] Deleuze's interpretation is akin to several other readings of Kant (notably, the work of Jean-François Lyotard) that, collectively, might be viewed as the "poststructuralist" response to Kant.[20]

Kant's comparison of aesthetical and teleological judgment provides a framework for narrating how AI's original preoccupations with teleology and neglect of aesthetics caused a series of crises for the field in the mid-1980s that initiated an "aesthetic turn" in research, motivating AI scientists and designers to pay increasing attention to issues of the body, the senses, and physical and social environments.[21] While Kant's vocabulary provides a convenient means of describing the problems and achievements of AI, within the literature of AI Kant is rarely mentioned, or, if mentioned, then only represented as formative of AI's parent discipline, cognitive science.[22] Here it is argued that Kant's vocabulary of aesthetics (as "spoken" by poststructuralism) is equal to the task of describing many important research issues in AI. No argument is offered to support the opinion that some sort of "equivalence" exists between AI and Kant's critical project.

In conflict with rationalists like René Descartes, Kant argued for a limited role for teleological principles to supplement mechanical explanations.[23] Likewise, cyberneticians, in conflict with most behaviorists, argued for a limited use of teleology in coordination with the vocabulary of physics to describe the behavior of complex, nonlinear systems. In the 1950s, when AI took up the vocabulary of teleology ("final cause") from cyberneticians, what was repressed—or at least foreclosed for AI—was the problematic status of the posited goals and purposes used to understand the behavior of complex systems. For Kant, teleological principles were considered to have no explanatory significance.[24] Instead, teleological judgment in Kantian terms was seen as a response to an apparent purposelessness of aesthetic judgment: "purpose" is a projection of the cognitive subject on nature, not an intrinsic property of nature itself. In contrast to Kant's careful reintroduction of teleology within a nuanced discussion of aesthetics where teleology was seen as a *product of cognition,* but not necessarily an artifact useful for communication and explanation, AI researchers took teleology as a *basis for their scientific explanations of cognition,* problem solving, and learning. This difference of opinion concerning the explanatory significance of goals and purposes is so large that one might assume that any continued narration of AI as a type of "Kantianism" (as AI's history is here described) would be fruitless. However, the way in which AI has struggled with the questions of teleology (for whom do posited goals and purposes signify something meaningful?) is strikingly Kantian in AI's recurrent appeal to "common sense," a faculty of great importance to Kant's critical philosophy.

KANT AND COMMON SENSE

"Faculty" (a "faculty of common sense") is a crucial yet ambiguous term in Kant's writings. For present purposes, it suffices to say that a Kantian "faculty" is a potential or power to realize some end.[25] Computational approaches to philosophy, like those championed by AI, often equate "powers" to "computational processes" or, to use a less theoretical term, "computer programs." Thus, to draw an analogy between the writings of Kant and the writings of AI researchers, it is necessary to imagine that Kant's "facultie" could be re-expressed in a variant, textual form—as computer programs with specific data structures, data flow, and control flow. Although this metaphorical comparison of the human cognitive faculties to computer programs may seem outlandish to many, it is a hallmark not only of AI but also of all contemporary cognitive science.[26] To compare Kant's work to the research goals of AI, it is not necessary to believe that this metaphor (mind as machine) is "true." Rather, it is only necessary for the reader to be able to imagine that AI researchers consider this metaphor to be true; or, if not true, then at least extremely useful.

Kant discusses three cognitive faculties: understanding, reason, and imagination. In the terminology of AI, one might explain these faculties as classification (understanding), inference (reason), and schema or pattern matching (imagination). In addition to the three cognitive faculties, Kant describes three sorts of common sense: two legislated and one engendered.[27] The ways in which the three faculties Kant described (of understanding, reason, and imagination) interrelate with one another are referred to as (1) *logical common sense* and, (2) *moral common sense* when, respectively, (1) understanding, and (2) reason legislate over the two other complementary faculties. In contrast with these two legislated sorts of common sense, (3) *aesthetic common sense* is engendered when none of the faculties are regent, but when they all, nevertheless, work together even as they function autonomously and spontaneously. In the vocabulary of contemporary computer science, one might say that the differences between these three kinds of common sense are differences in "control structure"—differences concerning which (or whether) one computer program, program statement, or "faculty" is directing the others.

Kant's theories of *reflective judgment* (which includes both *aesthetic reflective* and *teleological reflective judgment*) function with the support of an engendered, aesthetic common sense. This common sense is engendered when, for example, the faculty of reason compels the faculty of imagination to confront its limits by attempting to schematize a perception of the formless or the deformed in nature (a state referred to as the *sublime*). According to Deleuze, the aesthetic common sense should not be understood as a supplement to logical and moral common sense but as that which gives them a basis or makes them possible since the faculties of understanding and reason could not take on a legislative role if it were not first the case (as in the accord of an aesthetic common sense) that they are each capable of operating in free subjective harmony.[28] The implications for AI of this conceptualization of common sense—like Kant's aesthetic common sense—will play an important role in the following discussion.

AI AND COMMON SENSE

The neo-Kantian Jean-François Lyotard draws an analogy between Kant's description of *reflective judgment* (a mode of thought that works from the particular toward the universal, as opposed to *determinant judgment*, which proceeds in the inverse direction) and AI researchers' (especially Marvin Minsky's) descriptions of "frame-based" thought and perception.[29] Minsky's "frames" proposal was an attempt to describe common sense thought in humans and its possibilities in computers. Minsky, McCarthy, their students, and colleagues in AI were concerned with this question about common sense: What is the structure and content of common sense such that it allows one to quickly draw useful conclusions from a vast array of existing knowledge and perceptual data?[30] One of the immediate outgrowths of this research was a series of "frame-based" computer programming languages with control structure statements very unlike previous programming languages.[31] From this AI point of view, common sense is a legislative faculty, a control (or controlling) structure that allows a system to turn its attention away from nonsense so that it can concentrate on the sensical, or what is implied by the commonsensical. In other words, in Kantian terms, AI's analysis of "common sense" was largely (and still is in some circles) limited to "legislated common sense," "logical common sense," and "moral ('reason-legislated') common sense"—and had, until recently, completely neglected "aesthetic common sense," an unlegislated state of relations between understanding, reason, and imagination.

AI AND NONMILITARY CONCERNS

Such was the case until the mid-1980s, when two "events" motivated a reappraisal within AI of the issues of aesthetics, including the role of the body and the senses in cognition. The first "event" was the commercial success of a genre of AI computer programs called "expert systems."[32] For the first thirty years of its existence in the United States, AI was primarily academic research funded by the military. Then, in the mid-1980s, business concerns began funding the development of expert systems to automate a variety of white-collar work. While the U.S. Department of Defense had been content to finance long-term research in which it was presumed that theoretical work might, one day, be of practical interest, the new benefactors of AI demanded empirically evaluated, immediate results. What soon became clear was that many expert systems were "brittle"—they performed competently within a narrow domain of problems, but if the problems were posed in a slightly different manner, or if slightly different types of problems were posed to the systems, the systems responded in erratic and erroneous ways. Moreover, users of the systems noted that the systems were difficult to communicate with: one needed to pose problems in a specially constructed, artificial language and often, after receiving a solution from a system, it was impossible to get the system to explain the rationale for its solution. Expert system adherents claimed the problem was simply that more rules needed to be added to the "brittle" expert systems to make them "flexible." Expert system opponents, often using a philosophical vocabulary of Martin Heidegger's phenomenology, claimed that rules were inadequate to the task of articulating the means of human expertise and, thus, no number of rules could allow a machine to match the skills of a human expert.

The second "event" was the U.S. military's loss of funding in the late-1980s as a result of the end of the Cold War with the Soviet Union. Both "events" pushed AI researchers to look for new funding sources and "applications" in finance, advertising, and entertainment.

TWO STRANDS OF AESTHETIC AI RESEARCH

This exodus from the isolated, military-industrial-funded laboratories fostered two strands of research. One strand is attributable to a diverse collection of researchers whom, for the purposes of this essay, I will call the "neo-Encyclopediaists." The second strand of researchers I will call the "computational phenomenologists." Both of these strands have longer histories of existence, even within the lifetime of AI itself, but they were given more funding and attention after the two events mentioned above. One of the major distinctions between these two strands of researchers is this: while the neo-Encyclopediaists (or at least their predecessors in symbolic AI; Minsky, for example) feel that "common sense" can be catalogued as a system of rules with intentional content,[33] the computational phenomenologists do not believe that "common sense" can be articulated in the structure of rules.

The "rules" under scrutiny by the computational phenomenologists can be understood as a certain specialized form of computer program articulated as a series of IF-THEN statements (for example "IF the water is steaming and bubbling, THEN its temperature is probably 100 degrees Celsius"). But, the term "rules" can also be understood as synecdochically referring to a larger class of computer programs (including, for example, Minsky's "frames," and what others have called "schemata," or "scripts").[34]

THE NEO-ENCYCLOPEDIAISTS

Motivated by the observation that most AI programs do not contain enough schemata or rules to deal with unforeseen circumstances (the "brittleness" of expert systems mentioned above), the neo-Encyclopediaists are attempting to produce huge catalogues of "common sense" in the form of computer programs and databases.[35] Some of these efforts are largely accomplished "by hand," whereby dozens of people are employed for years to encode myriad mundane details and rules (for example, "water is a liquid," "what goes up must come down"). Other efforts are aided by statistical and machine learning techniques to augment or build such catalogues. The most well known of these efforts has been a ten-year project called CYC (originally short for enCYClopedia), financed largely by corporate sponsors.[36] CYC and a handful of other efforts are the contemporary offspring of Minsky's and McCarthy's proposals for representing common sense, often referred to as "symbolic AI."[37]

While work in symbolic AI has always stressed the importance of teleological and "intentional" representation, however, newer work in "computational
linguistics" (a field that intersects with the AI subfield of "natural language
processing") contributes to the efforts of the neo-Encyclopediaists without
necessarily ascribing the same importance to teleology. Computational linguistic, neo-Encyclopediaist work is often described as the latest extension to
the long-standing field of lexicography, the discipline that has historically
been responsible for the construction of encyclopedias, dictionaries, and the-
sauri.[38] This turn away from teleology in recent neo-Encyclopediaist work
might be seen as a renewed interest in the freedom of the (Kantian) imagination and its power to schematize without any concept, that is, an interest in
the basis for an aesthetic common sense (taste).[39] One difference, however, is
the dependence of much recent computational linguistic work on the form of
very simple "schemata" or "rules" (the form and limitations of Markov models) versus the postulation of no schematic influence whatsoever by Kant.

THE COMPUTATIONAL PHENOMENOLOGISTS

While computational phenomenology can be understood to be in opposition to the project of the neo-Encyclopediaists, the neo-Encyclopediaists'
turn away from teleology (in favor of lexicography) makes it clear that this
opposition is more of a tension than an unbridgeable gap. In fact, the two
strands can both be understood as pursuing different forms of phenomenology, one inspired more by Edmund Husserl (transcendental) and the
other inspired more by Martin Heidegger (existential).

Disbelief in structured rules with intentional content has spawned several
different research paradigms, some of which will here be subsumed under the
label of "computational phenomenology." One paradigm, known as "connectionism," is an attempt to replace rules with digitally simulated "neural nets."[40]
Another paradigm, "situated action" or "behavior-based AI," couples the "neural nets" of connectionism to robotic (hardware and software) bodies with
sensors.[41] The research agenda of the latter group is, in many ways, a direct
descendant of cybernetics insofar as it insists on the employment of feedback
circuits and the disruption of internal representation versus external world
dichotomies created in and by early AI work. Finally, what is here labeled
"computational phenomenology" is also meant to encompass recent work in
"distributed AI" and "multi-agent systems";[42] such work takes its metaphors
of interaction from social systems (the systems of various scientific communities for the publication and archiving of journal articles) instead of the
metaphors of the isolated thinker preferred by early AI researchers.

THE AESTHETIC TURN

The work of the computational phenomenologists constitutes an "aesthetic turn" in AI research since they focus attention on the aesthetic dimensions of cognition, including the senses, the body, and the social and physical environment of perception. While the neo-Encylopediaists might be seen as an outgrowth of an older, "symbolic AI," computational phenomenology has been formulated in opposition to symbolic AI. Pivotal to the position of the computational phenomenologists has been their understanding of common sense as a negotiated process as opposed to a huge database of facts, rules, or schemata. This position is often repeated by the computational phenomenologists: "It should come as no surprise that the area in which [symbolic] artificial intelligence has had the greatest difficulty is in the programming of common sense. It has long been recognized that it is much easier to write a program to carry out abstruse formal operations than to capture the common sense of a dog. This is an obvious consequence of Heidegger's realization that it is precisely in our 'ordinary everydayness' that we are immersed in readiness-to-hand."[43] In other words, common sense is a faculty engendered by our encounters with "nature" and others—that said by Kant (according to Deleuze) to engender an "aesthetic common sense."

HUSSERL, HEIDEGGER, AND AI

The references to Martin Heidegger used by the computational phenomenologists can be seen as a contemporary manifestation of a debate between AI software designers that began as a philosophical debate initiated by Hubert Dreyfus.[44] Dreyfus and several of his colleagues (especially John Searle) have been critiquing AI (particularly symbolic AI) for more than thirty years. Dreyfus has pointed out the close philosophical affinities between the projects of symbolic AI and Husserl's transcendental phenomenology and its differences from a Heideggerian existential phenomenology.[45] In particular, Dreyfus details the relationship between Husserl's philosophical project and Marvin Minsky's "frames" proposal for encoding common sense.[46]

Given Husserl's deep intellectual debts to Kant, it is understandable that Lyotard would compare Minsky's proposal to Kant's idea of reflective judgment.[47] Thus, these philosophical critiques of AI (of Dreyfus and Lyotard) give one a means of seeing how symbolic AI's proposals to encode common sense (for example, Minsky's proposal) inherit the limitations of Kant and Husserl; and the critiques illustrate how Heidegger's critique of Husserl is reflected in the computational phenomenologists' critique of symbolic AI. However, despite the frequent citing of Heidegger's work within the literature of computational phenomenology, it is not clear whether computational phenomenology is a Heideggerian project. In many ways, computational phenomenology is a self-contradictory effort to "enframe" Heidegger's critique of Husserl in a set of technologies.[48]

AI AND CULTURAL DIFFERENCE

When AI has been dependent upon a Kantian-influenced vocabulary (the terms "schema," "common sense," and "teleology"), its inability to articulate cultural difference is reminiscent of Kant's own limitations or oversights (with respect to gender differences). For example, in AI discussions of common sense, few researchers have asked *whose* common sense is under consideration, preferring instead to assume that common sense is common to all humans and not culturally specific.

Even with the "aesthetic turn" in AI, practically no work has been done in AI on culture—the (re)production of differences of gender, sexuality, class, race, nationality. A belief in aesthetics as culturally invariant is obviously a useful one for a liberal, Enlightenment politics to which Kant's theories of universal subjectivity contribute. AI and cognitive science in general are very much in the vein of Kant's cosmopolitan universalism in their hypothesis of universal cognitive mechanisms "executable" on all sorts of (silicon- and carbon-based) "hardware." What this hypothesis of a universal subjectivity leaves unthought is that significant differences between people do exist and, furthermore, the introduction of powerful technologies like AI can change people even more by changing their day-to-day lives. As a result, AI and its critics have largely been blind to the ethical implications of AI and its implications for post-Kantian aesthetics.[49]

Nevertheless, some AI work has addressed what could be *interpreted* as cultural difference. For instance, ideological difference has been modeled as a difference of teleology (a difference of goals and the interrelationships between goals);[50] expert/novice differences in education and learning have been modeled as differences of number, detail, type, and interrelationships of rules and schemas;[51] and differences between the mentally healthy and the mentally ill (Kenneth Colby's simulation of a paranoid mind) have been computationally modeled as differences of beliefs and intentions.[52] Although such work does engage the problematics of such important cultural phenomena as ideology, education, and mental illness, it implicitly assumes that differences of culture are personal differences by attempting to represent them exclusively with "mental," "internal" constructs like goals, plans, beliefs, and intentions. Such work reduces the public to the private by ignoring the ways in which social interaction can be (re)productive of cultural difference.

This weakness of AI is not surprising given that the central metaphor of the discipline has been—not *minds*—but *mind*-as-machine. Marvin Minsky's work stretches this metaphor by hypothesizing that a mind is composed of a society of "agents."[53] This work is a shift away from a Kantian vocabulary to a vocabulary of psychoanalysis.[54] Other, newer work in distributed artificial intelligence, multi-agent systems, artificial life, computational models of discourse, and computer-supported cooperative work stretches the central metaphor of AI further by making groups and communities the object of study (rather than the mind of a single individual).[55] Increasingly these new offshoots of AI are not simply stretching the boundaries of AI but, rather, are creating independent disciplines.

Even within these newer disciplines, however, little attention has been paid to the issue of cultural difference. Instead, what is predominantly stressed is consensus and questions such as the following: Within a community of agents, how can significant difference and miscommunication be overcome to allow for coordination, agreement, and "common knowledge"?[56]

TURING'S IMITATION GAME

Ironically, cultural difference (specifically gender) is central to what is considered by most AI researchers to be the founding essay of AI. In "Computing Machinery and Intelligence," Alan Turing proposes a Wittgensteinian language game, the "imitation game," to replace the (what he sees as meaningless) question of "Can machines think?"[57] Turing's "imitation game" includes a proposal to program a computer to play the role of a man attempting to imitate a woman, an intriguing proposal concerning the reproduction and representation of gender difference in computational, networked media. The "game" is usually renamed in the literature of AI as the "Turing Test" and re-narrated to exclude any mention of gender difference.[58] Turing describes the imitation game like this:

> It is played with three people, a man, a woman, and an interrogator who may be of either sex. The interrogator stays in a room apart from the other two. The object of the game for the interrogator is to determine which of the other two is the man and which is the woman. . . . It is [the man's] object in the game to try to cause [the interrogator] to make the wrong identification. . . . The object of the game for [the woman] is to help the interrogator. . . . We now ask

the question, "What will happen when a machine takes the part of [the man] in this game?" Will the interrogator decide wrongly as often when the game is played like this as he does when the game is played between a man and a woman? These questions replace our original [question], "Can machines think?"[59]

Within the literature of AI, discussions of Turing's imitation game have focused on the role of the machine and the role of the interrogator. The role of the woman has been almost entirely ignored. Yet, if one looks more closely at the woman's role in Turing's game, it is clear that variants of this role have been reiterated in popular art and performance for thousands of years. The woman's role in Turing's game is to compete with the machine for an identity that is properly hers to begin with (the role of "woman"). The frequently reiterated, popular fears surrounding AI and its cultural and specifically artistic precedents are the fears of this sort of role: the fears of loss of identity, fears of replacement by machine, fears of disfiguration, dismemberment, and death.

AI AND THE AESTHETICS OF THE UNCANNY

In short, these fears of an AI machine are, specifically, the fears of the "double" as it has been explored in psychoanalytic theory and in the arts, for instance, in literature and film.[60] More generally, these fears can be described as those associated with the *uncanny aesthetic* discussed by Sigmund Freud and others.[61] Fears of the uncanny are often associated with machines, automata, and artificially produced "doubles."

Julia Kristeva has written that "uncanniness occurs when the boundaries between imagination and reality are erased."[62] Some AI researchers have tried to disavow association between their "real" work and the imaginative, artistic tradition that explores the fears of uncanny aesthetics.[63] Yet, any review of AI and aesthetics would certainly be incomplete without mentioning AI's relationship to the aesthetics of the uncanny because popular perception (as reflected in film, television, literature, and journalism about AI) is often dominated by questions of "doubling:" Will machines replace people?

Limits of the Uncanny

A poststructuralist view of Kant provides a means of understanding some of the relationships between aesthetics and issues central to AI research (common sense and teleology). Newer offshoots of AI research tend to engage a larger variety of post-Kantian, philosophical, and critical vocabularies (those of Heideggerian phenomenology and psychoanalysis). Nevertheless, while newer work might move AI outside the limits of a Kantian-inspired aesthetics, the newer work is *not* independent of a larger discourse of aesthetics that includes issues beyond the beautiful and the sublime (the uncanny).

In fact, the above exploration of the connections between the commonsensical and the aesthetic shows a number of dependencies between seemingly different approaches to designing (AI) software and hardware. The first set of technologies discussed are based upon the assumption that common sense can be coded, articulated, stated, or at least reasoned about prior to the use of the technology. "User-friendly" software presumes a set of associations that are either coded into the software so that it behaves intelligently, or a set of associations that the user will make in trying to figure out and operate the software's interface. A second set of technologies—those of the so-called computational phenomenologists—is built with the aim that commonsensical behavior is negotiated between an agent and its environment. Thus, in this case the associations of common sense—Minsky's example of how a suitcase, in certain circumstances, might be categorized as something to stand on rather than as a piece of luggage—emerge from a combination of what is perceived and what is known.

Both the symbolic AI and computational phenomenologist perspectives, however, assume that there does exist a set of associations (either a priori or negotiated) that can be labeled commonsensical. Likewise, so does the uncanny perspective on technology assume a background of the commonsensical. Art and design that intends to produce an uncanny, alienating effect is an attempt to unravel the associations of the familiar and commonsensical. The Russian Formalist Viktor Shklovsky states that the purpose of art is to work against habitualization, familiarization, and automatization: "Habitualization devours works, clothes, furniture, one's wife, and the fear of war. . . . Art exists that one may recover the sensation of life; it exists to make one feel things. . . . The technique of art is to make objects 'unfamiliar,' to make forms difficult, to increase the difficulty and length of perception because the process of perception is an aesthetic end in itself and must be prolonged."[64]

This approach to art, and the common popular presentation of AI technologies (in Hollywood films) as uncanny, attempts the exact opposite of the aims of user-friendly, commonsensical, "homey" (canny) design because it specifically makes the designed artifact unfriendly, unsettling, even scary:

> But it is this very confrontation with social and political practice that the aesthetic theory of estrangement finds an apparently intractable and unyielding

test. The formal and critical expression of alienation, as the first avant-gardes found to their chagrin, does not always neatly correspond to the work of transforming or even ameliorating such conditions in practice. Formal explorations of defamiliarization based on carnivalesque reversals of aesthetic norms, substitutions of the grotesque for the sublime, the uncanny for the domestic, can all too easily be construed as decoration or caricature.[65]

As Anthony Vidler's comment makes clear, even though this different kind of design is intended to produce scary, unsettling artifacts, sometimes it just produces silly kitsch. Ironically, these aesthetic failures might have the same flaw as the unworkable technologies that were supposed to be immediately recognizable as familiar and user-friendly: it is impossible to determine what, for all people in all circumstances, will be interpreted to be familiar and commonsensical.

NETWORK AESTHETICS:
AFTER THE UNCANNY AND THE COMMONSENSICAL

Internet-based interactions are often electronic exchanges open to cross-cultural and multicultural exchanges. Consequently, a design practice that assumes that the common sense of Internet participants can be predicted and/or preenumerated is an untenable approach. I have devoted the bulk of this essay to an illustration of how previous software design approaches (especially those of AI) are closely tied to a *common-sense aesthetics,* an aesthetics that presumes a common sense, a predictably emergent common sense, or the uncanny interference of the common-sense world. An alternative to these approaches must be found if we are to design for the Internet, where a potential, or virtual, common sense is contingent upon the possible (but not necessarily probable) emergence of a community of people who create their own stable linguistic and social structure through continued interaction on the Internet. This new aesthetics, therefore, must be useful for the practices of designing for emergent communities.[66]

I am especially concerned with conversational interactions because Internet communities are usually founded on e-mail exchange, chat, Web-blogging activities, or other networked-based forms of conversation. I call these networked conversations "very large-scale conversations" (VLSC) because they are often a form of conversation that involves many more people in far more complicated social and semantic dynamics than earlier forms of conversation and dialectic.[67] The term "dialectic" originates from the Greek expression for the art of conversation.[68]

It is worth remembering that a variety of aesthetic practices from art and design have been dependent upon an understanding of conversation or, more particularly, an understanding of dialectics. The conviction that the common sense and stereotypes of mainstream media can be challenged through design of new media has been the foundation for many philosophical and artistic-design projects produced to find new material forms for some recent theory of dialectics. At least since Socrates' time, artists, designers, and philosophers have been inventing new dialectical processes to unravel the forms of each new medium and each new common sense. New theories of dialectics were developed by Plato, Aristotle, Kant, Hegel, Karl Marx, Theodor Adorno, and others. Artists and designers have elaborated these dialectical processes for new and existing media. For example, a variety of artistic processes were developed in the early twentieth century that can be seen as media-specific instantiations of Marx's theory of dialectics.[69] Among these processes might be mentioned Sergei Eisenstein's then-new techniques of editing and film montage.[70] Eisenstein's frequent collaborator, the Russian Formalist Viktor Shklovsky, described a set of devices used in poetry for making the unconscious conscious by making the familiar strange.[71] Shklovsky's notion of "making strange" *(ostranenie)* with poetry is comparable to Bertolt Brecht's theory of the "estrangement-effect" *(Verfremdung)* in epic theater.[72] Analogous phenomena and devices called *faktura* were researched by the Russian Constructivists for media as diverse as architecture, painting, sculpture, and collage.[73]

However, each of the artistic design practices mentioned differs according to the medium in which it was practiced and according to the theory of dialectics—or conversation—that it incorporated or made into material form. Obviously, as soon as conversation becomes something completely different, the aesthetics of a "dialectic" practice must also renew itself. The question is, therefore, What is the new aesthetics for interpersonal interactions on the Internet?

Dialectics has always been a form of conversational interaction, but also a procedure for division or repeated logical analysis of genera into species. Essentially, the division of objects into kinds and their ordering is one of the main activities of computer sciences, especially the area of computer science that concerns the construction of databases. Thus, the recent approach to what artist and designer Victoria Vesna calls "database aesthetics" is one vision of a new form for dialectical aesthetics: "Artists working with the net are essentially concerned with the creation of a new type of aesthetic that involves not only a visual representation, but invisible aspects of organization, retrieval, and navigation as well. Data is the raw form that is shaped and used to build architectures of knowledge exchange and as an active commentary on the environment it depends on—the vast, intricate network with its many faces."[74]

I agree with Vesna, but I think that two aspects of her proposal need to be amplified and extended. First, it is important to remember that data, especially the data of interpersonal interaction on the Internet, are never raw. They are always the result of the writing or speaking activities of some participant in conjunction with one or more "invisible" computation procedures of organization, retrieval, or navigation. Ever since the invention of things like Social Security numbers, the organization and indexing of databases has been about the organization and indexing of people as well as data. Like all dialectic, or conversational processes, VLSC is a process in which people are organized. If a democratic design is pursued, then the VLSC can be about the self-organization, the self-governance of people. In Michel Foucault's terms, it can be a *technology of the self* rather than a *technology of power*.

Second, the "invisible aspects of organization" are only invisible if design aesthetics adopts a point of view that puts those aspects over the "horizon line" of vision or inspection. In other words, I think a new aesthetics of conversation must have an affinity with many of the older dialectically motivated aesthetics insofar as they were attempts to make the invisible visible.

To mark these amendments to Vesna's proposal, I will refer to this new aesthetics as a "network aesthetics" to emphasize the focus of such an approach. The focus should be to show the production and reproduction of connections and associations between people and data and their interminglings (in, for example, the form of a *social cohesion,* or the emergence of a common sense or shared set of metaphors or definitions).

There is a well-worked-out philosophy of what I am calling network aesthetics. It is the descriptions of rhizomes, networks, desiring machines, and intensities articulated by Gilles Deleuze and Félix Guattari.[75] However, it is difficult to articulate that philosophical approach to aesthetics when the domain of analysis is the new media technologies of information-processing machines and networks (rather than, for example, older media like painting, architecture, or film). Deleuze and Guattari's lexicon was largely influenced by the vocabularies of nonlinear system dynamics, cybernetics, and other technical artifacts that now need to be redesigned with this new aesthetics. In short, it is hard to distinguish the figure from the ground, and many people, even the experts in this philosophical lexicon, fail to distinguish the vocabulary from the domain of analysis.

Various writers have noted a convergence between Deleuze's work and
the scientific theories of complexity and chaos (developed in fields such
as physics and computer science). Brian Massumi, the English-language
translator of Deleuze and Guattari's book *Thousand Plateaus,* said: "[Gilles
Deleuze's] work . . . could profitably be read together with recent theories of
complexity and chaos. It is a question of emergence, which is precisely the
focus of the various science-derived theories which converge around the
notion of self-organization (the spontaneous production of a level of reality having its own rules of formation and order of connection)."[76]

Manuel De Landa, in his book *War in the Age of Intelligent Machines,*
meticulously expounds on how Deleuze's work intersects with theories of
complexity, chaos, and self-organization.[77] Indeed, Deleuze emphasizes his
own mathematical and scientific "borrowings" in such work as chapter 15 of
his book *Logic of Sense.*[78]

CONCLUSIONS

Rather than presume a sort of common sense aesthetics to design for the
Internet, a new approach must be developed. This is true because the Internet is meant to be multicultural and cross-cultural in composition, so there
is no one common sense that can be identified a priori. Instead, the new
approach must be based on the understanding that communities can emerge
through network communities so new social and semantic relationships
can be produced, reproduced, and transformed. It is possible to visualize
these emerging communities and linguistic possibilities as the growth and
change of networks or rhizomes.

Yet, to visualize them as such is problematic or at least overdetermined.
When one thinks, for instance, of "network," is it not that the Internet itself
forces all other ideas of networks out of one's head? Obviously this is not
the case for everyone, but for the many for whom this is the case, the quick
association between any mention of network and the Internet creates a problem for a *network aesthetics.* How can network aesthetics be a new vocabulary for the design of network technologies if the vocabulary is immediately
conflated with the object of study and design?

Perhaps this concern for a more abstract theoretical language to describe
a more material design practice is simply another misplaced nostalgia for
an older kind of aesthetics. John Rajchman puts this counter into play:

> What is then abstract? Today the question arises in relation to what is known
> as the "information" age. Perhaps some new pragmatist will apply the critique

of abstractions found in Bergson and James to the very idea of information and the computational paradigm to which it belongs. Two related postulates might be distinguished. The first says that information is independent of the material medium through which it is transmitted; the second says that simulation and reality come to the same thing. Thus, one "abstracts" from material support and, by replicating processes, abstracts them from the particularities of their real existence; even "life" becomes only abstract information, which can be replicated and so made artificially. The two postulates of immateriality and irreality then combine in the great conceit of the info era: that electronic devices will abolish real or material space and time and transport us all into another abstract, bodiless "space" or "reality," consummating the triumph of silicon over carbon.

By contrast, in Deleuze one finds an abstraction concerned not with extracting information from things (as though the material world were so much clumsy hardware) but rather with finding within things the delicate, complicated abstract virtualities of other things. Such abstractions don't entail independence or transferability from material support and don't operate according to a logic of simulation. Rather inherent in materials it supposes the subsistence of connections that exceed the messages of a medium and ourselves as senders and receivers of them.[79]

To summarize, an aesthetics for the Internet needs to focus on producing the means for visualizing and understanding how social and semantic relations intertwine and communities and common sense emerge. It may be the case that the theory and the phenomena of these kinds of self-organizational productions and reproductions are both network-based and thus conceptually and materially, mutually recursive in definition—an unsettling but perhaps workable perspective.

NOTES

1. Ben Schneiderman, *Designing the User Interface: Strategies for Effective Human-Computer Interaction* (Reading, Mass.: Addison-Wesley, 1987).

2. Nicholas Negroponte, *Being Digital* (New York: Alfred A. Knopf, 1995).

3. Claudia Dreifus, "A Conversation with Dr. Marvin Minsky: Why Isn't Artificial Intelligence More Like the Real Thing?" *New York Times,* July 28, 1998; or see http://www.nytimes.com/library/national/science/072898sci-minsky.html.

4. Roger Fowler, *Linguistic Criticism,* 2nd ed. (New York: Oxford University Press, 1996), 27.

5. Antonio Gramsci, *Selections from the Prison Notebooks* (London: Lawrence and Wishart, 1971), 326, as cited in Stuart Hall, "The Rediscovery of 'Ideology': Return of the

Repressed in Media Studies," in *Culture, Society, and the Media,* ed. Michael Gurevitch, Tony Bennett, James Curran, and Janet Woollacott (New York: Routledge, 1982), 73.

6. Ibid. According to Stuart Hall, Anglo-American media studies of the early twentieth century saw the media (newspaper, television, etc.) as producers of content that "reflected" the "common sense" of the larger public. The media was said to objectively write down and distribute the consensus, or "sensus communus," that was produced by the public independent of the media. Hall argues that later, media studies came to recognize the media's role in producing, rather than simply reflecting, community values and common sense. By being the only "voice" that could reach across the nation and even across the world, the electronic and print media framed public discourse, and thus public "common sense," simply through the editorial choice of which stories should be broadcast and which should be left untold.

7. Howard Gardner, *The Mind's New Science: A History of the Cognitive Revolution* (New York: Basic Books, 1985).

8. Stuart C. Shapiro (editor in chief), *Encyclopedia of Artificial Intelligence,* 2nd ed. (New York: John Wiley and Sons, 1992).

9. See Gardner, *The Mind's New Science.*

10. See Pamela McCorduck, *Machines Who Think: A Personal Inquiry into the History and Prospects of Artificial Intelligence* (San Francisco: W. H. Freeman, 1979), 3–29.

11. Terry Winograd and Fernando Flores, *Understanding Computers and Cognition: A New Foundation for Design* (Norwood, N.J.: Ablex, 1986).

12. See B. F. Skinner, *Science and Human Behavior* (New York: Macmillan, 1953); and Norbert Wiener, *Cybernetics; or, Control and Communication in the Animal and the Machine* (New York: John Wiley and Sons, 1955).

13. Sherry Turkle, "Artificial Intelligence and Psychoanalysis: A New Alliance," *Daedalus* 17, no. 1 (Winter 1988).

14. Gardner, *The Mind's New Science.*

15. Steve Heims, *The Cybernetics Group* (Cambridge, Mass.: MIT Press, 1991), 15.

16. Alan Newell, J. C. Shaw, and Herbert A. Simon, "GPS, A Program That Simulates Human Thought," in *Computers and Thought,* ed. Edward A. Feigenbaum and Julian Feldman (New York: McGraw-Hill, 1963), 279–93.

17. J. Martins, "Belief Revision," in *Encyclopedia of Artificial Intelligence,* 2nd ed., ed. Stuart C. Shapiro (New York: John Wiley and Sons, 1992), 111.

18. Herbert A. Simon, *The Sciences of the Artificial,* 3rd ed. (Cambridge, Mass.: MIT Press, 1996).

19. Gilles Deleuze, *Kant's Critical Philosophy: The Doctrine of the Faculties,* trans. Hugh Tomlinson and Barbara Habberjam (Minneapolis: University of Minnesota Press, 1984).

20. Jean-François Lyotard, *Lessons on the Analytic of the Sublime: Kant's Critique of Judgment,* trans. Elizabeth Rottenberg (Stanford: Stanford University Press, 1994).

21. Immanuel Kant, *Kritik der Urtheilskraft,* in Kant's *Gesammelte Schriften,* vol. 5 (Berlin: Bey Lagarde und Friederich, 1790), 165–485. Warren Sack, "Artificial Human Nature," *Design Issues* 13 (Summer 1997): 55–64.

22. Gardner, *The Mind's New Science;* see also Andrew Brook, *Kant and the Mind* (Cambridge: Cambridge University Press, 1994).

23. Howard Caygill, *A Kant Dictionary* (Cambridge, Mass.: Blackwell Reference, 1995), 388.

24. Kant, *Kritik der Urtheilskraft*, 61.

25. Caygill, *A Kant Dictionary*, 190.

26. Gardner, *The Mind's New Science*, 6.

27. Deleuze, *Kant's Critical Philosophy*, 49–50.

28. Ibid., 50.

29. Jean-François Lyotard, *The Inhuman: Reflections on Time*, trans. Geoffrey Bennington and Rachel Bowlby (Stanford: Stanford University Press, 1991), 15.

30. Marvin Minsky, "A Framework for Representing Knowledge," in *Mind Design: Philosophy, Psychology, Artificial Intelligence*, ed. John Haugeland (Cambridge, Mass.: MIT Press, 1981). John McCarthy, *Formalizing Common Sense: Papers by John McCarthy*, ed. Vladimir Lifschitz and John McCarthy (Oxford: Intellect, 1998).

31. See R. Bruce Roberts and Ira P. Goldstein, *The FRL Manual* (Cambridge, Mass.: Massachusetts Institute of Technology, 1977).

32. Edward A. Feigenbaum and Pamela McCorduck, *The Fifth Generation: Artificial Intelligence and Japan's Computer Challenge to the World* (Reading, Mass.: Addison-Wesley, 1983).

33. See Hubert L. Dreyfus with Harrison Hall, eds., *Husserl, Intentionality, and Cognitive Science* (Cambridge, Mass.: MIT Press, 1982), 23.

34. Roger C. Schank and Robert P. Abelson, *Scripts, Plans, Goals, and Understanding: An Inquiry into Human Knowledge Structures* (New York: John Wiley and Sons, 1977).

35. The first Encyclopediaists were Denis Diderot, Jean Le Rond d'Alembert, and their colleagues, who wrote and published the *Encyclopédie* from 1751 until 1772.

36. Douglas Lenat and R. Guha, *Building Large Knowledge-based Systems: Representation and Inference in the Cyc Project* (Reading, Mass.: Addison-Wesley, 1990).

37. Minsky, "A Framework for Representing Knowledge"; and McCarthy, *Formalizing Common Sense*.

38. Yorick A. Wilks, Brian M. Slator, and Louise M. Guthrie, *Electric Words: Dictionaries, Computers, and Meanings* (Cambridge, Mass.: MIT Press, 1996).

39. Kant, *Kritik der Urtheilskraft*, 35.

40. James L. McClelland and David E. Rumelhart, eds., *Parallel Distributed Processing: Explorations in the Microstructure of Cognition*, 2 vols. (Cambridge, Mass.: MIT Press, 1986).

41. Philip E. Agre and David Chapman, "Pengi: An Implementation of a Theory of Activity," in *Proceedings of the Fifth National Conference on Artificial Intelligence* (Seattle: Morgan Kaufmann, 1987), 268–72. Rodney Brooks, "Intelligence Without Representation," *Artificial Intelligence* 47 (1991): 139–60.

42. Les Gasser, "Social Conceptions of Knowledge and Action: Distributed Artificial Intelligence and Open Systems Semantics," *Artificial Intelligence* 47 (1991): 107–38.

43. Winograd and Flores, *Understanding Computers*, 98.

44. Hubert L. Dreyfus, *What Computers Can't Do: A Critique of Artificial Reason* (New York: Harper and Row, 1972).

45. Hubert Dreyfus and Harrison Hall (contributor), *Heidegger: A Critical Reader* (Williston, Vt.: Blackwell Publishers, 1992), 2–27.

46. Ibid., 19–22.

47. Lyotard, *The Inhuman*, 15.

48. See Richard Coyne, *Designing Information Technology in the Postmodern Age* (Cambridge, Mass.: MIT Press, 1995), 177. Martin Heidegger, *The Question Concerning Technology*,

and Other Essays, trans. William Lovitt (New York: Garland, 1977). See Dreyfus, *What Computers Still Can't Do.*

49. Sack, "Artificial Human Nature."

50. See Robert P. Abelson and J. D. Carroll, "Computer Simulation of Individual Belief Systems," *American Behavior Scientist* 8 (1965): 24–30; Jaime Carbonell, "Subjective Understanding: Computer Models of Belief Systems" (Ph.D. diss., Yale University, 1979).

51. See Etienne Wenger, *Artificial Intelligence and Tutoring Systems: Computational and Cognitive Approaches to the Communication of Knowledge* (Los Altos, Calif.: Morgan Kaufmann, 1987).

52. Kenneth Mark Colby, "Modeling a Paranoid Mind," *Behavioral and Brain Sciences* 4 (1981): 515–34.

53. Marvin Minsky, *The Society of Mind* (New York: Simon and Schuster, 1986).

54. For a description of "agents" and Freud's "realist" model of the ego, see Elizabeth A. Grosz, *Jacques Lacan: A Feminist Introduction* (New York: Routledge, 1990).

55. See A. H. Bond and Les Gasser, eds., *Readings in Distributed Artificial Intelligence* (Los Altos, Calif.: Morgan Kaufmann, 1988). For multi-agent systems, see Ronald Fagin, J. Y. Halpern, Y. Moses, and M. Y. Vardi, *Reasoning About Knowledge* (Cambridge, Mass.: MIT Press, 1995). See Rodney Brooks and Pattie Maes, eds., *Artificial Life IV: Proceedings of the Fourth International Workshop on the Synthesis and Simulation of Living Systems* (Cambridge, Mass.: MIT Press, 1994). For computational models of discourse, see Barbara Grosz and Candace Sidner, "Attention, Intentions, and the Structure of Discourse," *Journal of Computational Linguistics* 12, no. 3 (1986): 175–204. For computer-supported cooperative work, see Winograd and Flores, *Understanding Computers.*

56. See Fagin et al., *Reasoning About Knowledge.*

57. Alan Turing, "Computing Machinery and Intelligence," *Mind* 59, no. 236 (1950): 433–60. Turing's essay has been intensely discussed for half a century and yet few of these discussions link Turing's method of rephrasing the question "Can machines think?" as a (language) game to the methodology that Wittgenstein used more generally to reanalyze the so-called problems of philosophy as language games. Two sorts of evidence make this link between Turing's thinking and Wittgenstein's plausible. First, several scholars tell of Turing/Wittgenstein interactions. See, for instance, Otto Neumaier, "A Wittgensteinian View of Artificial Intelligence," in *Artificial Intelligence: The Case Against,* ed. R. Born (London: Croom-Helm, 1987); see also Andrew Hodges, *Alan Turing: The Enigma* (New York: Simon and Schuster, 1983). But second, and most interestingly I believe, some of Wittgenstein's own writings seem to foreshadow by almost twenty years the approach Turing takes: "This objection is expressed in the question: 'Could a machine think?' I shall talk about this at a later point, and now only refer you to an analogous question: 'Can a machine have a toothache?' You will certainly be inclined to say 'A machine can't have toothache.' All I will do now is to draw your attention to the use you have made of the word 'can' and ask you: 'Did you mean to say that all our past experience has shown that a machine never had a toothache?' The impossibility of which you speak is a logical one. The question is: What is the relation between thinking (or toothache) and the subject which thinks, has toothache, etc.?" Ludwig Wittgenstein, *The Blue and Brown Books: Preliminary Studies for the "Philosophical Investigations"* (New York: Harper Torchbooks, 1958), 16. Thanks to Joseph Dumit for pointing out this passage in Wittgenstein's writings.

58. Judith Genova, "Turing's Sexual Guessing Game" *Social Epistemology* 8, no. 4 (1994): 313–26. See also Warren Sack, "Painting Theory Machines," *Art and Design* 48 (May 1996): 80–92.

59. Turing, "Computing Machinery," 433–34.

60. For example, Otto Rank, *The Double: A Psychoanalytic Study,* trans. Harry Tucker Jr. (Chapel Hill: University of North Carolina Press, 1971). For example, E. T. A. Hoffmann, "The Sandman," in *Hoffmann's Strange Stories,* trans. L. Burnham (Boston: Burnham Brothers, 1855). See *The Student of Prague,* written by Hanns Heinz Ewers and directed by Paul Wegener, 1912.

61. Sigmund Freud, "The 'Uncanny,'" in *The Standard Edition of the Complete Psychological Works of Sigmund Freud,* vol. 17, trans. James Strachey (London: Hogarth Press, 1919). Julia Kristeva, *Strangers to Ourselves,* trans. Leon S. Roudiez (New York: Columbia University Press, 1991); Anthony Vidler, *The Architectural Uncanny: Essays in the Modern Unhomely* (Cambridge, Mass.: MIT Press, 1992).

62. Kristeva, *Strangers to Ourselves,* 188.

63. See Patrick Hayes and Kenneth Ford, "Turing Test Considered Harmful," in *Proceedings of the International Joint Conference on Artificial Intelligence* (Los Altos, Calif.: Morgan Kaufmann, 1995), 972–77.

64. Viktor Shklovsky, "Art as Technique," in *Russian Formalist Criticism,* ed. L. T. Lemon and M. J. Reis (Lincoln: University of Nebraska Press, 1965), 11–12.

65. Vidler, *The Architectural Uncanny,* 12–13.

66. These emergent communities might, in the lexicon of Gilles Deleuze and Félix Guattari, be called "minorities." See Gilles Deleuze and Félix Guattari, *A Thousand Plateaus: Capitalism and Schizophrenia,* trans. Brian Massumi (London: Athlone Press, 1988), 469–71.

67. Warren Sack, "What Does a Very Large-Scale Conversation Look Like?" in *Leonardo: Journal of the International Society for Arts, Sciences, and Technology* 35, no. 4 (August 2002): 417–26.

68. Paul Edwards, ed., "Dialectics," in *Encyclopedia of Philosophy,* vol. 2 (New York: Macmillan and The Free Press, 1967), 385.

69. See, for instance, Karl Marx, "Critique of Hegel's Dialectic and General Philosophy," in *Karl Marx: Early Writings* (New York: McGraw-Hill, 1983), 379–400.

70. Sergei Eisenstein, ed., *Film Form: Essays in Film Theory,* trans. Jay Leyda (New York: Harcourt, Brace, 1949).

71. See Fredric Jameson, *The Prison-House of Language: A Critical Account of Structuralism and Russian Formalism* (Princeton: Princeton University Press, 1972), 61. Victor Erlich, *Russian Formalism: History, Doctrine,* 3rd ed. (New Haven: Yale University Press, 1965).

72. Jameson, *The Prison-House of Language,* 58. Bertolt Brecht, *Brecht on Theatre: The Development of an Aesthetic,* ed. and trans. John Willett (New York: Hill and Wang, 1964), 70–71.

73. "The Russian term 'faktura' literally means texture but this is inadequate to convey the ideological and artistic overtones which it carries in Russian. Faktura suggests the working of the surface of materials." From Christina Lodder, *Russian Constructivism* (New Haven: Yale University Press, 1983), 280. See also Benjamin Buchloh, "From Faktura to Factography," *October* 30 (Fall 1984).

74. Victoria Vesna, "Database Aesthetics: Of Containers, Chronofiles, Time Capsules,

Xanadu, Alexandria, and the World Brain," *Journal of Artificial Intelligence & Society* (Fall 1999).

75. See Deleuze and Guattari, *A Thousand Plateaus;* see also *Anti-Oedipus: Capitalism and Schizophrenia,* trans. Robert Hurley, Mark Seem, and Helen R. Lane (Minneapolis: University of Minnesota Press, 1983); Gilles Deleuze, *Cinema 1: The Movement-Image* and *Cinema 2: The Time-Image,* trans. Hugh Tomlinson and Barbara Habberjam (Minneapolis: University of Minnesota Press, 1986).

76. Brian Massumi, "The Autonomy of Affect," *Cultural Critique (The Politics of Systems and Environments, Part II)* 31 (Fall 1995): 93.

77. Manuel De Landa, *War in the Age of Intelligent Machines* (New York: Zone Books, 1991), 234–37.

78. Gilles Deleuze, *Logic of Sense,* trans. Mark Lester, ed. Constantin V. Boundas (New York: Columbia University Press, 1990), chap. 15.

79. John Rajchman, "What Is Abstraction?" in *Constructions* (Cambridge, Mass.: MIT Press, 1998).

10. Game Engines as Embedded Systems

ROBERT F. NIDEFFER

Starting Points

The attention, time, and resources expended in relation to computer games and gaming emerge out of long-standing and diverse cultural traditions rooted in fundamental human needs related to the importance of play, interactivity, and creative experimentation in our social lives. In 2002, roughly 60 percent of Americans older than six years of age (about 145 million people) reported playing computer and video games. More than 221 million computer and video games were sold, almost two games for every American household. By 2006, U.S. computer and video game software sales grew 6 percent in 2006 to $7.4 billion—almost tripling industry software sales since the mid-1990s. The average game *player* is thirty-three years old and has been playing games for twelve years. Approximately 35 percent of American parents say they play computer and video games, while 80 percent of gamer parents say they play video games with their kids. Of all game players, 38 percent are reportedly women, and, in fact, women over eighteen represent a significantly greater portion of the game-playing population (30%) than boys seventeen years or younger (23%). By 2005, 25 percent of Americans over the age of five played video games, an increase from 9 percent from the late 1990s.[1] In the past decade, computer games and gaming have exploded from a niche market dominated by a particular youth demographic to a much more diversified audience.

Games have been at the forefront of major hardware and software advances in institutions as diverse as education, entertainment, government, and the military. The first CRT display was an old oscilloscope converted to display *Spacewar,* one of the earliest computer game examples. *Spacewar* was designed and implemented by a group of graduate students working at MIT in the early 1960s, in a lab funded by the military for calculating missile trajectories.[2]

Spacewar also catalyzed the development of the first joystick as a controller, modeled after a control device used by the MIT Tech Model Railroad Club. Legend has it that the UNIX operating system was developed by Ken Thompson on a PDP-1, largely out of a desire to play the game in a locally networked environment.[3]

The connection of games and gaming to the military runs deep. It is common knowledge that the military prepared for "Operation Desert Storm" by doing simulation strategy exercises in Florida before the invasion of Iraq, and that the U.S. military continues to pump large amounts of capital into figuring out how to appropriate gaming principles for battle

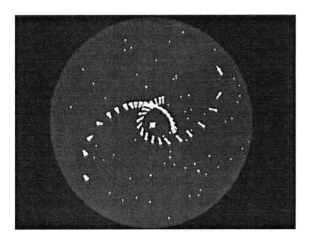

FIGURE 10.1.
SPACEWAR, 1961.
COPYRIGHT 1981.
CREATIVE COMPUTING
MAGAZINE.

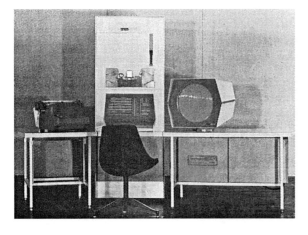

FIGURE 10.2. *SPACEWAR*
HARDWARE, 1961.
COPYRIGHT 1981.
CREATIVE COMPUTING
MAGAZINE.

training in massive multi-user SimNet environments. Such synchronicities between games, military preparedness, and academically driven research and development achieved new heights (or plunged to new depths, depending upon your point of view) in 1999, when the U.S. Army awarded a five-year contract to the University of Southern California to create the Institute for Creative Technologies (ICT).

As described on its public Web site, "The ICT's mandate is to enlist the resources and talents of the entertainment and game development industries and to work collaboratively with computer scientists to advance the state of immersive training simulation."[4] Essentially the military wants to implement training environments that have a narrative and emotional impact on par with the best that Hollywood has to offer. One thing that this alliance clearly indicates is the degree to which technology research and development within the private sector, and specifically the commercial games industry, has outpaced what goes on in the government-sponsored labs of academia and the military. The ICT, by its mere existence, is an explicit acknowledgment of this transition.

It doesn't take a rocket scientist to see that electronic gaming not only is transforming the entertainment marketplace but is increasingly dominating the time and attention of children and adults. What analog film and television represented at the close of the twentieth century, computer games and interactive entertainment represent at the dawn of the current century. While entertainment will continue to exist in myriad forms and fashions, it is not difficult to see that we are shifting from relatively passive media experiences to more interactive ones, from being simple consumers of digital media products to playing active roles in the creation of those products, and from computing in small-scale individually isolated domains to computing in large-scale collectively networked ones.

As we undergo these shifts, we must begin critically situating computer games in relation to the cultural milieu in which they are produced, distributed, and consumed—giving them the same kind of attention and analysis that we give to art, literature, and film. This process entails developing methodologies and theoretical vocabularies that recognize the uniqueness of the medium, while at the same time placing it in the context of the social conditions that produce it. In this light, one of the most important things to consider is how technical infrastructure can influence, or even dictate, form and content for games as well as for other creative work that incorporates game design principles, metaphors, and technology.

ENGINES OF CREATION

What exactly is a game engine and how does it work? Simply put, a game engine is a piece of software that provides the technical infrastructure for games. As pointed out in an informative essay published by Steven Kent in *GameSpy,* the game engine is responsible for rendering everything you see and interact with in the game world.[5] Game engines not only provide the rendering, but they also can provide the physics models, collision detection, networking, and much of the basic functionality the player experiences during game play. The game engine should not, however, be confused with the game itself. This would, as game developer Jake Simpson points out, be analogous to confusing the car engine with the entire car. A key difference is that "you can take the engine out of the car, and build another shell around it, and use it again."[6] The same holds true, more or less, with game engines and game applications. However, the customization needs of particular titles, coupled with the proprietary interests of publishers, often dictate that developers code their own engines in-house, or significantly modify licensed ones to suit their specific interests. In either case, considerable amounts of hard-core sweat, tears, and programming are usually involved.

In the last several years, game engines have advanced rapidly in terms of memory management, processing power, optimization procedures, networking capabilities, and pushing polygons to screens. Remembering the early days of 3D computer games, characters like those found in *Castle Wolfenstein* (circa 1992) had polygon counts of several hundred (if that), whereas now it is not uncommon for characters to have polygon counts in the thousands. *Doom III,* with the source models (often used for promotional materials and transitional animations during play), has polygon counts in the millions.[7]

Concerning 3D game engines, until recently polygons remained developers' primary concern. How many polygons an engine allows you to use efficiently largely determines the perceived realism of the environments created. However, one of the interesting things happening as engines and hardware evolve is that "most designers agree that raw polygon counts—so important in generations past—are no longer the main measure of a graphics engine. Instead, more and more computing power is needed to realistically light, shade, and texture those polygons to make objects appear even more real." Legendary game-engine programmer John Carmack, who has played a pivotal role in the development of the game genre known as the "first-person shooter" (and is the programming mastermind behind *Castle*

Wolfenstein, Doom, and *Quake*), reinforced this notion in Kent's article when he stated that what he wanted wasn't more polygons, but *more passes* per polygon. This is because with each "rendering pass" a computer makes, more and more detail can be added before displaying the graphics.[8]

RENDERING AND THE HOLY GRAIL OF REALISM

As Kent and others have pointed out, improved lighting, increasingly accurate physics models, and more believable artificial intelligence (AI) are seen as the next frontier for game engines by many in the industry. For anyone who attends meetings like the Game Developers Conference (GDC), the

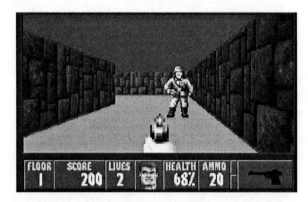

FIGURE 10.3.
CASTLE WOLFENSTEIN,
1992.

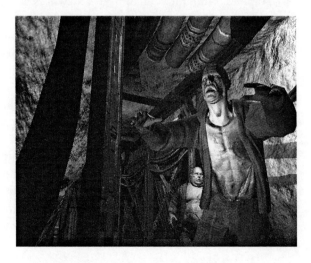

FIGURE 10.4.
DOOM III, 2003.

Electronic Entertainment Expo (E3), or SIGGRAPH, it quickly becomes apparent that these concerns are voiced almost exclusively from the desire to enhance the game world's realism.

Game AI is particularly interesting to think about in these terms. In the game world, AI tends to be associated with what are called NPCs, or Non-Player Characters. NPCs are prescripted machine-controlled characters with which the player-controlled character interacts. Good NPC AI will allow the NPC to function, or even more important, to *learn* how to function, in context-specific ways, adding impressive texture to the game play. The behavioral models applied to the complex coding of this kind of context-specific conduct, not surprisingly, come from careful observational studies of human interaction and human learning. Thus even inappropriate or random behaviors or mistaken responses may be hard-coded into the system to more accurately mimic human interaction.

There is a consensus that in order for the game development community to expand beyond the niche market it currently occupies, although that market is incredibly lucrative, it will need to diversify genre and content and make more compelling characters and narratives. As game engines and hardware platforms become capable of in-game photo realism, or even what is called "enhanced realism" (that which is beyond photo-realistic), it is assumed that players will more readily be immersed and identify with character and story—as tends to be the case with good literature, films, and television—making for a deeper and more meaningful media experience.

In many ways, this cultural moment within the game development and graphics community can be likened to what was happening in the arts, particularly within the domain of portrait and landscape painting, before the advent of photography. There were huge commissions, and the more detailed and realistic the work, the more value it had, and the more compelling, beautiful, and aesthetically pleasing it was deemed to be.

Then along came the camera. Artists had been using camera obscuras of various kinds throughout the sixteenth, seventeenth, and eighteenth centuries in order to form images on walls in darkened rooms that they could trace. However, it was a combination of André Adolphe Disderi's development of *carte-de-visite* photography in Paris circa 1854, leading to a worldwide boom in portrait studios for the next decade, the beginning of the stereoscopic era in the mid-1800s, and the subsequent popularization of photographic technology developed in the late 1800s and early to mid-1900s that heralded a new era. The camera was the most faithful documentarian imaginable. No longer was it necessary to so faithfully attempt to mimic an external reality

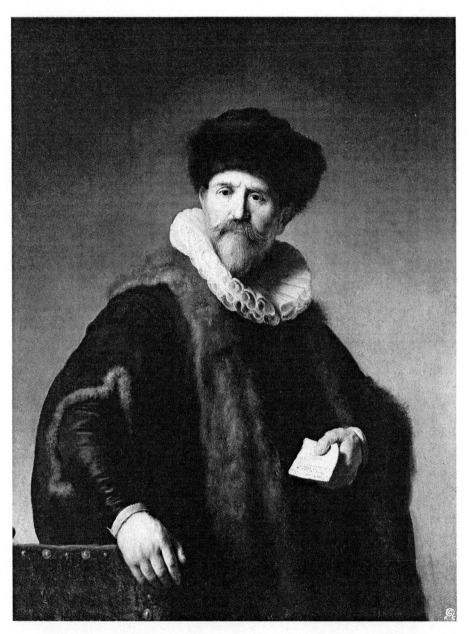

FIGURE 10.5. REMBRANDT VAN RIJN, *NICOLAES RUTS,* 1631, OIL ON MAHOGANY PANEL, 118.5 x 88.5 CM. COPYRIGHT THE FRICK COLLECTION, NEW YORK.

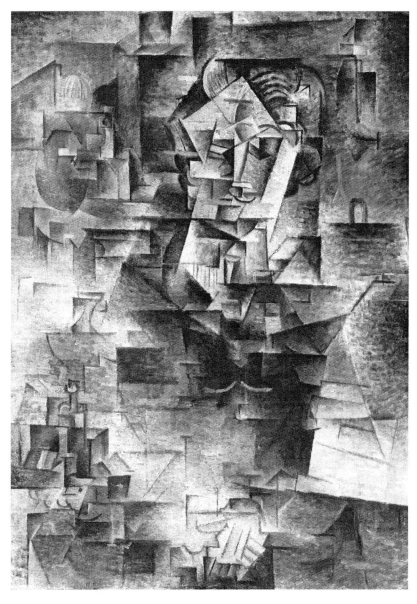

FIGURE 10.6. PABLO PICASSO, *DANIEL-HENRY KAHNWEILER*, 1910, OIL ON CANVAS, 101.1 X 73.3 CM. THE ART INSTITUTE OF CHICAGO, GIFT OF MRS. GILBERT W. CHAPMAN IN MEMORY OF CHARLES B. GOODSPEED, 1948.561. COPYRIGHT THE ART INSTITUTE OF CHICAGO.

with paint. From a conceptual and creative standpoint, artistic representation started to get more interesting.

Artists began to experiment more boldly with shape, color, light, texture, and form and, as a result, some of the most influential art movements of the twentieth century evolved from this new exploration: impressionism, postimpressionism, and pointillism (1870s–1880s), fauvism (1905–1908), Die Brucke (1905–13), Der Blaue Reiter (1911–14), expressionism (1905–25), cubism (1907–on), Dadaism (1916–22), surrealism (1924–30), de Stijl (1917–31), abstract expressionism (1940–50), color-field (1945–50), pop art (1950s), minimalism (1958–on), op art (1965–on), and so on.[9] The list could continue. The point here is that with the introduction and adoption of a specific technology, the camera, the aesthetic sensibilities of the dominant art-world culture shifted and diversified, and whole new horizons of possibility opened up to experimentation and creative exploration. The same type of conceptual shift needs to happen in the context of computer games and game engines.

DATABASE INTERFACES

We might think of the game engine as a database interface, a mechanism through which a predetermined, relatively constrained collection of procedures and protocols are used to render a world and make it navigable in context. If we wish to look at the game engine as a cultural artifact that circulates within a specific social domain, then we must extend the boundaries of what strictly constitutes the game engine and posit the game player as not only a functional requirement of the engine, but also as its key constitutive element. Without the player, the engine effectively ceases to exist. Once the player is positioned as an integral part of the game engine, a pivotal question becomes, What, then, constitutes the database used in the game engine's rendering of the game world?

The classical computer science definition of database refers to any organized store of data for computer processing. Data are taken to be items upon which operations may be performed within a computing environment. It is not too much of a stretch, then, to claim that any of a game's resources—the images, models, textures, sounds, interfaces, and code base—can be thought of as elements of the database, as they are all part of an organized store of data upon which the game engine performs operations, primarily—though not exclusively—in relation to the user input. The methods used to extract resources from the database play a big role in the generation of contextually specific meaning, a generative process that is required for goal-oriented interaction to occur. The more resources there are to pull from, and the more robust the methods for pulling, the greater the amount of context that can be provided, and the richer the potential exchange. Without such additional context, we run the risk of less functional interpretation, navigation, and orientation to the mental and physical space we occupy.

It is equally important to reflect on the process of populating (asset creation), accessing (asset management), rendering (asset visualization), manipulating (asset modification), and playing a given game if we want to try to tell a tale about the underlying logic. That underlying logic, however, particularly with regard to complex technical infrastructures, can usually be uncovered to a limited degree. Knowledge, and the narrative (or meaning-making), mapped upon experience in relation to that presumed knowledge is always situated, contextual, and partial. This partial awareness is compounded by the fact that the dominant paradigm in software engineering is to keep the inner workings of the infrastructure hidden from the end user.

For example, imagine kanji, the character set of the Chinese and Japanese language, as a database. Within kanji, there are more than fifty thousand unique characters. Roughly two thousand or so are used in daily conversation. Let's assume that you have been studying the language and know about three hundred of those characters. You could probably get by reasonably well if you visited China or Japan and do things like read bits of the newspaper, order in restaurants, find your way to the bathroom, and so on. However, your relationship to the culture would be superficial because your contextual understanding—the ability to make connections between ideas, appreciate subtle nuances, wordplays, humor, sophisticated concepts, and analogies—would be severely limited. In other words, you would not be a very robust interface to the database.

We also need to ask, and this is critical, what constitutes the database *of the player,* where does it begin and end, and how is it rendered during play? To begin answering this question, a concept proposed by Berkeley sociologist Ann Swidler, who advanced the notion of "culture as a toolkit," is useful. From Swidler's perspective, individuals draw on cultural tools to solve problems and interpret their social worlds. There are any number of different cultural values and beliefs in an individual's cultural toolkit, depending upon the various environments and experiences in which the individual is situated.[10]

For our purposes, think of the player's cultural toolkit as a kind of database. Then, in addition to values and beliefs, include things like personal history, geographic location, language, education, race, class, and ethnicity as constitutive elements of that database, all of which influence the way meaning-making happens not only during the gaming experience but also during the development of the infrastructure designed and implemented to support that experience.

Every game has its set of rules, grammar, and logic. Together these constitute the language or narrative of the game, a language or narrative that must be learned in order to gain experience, increase levels, acquire power, or make meaning within the given system. Interpretation of the world must happen continually in order to negotiate action within it. Thus, players as well as developers inescapably function as indexical pointers to their respective cultural toolkits or databases at all phases of game-engine and game-application production, distribution, and consumption.

GIVE A BOY A HAMMER . . .

The metaphor of the cultural toolkit provides a useful mechanism for thinking about how we can extend the idea of the database into the social domain. It also allows us to examine how the relevant attributes and elements of the database can mutate in relation to context. Yet, for all its utility, the toolkit analogy is not as useful in explaining why certain gaming designs, aesthetics, and experiences are consistently chosen or privileged over others, or why certain constraints are continually coded into software. Frame theory provides a more useful theoretical scaffold for addressing these concerns. A core concept of frame theory is "frames of reference," defined in the *Dictionary of Modern Thought* as "the context, viewpoint, or set of presuppositions or of evaluative criteria within which a person's perception and thinking seem always to occur, and which constrains selectively the course and outcome of these activities."[11] A wide range of theoreticians within the social sciences have, in varying degrees, mobilized this concept to explain human behavior within the disciplinary domains of psychology, sociology, and anthropology.[12] Admittedly, there is some slippage in the usage of the terms "framing" and "ideology." At the risk of opening Pandora's box, let's postulate ideology as a complex web of systematically and institutionally related ideas, values, and norms that is often seen as having a material basis as it articulates the social world and positions subjects within it. On the one hand, ideological systems have tended to be theorized as inflexible and resistant to change. On the other hand, framing more readily allows a give-and-take to be injected into rigid and unidirectional understandings of ideology so characteristic of the earlier literature on the topic. As such, frames can become tactically and strategically mobilized when consciously used in efforts to realign prior framings that have become relatively fixed and stabilized.[13] Good frames (the objects), and effective framings (the objects put into action), have a cultural resonance, meaning they are in synchrony with a collective or shared belief about how the world works, albeit a belief that is often hidden and taken for granted until exposed or threatened with a competing frame.

Arguably, in order for game play to be successful and resonate with the player in the ways anticipated and intended by the developers, the proper cultural toolkits and frames of reference need to be available to the player in order for appropriate character identification, narrative and environmental navigation, and contextual meaning-making to occur. However, it should not be assumed that there is a one-to-one correlation between the cultural toolkits and frames of reference drawn on by the producers of the game, and those employed by the consumers of that game, in order for a game to be perceived successful in terms of design or economics or, at a minimal level, simply as fun. It does, however, imply that if more tools are shared, and the frames of reference deployed within the game space are meaningful to the player, the game play experience will have a far more profound emotional, psychological, and physiological impact. This implication holds particularly true as game concepts, technology, and industries mature and diversify.

Similarly, in order for the success of the game engine to be maximized within the developer community, it also must resonate with the popular frames of reference consistently mobilized within that domain of interest. In other words, when developers, and by extension players, have reasonably consistent values, beliefs, and expectations with regard to what qualities are important for engines and the applications wrapped around them to possess, a game, and the engine supporting it, will have popular appeal. In addition, when those values, beliefs, and expectations are not shared, the appeal will be far less. This dynamic can easily be seen in the many failed efforts to market games cross-culturally, particularly when there is little sensitivity to the specificities of a region's people and history. Although it is beyond the scope of this essay, the converse situation is perhaps even more interesting: How do we explain the cross-cultural success of particular game titles that have little to do with or even run counter to the particularities of the people and places in which they get played, and what significance do we make of it? This is of course a variation on a theme that has been relevant to the study of media hegemony from its inception.

Granted, the purpose of this essay is not to explicate the various toolkits, frames, and framings that have been present within the computer game development community over the past several decades, particularly as they percolate up and manifest at the level of the game application. The goal here is simply to present the concept in the effort to explain how and why certain functionality gets consistently coded into software, and the difficulty of creatively modifying that functionality once it has been embedded into infrastructure. It is also to begin to provide a theoretical foundation that can be useful for deliberately thinking through alternative frames and framings in the effort to enhance creative production and consumption possibilities, diversify the rapidly expanding media ecology tied to games and gaming, and effect responsible social change.

AND THE WORLD BECOMES A NAIL

What are some of the key functionalities that are perceived necessary within the development community in order to provide the game designer with the requisite tools for efficient and successful product as it hits the competitive marketplace? To address this question, we'll restrict the discussion to 3D game engines, though much of what follows could be as readily applied to 2D engines, by looking at it in the context of the Electronic Entertainment Expo (E3), held annually in Los Angeles, California, to showcase the latest in games technology.

One of the most noticeable things when walking around the exhibition floor of E3 is the remarkable functional and aesthetic resemblance between titles using 3D engines.

- Usually an animate "thing" rendered to a display device gets situated in a recognizable wire-framed and texture-mapped environment.
- Its movement is controlled through a hardware interface such as a joystick, keyboard, or game pad and it has a predictable real-world physics model attached to it.
- It is proximately aware of other things around it or that it comes into contact with.
- There are other "things" similar to it that are either remotely controlled by other players within a networked social space or are precoded entities.
- It has ambient and event-based sounds, lighting, and particle effects tied to its location and action.
- It gains power and privilege in the system over time with successful manipulation of objects and completion of goals and objectives.

- Temporally and spatially sensitive state information can be saved on it so that it is possible to stop and start again from where the player last left off.

Clearly this list could continue at great length. Why are these attributes seemingly so entrenched? Arguably, it has less to do with technical limitations than it does with conceptual ones.

Granted, we can push more pixels to the screen, have higher resolution, static and dynamic imagery, navigate more complex environments, and move around in 3D. And while we can see considerable variation with the game shell—the game content wrapped around the engine—there still has been surprisingly little experimentation at the level of the functional attributes assumed integral to the successful 3D game engine. Moreover, without that flexibility at the level of the infrastructure, it is difficult, if not impossible, to see radical transformation happen at the level of the application hooked into that infrastructure. These things look and feel strikingly similar.

Even in the realm of the MMORPG (Massively Multiuser Online Role-Playing Games), most of what we find can be linked directly back to the text-based MUDs (Multi-User Dungeons or Domains) and MOOs (Multi-user Object-Oriented domains) that had impressive popularity in the 1980s and early 1990s. MMORPGs like *Everquest, Ultima Online, Asheron's Call,* and the *Sims* can functionally and conceptually be thought of as extended versions of MUDs and MOOs that have been given a graphical front end.

There are many reasons for this lack of structural experimentation. Some of the reasons have to do with *generic convention*—the tendency toward inertia once something establishes itself as successful in the marketplace. In addition, bigger budgets and longer production times are required to remain competitive as the industry expands. This of course leads to an aversion to risk-taking, particularly in less-established production houses. Blockbuster Hollywood filmmaking is an excellent example of what happens when the

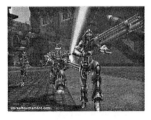 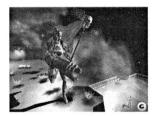 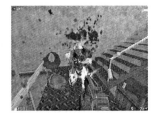

FIGURE 10.7. FIRST-PERSON SHOOTERS.

economics of production start to put a stranglehold on creative experimentation. The games industry is rapidly following suit, to the consternation of
many developers, publishers, and players.

Other reasons are related to the relative openness and ease of use of the
software and hardware required to implement a working game, let alone
modify or creatively explore the confines of an existing one, either at the
level of the application or the underlying engine driving it. And of course
perhaps paramount are the constraints that result from the use of specific
cultural toolkits, frames, and framings.

As an illustrative example, imagine a "Repetition in Game Engines and
Game Design" continuum, where on one end you plot "Materialist Reasons"
and on the other "Ideational Reasons" for why commercial (as well as independently produced) products look and feel so similar. Game industry economics and the openness of software and hardware would be positioned
toward the materialist end of the continuum, while cultural toolkits, frames,
and framings would be positioned toward the ideational. Predictably, as is
the case when the material and the ideational are working in concert, change
is quite difficult to achieve, and we cannot expect to find much diversity or
heterogeneity.

For instance, take the *idea* that modeling game physics after real-world
physics is necessary in order for game play to be fun, or that characters need
to be recognizable and anthropomorphic for identification to happen more
intensively, or that photo-realism allows for increased immersion in the
game world. Couple that with awareness that all of these functional attributes are present in the most economically profitable titles and it makes
sense that that would be an exceedingly difficult decision for a designer to
diverge from the prevailing codes and conventions. This holds true for both
commercial developers and independent producers. However, there are
some small but significant indications that the tide may be turning.

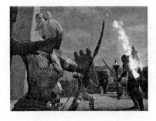 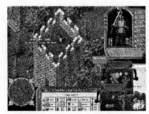 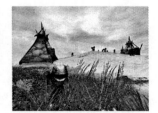

FIGURE 10.8. MMORPG.

CRACKS IN THE EDIFICE

Something interesting has started to happen in the gaming industry recently. Tools that had been used exclusively by title developers are now being released to the public in order to allow players to customize and/or radically modify their game environments. The capacity to create changes by the player within the confines of existing games—"modding"—has become a widespread phenomenon within the videogame community. Game modding tends to consist of players who possess a facility for programming, and who create custom level maps, character skins, and weapon types and retool various other objects and items that are part of the game.

As veteran games programmer and author Jake Simpson points out, game mods evolved from editing programs that enabled gamers to modify the original. WAD files for *Doom* are a good example. These files contain all the information about the graphics, sound, and level maps for the game, and they supply their own level designs and textures. Gamers started playing with these custom-built tools and found that they, too, could produce levels that other people wanted to play. It was not long before game companies, notably ID software, noticed this trend and took it a stage further with the *Quake* series of engines, designing the game so that it was eminently user-modifiable. ID even went so far as to release its own design tools, instructions, and code samples, so aspiring game programmers could tweak the *Quake* universe.[14]

Other companies soon followed suit and started building modification tools into their own game titles in order to see what players would do, and to assess where future development efforts might be focused. Games like *Doom, Quake,* and *Unreal Tournament* are all now able to bring out users' creativity by providing level editing, mod authoring, and server tools to players. The hope is that eventually the movement will take off on its own momentum.[15]

One of the most interesting examples of just how far the game mod can go is the game *Counter-Strike. Counter-Strike* is a modification to another counter-terrorism game, *Half-Life.* It modifies the multiplayer aspects of *Half-Life* to bring to it a more team-oriented game play. As of March 2003, *Counter-Strike* had the largest service footprint of any online action game with roughly 35,000 servers generating more than 4.5 billion player minutes per month.[16] What is even more impressive than the sheer volume of traffic these numbers indicate is that *Counter-Strike* became far more successful than *Half-Life,* the game from which it was originally modified. In fact, it became so successful that Valve, the parent company of *Half-Life,* shrewdly decided to acquire *Counter-Strike* and continue developing it in-house.

Another development worth watching is the introduction of a whole new genre of real-time moviemaking called "Machinima," which uses 3D multiplayer game engines as the primary authoring platform. Similar to the modding phenomenon, developers are now designing custom tools to support this highly creative and entirely unintended use of the game space, which is a blend of film, animation, and gaming. Filmmakers with a home PC work exclusively within a digital realm to create feature-length movies that just a short time ago would have required millions of dollars to make using traditional computer graphic techniques. Once the film is made, Machinima productions can be distributed over the Internet and rendered on any viewer's computer.[17]

Many of today's game gurus came from this early modification experience, and entirely new industries have been spawned in response to the modding community. Additionally, modding competitions have begun cropping up, art exhibitions themed around game hacking and modding have been created, and "how-to" courses, panels, and workshops on modding are being conducted at universities and conferences around the country. The proponents of this "revolutionary" medium are so full of hope and optimism that an Academy of Machinima Arts & Sciences has formed (currently headquartered in New York) and played host to the 2003 Machinima Film Festival.[18]

But let's be real for a moment. The film community has little to fear at this point. Even the best Machinima films are so severely constrained by the technical infrastructure, and struggle so desperately against what has been coded into the system, that it often becomes painful to watch. So far, making compelling movies with a game engine is like trying to perform *Swan Lake* with a SWAT team. No matter how much effort is put into the production, if you are expecting classical ballet, you won't be very satisfied.

Granted, Machinima may be interesting on other levels, such as the methods and modes of production and distribution, or the intentional misuse of technologies intended for other purposes. The current fascination, however, has more to do with the *idea* of using a game engine for moviemaking than the *reality* of what is produced. The only logical way to understand the hype is to assume that it comes from folks who have never sat and tried to download and watch a Machinima movie.

That said, it is impressive to see what people are capable of doing with tools that until very recently were never meant to support the use to which they are being put. While modding and Machinima may provide a glimmer

of hope for those who aspire to creatively play with game designs and technologies in a deeper way, the larger issue remains one of how open-ended
and far-reaching the tools facilitating that experimentation actually are.

WINDING UP AND DOWN AND BACK AROUND

In the history of the arts, the most inspiring, uncomfortable, and transfor-
mational moments have tended to be those that radically broke with tradition and were subsequently associated with being part of an avant-garde.
They were moments that catalyzed more than simple variations on preestab-
lished practice and content; instead, they were somehow able to dig deeper
and to fundamentally alter form. This also has consistently meant that they
would be perceived as threatening to those who occupied seats of institutional power and prestige. The result was that the institutions and cultural
gatekeepers either shifted to accommodate and appropriate the avant-garde
or they collapsed and were replaced.

Developing the ability to maintain a critical distance in relation to work
and play, keeping one's own cultural practices and frames of reference "an-
thropologically strange" (meaning to reflect consciously to whatever degree
possible upon one's embedded behaviors, values, and beliefs as "foreign" or
"other"), enables a type of creative production that disrupts social space in
the interest of rendering visible the invisible structures of language, meaning, and power. Of course, in the commercial world such critical consciousness is not necessarily so openly embraced—at least not until it is seen as
useful in marketing to an underexploited consumer base. Regardless, even
when the goals are not so overtly political, cultivating this awareness allows
for far more responsible, subtle, and sophisticated output. This holds especially true when thinking about infrastructure design, where the primary
desire has been to actively code to support transparency and intuitive interface at every level during the game's development process.

It takes a lot of effort to cast light on the internalized dynamics motivating and enabling meaningful action in the world. Nevertheless, once those
dynamics start to be revealed and situated in a way that speaks persuasively
to the heart and the mind, change becomes possible at an individual level,
as well as at an institutional one. We need to develop tools and techniques
that facilitate that process of uncovering in the interest of strategically assess-
ing the past, consciously being in the present, and responsibly diversifying
the array of possibilities in the future. From the beginning of human history, play and games have been a key way in which we learn about the rules
and regulations that govern our social lives.

I hope that it has become clear that the game engine is not simply software; it is software that reflects and embodies the cultural conditions symptomatic of the developers of the system, as well as the end users of that system. Moreover, when players are positioned as integral components of the system, the question of database, what it is or where it begins and ends, is radically transformed. The database, and the aesthetic manifest through the game application in relation to the database as it gets rendered by the engine, consists not only of the more traditionally conceived content of the game—the images, models, textures, sounds, interfaces, and code base—but of the cultural toolkits and frames of reference brought to bear on the design, implementation, and play of the game as well.

The greater the degree to which one's cultural conditions are brought into critical consciousness, and the more abstracted, accessible, and flexible the interplay between the software, hardware, and player is made, the richer the creative power and possibilities will be when that infrastructure is put to use. The problem is that reflexivity in relation to the ways that ideological systems get coded into infrastructure is practically nonexistent. Clearly we have a lot of work to do.

NOTES

1. Entertainment Software Association: Top 10 Industry Facts. http://www.theesa .com/facts/top_10_facts.php.

2. J. M. Graetz, "The Origin of Spacewar," reprinted online from *Creative Computing Magazine* (now defunct), August 1981 at http://www.wheels.org/spacewar/creative/ SpacewarOrigin.html.

3. Ibid.

4. Welcome to the ICT, 2003. http://www.ict.usc.edu/disp.php?PHPSESSID =869044eb898e4f396222ffde8c5c179f.

5. Steven L. Kent, "Engines and Engineering: What to Expect in the Future of PC Games," *Gamespy,* October 31, 2002.

6. Jake Simpson, "Game Engine Anatomy 101, Part I: Intro to Game Engines, The Renderer, and Creating a 3D World." http://www.extremetech.com/article2/0,3973,594,00 .asp (accessed April 12, 2002).

7. Kent, "Engines and Engineering."

8. Ibid.

9. Philip Greenspun, "History of Photography Timeline," http://www.photo.net/ history/timeline.

10. Ann Swidler, "Culture in Action: Symbols and Strategies," *American Sociological Review* 51 (April 1986): 273–86.

11. *The Fontana Dictionary of Modern Thought,* 2nd ed., ed. Alan Bullock, Oliver Stallybrass, Stephen Trombley, and Bruce Eadie (London: Fontana Press, 1988), 221.

12. See Gregory Bateson, *Steps to an Ecology of Mind* (London: Paladin, 1972); Julian

Hochberg, "Gestalt Theory," in *Oxford Companion to the Mind,* ed. R. L. Gregory (Oxford: Oxford University Press, 1987); Jean Piaget, *The Child's Conception of the World* (London: Paladin, 1973); Phillip G. Zimbardo and Michael R. Leippe, *The Psychology of Attitude Change and Social Influence* (New York: McGraw-Hill, 1991); Robert Benford and David Snow, "Framing Processes and Social Movements: An Overview and Assessment," *Annual Review of Sociology* 26 (2000): 611–39; William A. Gamson, David Croteau, William Hoynes, and Theodore Sasson, "Media Images and the Social Construction of Reality," *American Review of Sociology* 18 (1992): 373–93; Erving Goffman, *Frame Analysis* (Harmondsworth: Penguin, 1975; Alfred Schutz, *Collected Papers,* vols. 1–3 (The Hague: Martinus Nijhoff, 1962–66); Benjamin L. Whorf, *Language, Thought, and Reality* (Cambridge, Mass.: MIT Press, 1956). For more detailed discussion, see James Atherton, "On Learning to 'See,'" http://www.doceo.co.uk/tools/frame.htm (accessed 2002).

13. Hank Johnston and Pamela Olivia, "Mobilization Forum: A Reply to Snow and Benford," *Mobilization: An International Journal* 5, no. 1 (2000): 61–63.

14. Simpson, "Game Engine Anatomy 101."

15. Stonewall, "RPOV Interviews," interview with Tim Sweeney, founder and president of Epic Games. http://www.r-pov.com/interviews/tsweeney2.html (accessed March 21, 2000).

16. Official *Counter-Strike* Web site, "Valve Opteron Support." http://www.counter-strike.net/news.html (accessed March 9, 2003).

17. Introduction to Machinima. http://www.machinima.com/Whatis/intromach.shtml.

18. Academy of Machinima Arts & Sciences. http://www.machinima.org/ (accessed 2002–3).

11. *Stock Market Skirt:*
The Evolution of the Internet,
the Interface, and an Idea

NANCY PATERSON

Dedicated to Brenda Laurel (who asked if she could wear it), this cyberfeminist fashion statement is my response to the convergence of technology, fashion, and feminism. The potential of IPV6 and wireless access were among the motivating issues underlying this project. Like many of my other media works, *Stock Market Skirt* presents a tongue-in-cheek and intentionally ironic exploration of the relationship between the two most interesting, if not most important, expressions of late twentieth-century Western culture and individuality: lust and money.

A play on Desmond Morris's theory that the women's fashion industry responds to fluctuations in the equities market by hiking or lowering hemlines, *Stock Market Skirt* provides commentary on several levels. In an interview about the project with Matt Mirapaul for the *New York Times* "Cybertimes" review, Laura McGough, an independent curator in Washington, D.C., stated that *Stock Market Skirt* can be read in so many ways. "It's playful, it's political, it's sexy. There's a lot for viewers to sink their teeth into."[1]

In describing this project as a cyberfeminist work, I draw on ideas that I have been formulating since the early 1990s, when I began working on the essay "Cyberfeminism." This essay was first e-published in early 1993 on Stacey Horn's ECHO (East Coast Hang Out) gopher server in New York City. I considered the possible parameters of a new philosophy—postgender/ transgender—that challenges popular culture's link between the erotic representation of women with the (often) terrible cultural impact of new electronic technologies: "Sex, danger, women, and machines: the plot of virtually every futuristic, sci-fi movie in which women play any role at all. Cyber-femmes are everywhere, but cyberfeminists are few and far between."[2] More important than contesting this representation of women, however, is challenging women to reclaim new technologies for themselves.

Technological convergence describes the unification of computers, television, and communications technologies. However, convergence describes much more than the evolution toward an environment in which electronic technologies are pervasive. Convergence is happening on more than a technological level—it is happening on a metaphysical level as well. Cultural convergence may be described as the meeting or merging of art and technology. Cyberfeminism is entering an arena in which much more than gender is up for grabs.[3]

On another level, *Stock Market Skirt* was designed to embody what many have chosen to describe as the emerging intelligence of the Internet. In an essay written for a catalogue on my work, "Remapping the Terrain," Randy Lee Cutler points out:

> It is the Internet, the posthuman flow of information that drives *Stock Market Skirt*. Women's bodies are often used as a sign of technology and desire. *Stock Market Skirt* makes manifest the libidinal economy of technology, money and gender. . . . [It is] driven by the collective unconscious of human greed and illuminated through an appetite for fashion.[4]

Alfred Korzybski coined the phrase "the map is not the territory" in *Science and Sanity,* his book about general semantics.[5] However, the task of distinguishing between artificial maps and the reality they are intended to construe, which is Korzybski's point, is rendered impossible by the fact that in mapping digital data both the "reality" and the map itself are in a state of constant flux. In *Stock Market Skirt,* the fluctuating data that are collected are grounded in experience through the manipulation of a physical object. There is a difference between this project and others, where changing data (stock market data, weather patterns, seismic data) control 3D or 2D representations. Mapping is perhaps an inadequate metaphor as we expect a map to present some pretence of permanence; the Internet is clearly not a closed system any more than it is a "place."

In the context of a presentation that I made at Carnegie Mellon's Robotics Institute, *Stock Market Skirt* was described by engineers in the audience as a tele-robotic project. Yet, unlike the majority of tele-robotic works, *Stock Market Skirt* has the potential to be interactive with the global flow of information by responding to a dynamic feed of data (rather than being interactive through the Internet as a pipeline). Using a computer program to pick stocks used to be the ultimate in investing sophistication. As this became commonplace, "quant" methods evolved to describe the use of computer models based on complex algorithms to implement arcane trading strategies. A pure quant approach takes the human element (and related emotional factors) out of the stock-buying decision altogether. *Stock Market Skirt* illustrates the rise of algorithmic and statistical techniques to choose and implement trading strategies as well as tracking the volatility of the market.

In the Gallery, *Stock Market Skirt* is displayed on a dressmaker's mannequin, or "Judy," located next to a computer and several monitors of varying sizes. In large white type against a blue background (matching the blue of the taffeta skirt), the stock ticker symbol and constantly updated price scroll from right to left in simulation of the pixel board displays used to track stock values on traditional exchange-room floors. Stock quotes are retrieved at least once per second (depending on the speed of connection) from stock-quote pages online, with the hemline moving in response to the changing values. Custom-designed PERL scripts running under Linux retrieve and parse the code. These data are sent to a custom-designed controller that accordingly sends positive or negative pulses to the stepper motor mounted up and under the skirt. A bullish market triggers the hemline to be seductively raised, and the hemline is lowered to correspond to falling stock prices. There is a range of six hundred steps between the skirt at its most mini and at its most modest length.

Written into the program is a script that sets parameters for the present

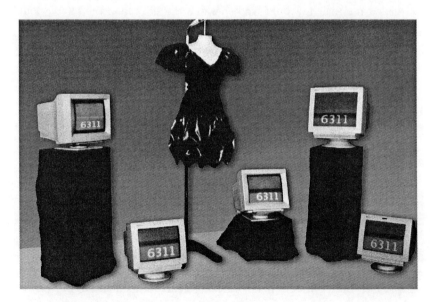

FIGURE 11.1. PUBLIC EXHIBITION OF STOCK MARKET SKIRT, BELL CENTRE FOR CREATIVE COMMUNICATIONS, 1998.

day's range of movement based on the previous day's performance of the selected stock. This range is monitored throughout the day, and is automatically adjusted if necessary. Furthermore, *Stock Market Skirt* is capable of being configured to track the price of any stock on any exchange that provides online updates: North American, European, Asian, and so forth. At the end of the trading day, *Stock Market Skirt* is programmed to switch to the next time zone to continue tracking a select stock in real time. When all the exchanges are closed, it switches to historical data until a market opens.

This media work also uses a Web cam to capture and display real-time images of the hemline as it fluctuates. A Web site simultaneously displays these images as well as the stock market quotes, which are controlling the length of the hemline. This site is made available in conjunction with the exhibition of this media work.

Developed during the boom market of the mid- to late 1990s, when the (high-tech) investment bubble first swelled and then burst, this project captured the imagination and attention of New Media journals and audiences (for example, *Flash Art* and *Tema Celeste*). *Stock Market Skirt* has also been featured in business and fashion magazines. During the first public showing of the work at the Centre for Creative Communications in Toronto (Centennial College, spring 1998), a stockbroker who had heard about the project e-mailed me that he would "rather watch the skirt than the DOW," and visionaries such as Sandy Pentland of MIT's Media Lab has described the project as "brilliant."[6] Inspired by the launch of the Hollywood Stock Exchange, the mutant offspring of celebrity culture and stock market fever, I had fleeting (though less than serious) thoughts of listing the project as an over-the-counter penny stock so that the hemline could track its own success.

Part of what inspired me to produce this project was the notion that bandwidth is political. *Stock Market Skirt* uses very little bandwidth, but connectivity is integral to the project. This has always seemed to epitomize for me the potential power of online resources. It is not always how big or fast your modem is; often what matters is what you choose to do with it. I am as mesmerized as the next New Media artist by the tools and technology that are often just beyond my reach. But as I wrote in "Technology (does not equal) Art,"[7] new media art is about more than the application of tools. Usenet is a case in point, and since it was my first experience with online resources, a description of its evolution is apropos.

In 1982, while I was a general arts and sciences student at the University of Toronto, I heard that Usenet accounts were being made available. The Internet as we know it now did not exist. I went across campus and was rewarded with an account; my user name was simply "nancy." In 1982, there were no PC graphical interfaces or friendly operating systems; the graphical Apple Macintosh would not emerge until January 1984.

When I signed up for the Usenet account, I was required to accept or refuse subscription to a list of News Groups. There were 429 groups available when I joined and I dutifully ticked off my preferences. Access to the network at that time meant that you could read and send messages relevant to the News Groups to which you belonged, as well as to other users. I recall I was not interested in science fiction, but I thought that astrophysics might be interesting as there were actual researchers in the field participating in online discussions.

Usenet had been born at Duke University in 1979, when graduate students Tom Truscott and Jim Ellis decided to create a computer network to link together those in the Unix community using simple shell scripts to have computers automatically call one another up and search for changes in the date stamps of files. Soon a network of three sites existed: "duke" at Duke University, "unc" at the University of North Carolina at Chapel Hill, and "phs" at the Physiology Department of the Duke Medical School. When the program connecting these three sites was found to be too slow, the code was rewritten in the C programming language, and, once this was debugged, the "Invitation to a General Access UNIX Network" was presented at the 1980 Usenix Conference in Colorado. Usenet was at that time commonly described as a "poor man's ARPANET."[8]

UCLA, Stanford, the University of California at Santa Barbara, and the University of Utah were among the first sites of ARPANET, which was originally funded under the U.S. Department of Defense's Advanced Research Projects Agency (ARPA). However, only those academic computers with DOD funding had the opportunity to the ARPANET. Enter Usenet, available to anyone who had access to the Unix operating system, available at very low cost to the academic and computer research community. Posting and participating in the network was essentially free, with users paying only for their equipment and telephone calls to receive or send Netnews. "Therefore, the joys and challenges of participating in the creation of an ever-expanding network, an experience available to an exclusive few via the ARPANET, became available via Usenet to those without political or financial connections—to the common folk of the computer science community."[9]

UTZOO, established by Henry Spencer at the University of Toronto in 1981, was the first viable international node on the network. Other University of Toronto departments, and other Canadian universities, followed suit when they realized that this networking, done intermittently at phone-line speeds, was an inexpensive and immediate alternative to the ARPANET access that they lusted after. Spencer went on to become well known in Usenet circles as the co-author of the software (C News), which would be used throughout the UUCP universe until UUCPnet itself was incorporated into the Internet.

But even after the Usenet backbone was replaced by Internet connections, the fringes of Usenet continued to communicate using UUCP links (and C News) that remained quicker, cheaper, and easier to install and maintain. Local UUCP sites remained the most common means of connecting to Usenet, and what was referred to generally as "the Net," well into the 1990s. In fact, UUCP was still the largest computer network in the world until the TCP/IP-based Internet finally overtook it in 1994.[10]

It was more than a year after I gained access to Usenet that I finally met someone outside of the university community I could e-mail, a colleague that I worked with on an exhibition, *Portrait of the Artist as a Young Machine,* at the Ontario Science Centre in Toronto in 1983.

After I left the University of Toronto and enrolled at the Ontario College of Art, I participated in the founding of the ArtCulture Resource Centre, Toronto's first video and new media facility, eventually returning to the University of Toronto to study with Northrop Frye. Following my graduation from the University of Toronto, I produced a wide range of video and interactive installations using custom-designed controllers and often laser-disc technology, the hot "new" format of the early 1990s.

In 1995, I began to work in earnest on *Stock Market Skirt,* a project that had occurred to me as I observed the transformation of the Internet from a purely academic, if not entirely serious, resource. In the days of ARPANET and Usenet, News Group subscribers could follow the discussions of astrophysicists comparing notes on research projects, occasionally even contributing to the ongoing debate. The nature and form of online discourse changed in the early 1990s as the graphical user interface became more common and technologies such as 3D entered the mainstream; the focus began to shift to entertainment and commercial applications. In public presentations I describe this shift: the Internet is like watching "Jeopardy," a thin veneer of information with no depth or context—a mile wide but only an inch deep. Current developments such as the "semantic web" are a more positive evolution. As the value of tech stocks began to soar, I reasoned, it would only be a matter of time before online trading became commonplace as well as accessible on a 24/7 basis.

Stock Market Skirt was conceived, and I began work on it long before the technology was available to make it a reality. When I began to think about my project, the only financial resources available online were expensive proprietary subscription services that provided stock quotes, such as Reuters, Star Data, and Bloomberg—services well beyond the financial reach of all but the wealthiest individual traders, who were primarily interested in corporate investment. With the Bloomberg service, for example, it was necessary to use a dedicated terminal that it supplied and the fee was in excess of $1,200 per month.[11]

In 1995, I was able to secure historical files from the Toronto Stock Exchange close-of-day data for the previous forty years, which I used to begin designing and testing a BASIC program that would compare values and send signals to a stepper motor. Steve Kee, director of Media Relations at TSX, generously provided these files. In 1996, the dress was designed and stitched, complete with a complex system of cables, loops, and weights sewn to the interior of the skirt to ensure that the hemline length changes could take place smoothly. With the next engineer who assisted with the project (there would be several before it was finally complete in 1999), I undertook

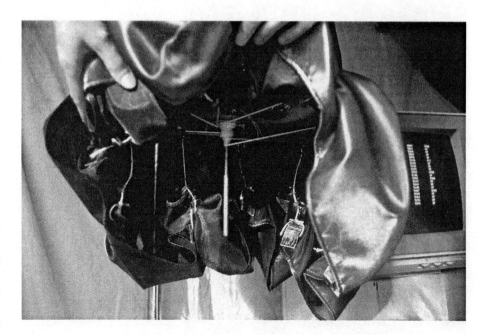

FIGURE 11.2. *STOCK MARKET SKIRT:* BASIC RUNNING WITH TSE DATA.

to run the project using Internet-based data, retrieved from online stock-quote services, which were just beginning to be popular. Yahoo was the first to make online financial quotes available, and out of gratitude, their stock symbol was selected as the first one I tracked: YHOO.

Initially I worked with Windows NT 3.5.1, then later NT 4.0, but found both to be extremely problematic because I was attempting simultaneously to run the controller for the stepper motor, a modem, and a large print program (for the display), which caused numerous conflicts. When I switched the OS to Linux, the project, which I had labored over for years, began working properly within a matter of days. As the project progressed, so did the availability of online data. By the time I went public with *Stock Market Skirt* in April 1998, I had my choice of sites that provided data that I could use

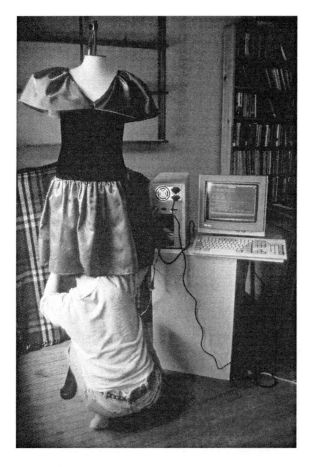

FIGURE 11.3.
STOCK MARKET SKIRT
UNDER DEVELOPMENT.

from markets across the globe. At that time, I was artist-in-residence at the Bell Centre for Creative Communications (Centennial College) and had access to its network and bandwidth.

As I was completing *Stock Market Skirt,* I was beginning work on a Millennium Arts project that fell into the opposite end of the bandwidth spectrum. Whereas *Stock Market Skirt* requires relatively low bandwidth, *The Library* is a fully navigable, multistoried 3D environment containing projects by select artists, which is available online at http://www.thelibrary2.com. Based on the beautiful rotunda of the Canadian Library of Parliament, the intention of this project was to create a metaphorical interpretation of a building selected for its architectural and cultural significance.

Three-dimensionality represents an opportunity to transform text and data from linear experiences into dynamic and interactive narratives. Exploring new means of collecting, storing, retrieving, and distributing information, creative approaches to navigation and way-finding emerged as guiding themes through the production of this project. In *Stock Market Skirt,* online data (stock prices) are sourced from the Internet in order to control the length of the skirt hemline. In *The Library* project, I used the Internet as an enormous database of information and images to be repurposed for my project. Proof of concept for this is my use of a constantly updated (every five minutes) satellite image of the earth's surface from space (available on the NASA Web site), retrieved, and used as the texture map for a rotating sphere (a world globe), which is the centerpiece in my 3D environment. A visitor to *The Library* environment who approaches the world globe sees a 3D representation of the earth, with the day/night line displayed in almost real time.

It was entirely appropriate that these two projects should be developed in parallel with the stock market crisis that occurred at the turn of the millennium. This crisis, due in part to the application of analog methods to digital culture, has perpetuated a flawed set of cultural priorities regarding bandwidth and interactivity. The bottleneck to creativity and productivity that has developed is the result of a mind-set and practice that limits the free and symmetrical exchange of data, the original promise of the Internet. Our challenge is to avoid replacing the limitations of the technology with the limitations of imagination.

NOTES

1. Laura McGough, as quoted by Matt Mirapaul in the *New York Times* "Cybertimes" review, February 5, 1998. http://www.vacuumwoman.com/MediaWorks/Stock/stockreview.html.

2. Nancy Paterson, "Cyberfeminism," in *Mediaworks* (Surrey, B.C.: Surrey Art Gallery, 2001), 59.

3. Ibid., 63.

4. Randy Lee Cutler, "Remapping the Terrain," in *Mediaworks* (Surrey, B.C.: Surrey Art Gallery, 2001), 25.

5. Alfred Korzybski, *Science and Sanity* (Brooklyn, N.Y.: Institute of General Semantics, 1994).

6. E-mail from Sandy Pentland to author, August 27, 1998.

7. Nancy Paterson, "Technology (does not equal) Art," *Fuse* 20 (Fall 1997).

8. Michael Hauben and Ronda Hauben, "Netizens: On the History and Impact of Usenet and the Internet." http://www.firstmonday.dk/issues/issue3_7/chapter2/.

9. Ibid.

10. CAnet Institute Report, *A Nation Goes Online* (Canet, 2001), 41.

11. Conversation between the author and a representative of the Bloomberg service, November 1995.

12. POCKETS FULL OF MEMORIES

GEORGE LEGRADY

According to the records of Centre Pompidou, approximately twenty thousand visitors viewed *Pockets Full of Memories* (PFOM), an installation on exhibit for four months, resulting in a contribution of more than 3,300 objects in the database archive.[1]

The archive consists of objects that museum visitors carried with them—for example, such common items as phones, keys, toys, fragments of clothing, personal documents, currency, and reading material. The size of the scanning box was the only limiting factor that determined what could be added to the archive. The expectation in the early stages of planning was that the majority of contributions would consist of everyday common objects, and the final result would provide an overview of the range of things people carry with them. Nonetheless, we hoped that some members of the public would be creative in their contribution choices, methods, and descriptions. A few objects went beyond the everyday, such as a marriage-proposal note. We were also aware that public interactive systems are testing situations to a segment of the audience who want to see how robust such systems are by trying to break through both the technical and conceptual limits of the project. One of the unexpected contributions to the archive included the numerous scans of body extensions (heads, hands, and feet)—contributions that increased exponentially once the initial examples entered the archive.

The overall quality of the archive is a consequence of the dialogue that occurred between the audience's perception of the archive's holdings, followed by a contribution that functions as a statement of participation and the desire to leave a trace of themselves behind. Contributing an image and descriptive information of one's personal object into an institutional environment such as a museum or database or archive certainly provides a sense of fulfillment, but the best trace left behind seems to be a direct image of one's body parts. The many scanned heads, hands, and feet have augmented

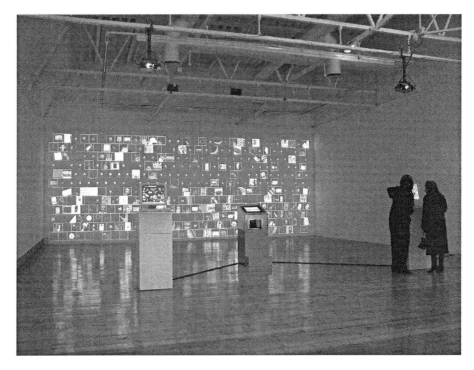

FIGURE 12.1. GEORGE LEGRADY, *POCKETS FULL OF MEMORIES*. INSTALLATION AT THE CORNERHOUSE GALLERY, MANCHESTER. COPYRIGHT 2005 GEORGE LEGRADY.

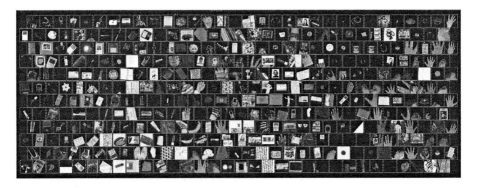

FIGURE 12.2. ALGORITHMICALLY ORGANIZED VISUAL MAP OF VISITORS' CONTRIBUTIONS OF OBJECTS AND THEIR DESCRIPTIONS. CORNERHOUSE GALLERY, MANCHESTER. COPYRIGHT 2005 GEORGE LEGRADY.

the archive from simply being a collection of objects to encoding it with the corporeal presence of the contributors transforming the digital data environment into a metaphoric extension of the human body.

ORDERING DATA AND THE SOM ALGORITHM

The database archive of objects is ordered by the Kohonen Self-Organizing Map before being projected in the gallery space and accessed online. Because of current bandwidth limitations and scale of the gallery projection, the map of objects has been limited to 280 objects, so a selection is first made out of the total database each time the SOM is activated (once per minute). The selection is based on a percentage sampling of the database's life, with priority given to the ten most recent entries. Timo Honkela describes the function of the SOM in this project:

> The Self-Organizing Map (SOM, also called Kohonen map) algorithm is the basic method that is used to create the "wall of objects." The SOM organizes the input items (contributed objects by the public) into an ordered display, a 2 dimensional map. On the map, two items tend to appear close to each other if they have similar input features. In this exhibition, the input features consist of attributes and keywords. The attribute values and keywords are given by the exhibition visitor. They are transformed into numerical form that can serve as inputs. The algorithm may start from a random state of the map. Through the process of iteratively (repeated recalculation) handling the inputs, it reaches an ordered state.[2]

The map consists of a collection of map nodes that can be thought of as places on the map landscape. On the map, nearby nodes tend to have similar items. Close to each, there may be items that have been given similar attribute values, or items that have been named similarly. Thus, all the items with a particular keyword are not necessarily next to each other if the other features vary. Moreover, even if the visual qualities of an image are similar, it may very well happen that two persons evaluate the item very differently based on their subjective point of view. There are also cases in which even the neighbors are rather far from each as there are occasionally dividing valleys and mountain ranges also in the natural landscapes.

The order of the final map is a consequence of all the inputs. The phenomenon is called emergence: the order is not determined beforehand, but rather emerges through audience contributions. The classification system is not specified by hand but is created through the large number of local interactions on the map. This is why the system can be called "self-organizing." Metaphorically, similar items look for each other without any centralized command.

SEMANTIC MEANING AND LINGUISTIC DESCRIPTION

Because the positioning of an object in the SOM map is completely dependent on the way the contributor describes them, the emphasis in this work shifts to the function of linguistic description and semantic interpretation, as opposed to the object's immediately recognizable literal or physical properties. Contributors engage in a creative process when they prescribe keywords and evaluate their object according to the questionnaire's attributes. Even though the map may contain numerous cell phones, watches, and hands, their positioning across the map reflects the contributor's perception of them and the choice of words used to describe them. One of the key experiences of the exhibition was watching the positioning of the object's image on the large-scale projection. After a short wait following data entry, the image appears on the screen highlighted with an orange frame to make it easier to identify. As the SOM processes the data every minute, it scans each line of the map and replaces or moves objects based on the new order. This process goes on continuously and provides the opportunity for comparison and reflection about the descriptive choices the contributor has made to define the object. Accessibility on the Internet further enhances study of the map as each object can be clicked on to see its properties and attached stories, resulting in comparisons to surrounding neighbors. Internet interaction has provided another means by which to extend the dialogue for visitors, as the museum and Internet audience have the opportunity to add comments and stories to any object, and from anywhere in the world. Many visitors who have traveled from other geographical areas have used this as a means to make contact with friends and family back home, who then have added their own responses.

VISUAL IDENTITY AND GRAPHIC AND INTERFACE DESIGN

All graphic design aspects of the PFOM project have been designed as a result of extensive dialogues about the meaning and function of all of the elements: the signage, the interactive questionnaire, the installation, and the Web site. The information environments within which data are organized and accessed impose a metalevel of meaning that redefine the content passing through it, much of which is implicit and necessitates extensive study of its functioning. I was very interested in handing over the design solutions to Projekttriangle because their work places emphasis on coherent systems and the development of a specific visual vocabulary determined by the needs of the project. The thematic repetition throughout all the design elements focused on the process of the production of meaning, beginning with the public's personal contributions and descriptions, which become synthesized into an institutional archive. The signage in the exhibition floor space exemplifies the three-phase transformative process from object to descriptive parameters to data. From the entrance to the scanning station, the floor was covered by graphic icons of objects physically guiding the public's movements to the various stages of the installation. Between the triangular space from the scanning station to the Web viewing stations, the floor markings changed to keywords that are also listed on the large wall to the right of the projected map. The projected map, consisting of ID numbers, was in front of the final stage of viewing.

FUTURE EXHIBITIONS AND NEXT-STEP DEVELOPMENTS

We have planned to exhibit the PFOM installation in a number of different cultural environments. We currently have a large database contribution that reflects the particular population that has visited the Centre Pompidou during summer vacation time. The questionnaire has provided descriptions of the contributors' backgrounds, and the data reveal a diversity of ages, nationalities, professions, and interests. The current research work on the semantic specificities of the contributed data of 3,300 objects in the archive is led by Dr. Steinheider. Once the data are analyzed, resulting in an evaluation of the overall archive, we will be able to present a cultural overview of how the members of this particular audience have described themselves through their object and description choices. These results will be meaningful in themselves, but they will be even more interesting when contrasted to the results of future collections assembled as the exhibition travels to other cultural regions.

The realization of the exhibition at the Centre Pompidou has made it possible for us to study its functioning and consequently we have identified a number of areas that could benefit from further development. These include data-collecting and datamining processes, dynamic feedback systems, and visualization methods.

NOTES

1. Production began in the summer of 2000, following funding by the Daniel Langlois Foundation for Art, Science & Technology grant, and continued until the opening of the

exhibition in April 2001. In addition to the contribution by the UIAH Media Lab team (Professors Timo Honkela, Timo Koskenniemi, and Petri Saarikko), an international team of specialists realized various components of the project. Márton Fernezelyi and Zoltán Szegedy-Maszák, from the C3 Center for Culture and Communication, Budapest, designed and constructed the scanning station unit consisting of touch-screen interactive software, an image digitizing system with image-processing software, the database and networks software, and the interactive station structure itself. The exhibition's visual identity, which included the exhibition design, scanning station designs, interface design for the questionnaire and Web site, was produced in Stuttgart by the Projekttriangle design team consisting of Danijela Djokic, Martin Grothmaak, and Juergen Spaeth. The Internet site providing access to the database and SOM algorithm was developed by Andreas Engberg at the CREATE Lab University of California, Santa Barbara. Dr. Brigitte Steinheider from the Fraunhofer Institute for Industrial Engineering contributed with the development of the data description questionnaire and is currently analyzing the data of the archive from a social science perspective. Detailed information about each contribution is available at http://legrady.mat.ucsb.edu/pfom_map_e.html. For the project description with images, see http://www.mat.ucsb.edu/~g.legrady/glWeb/Projects/pfom2/pfom2.html. For the database of all contributions, see http://tango.mat.ucsb.edu/pfom/databrowser.php.

2. Timo Honkela, Koskinen Ilpo, Timo Koskenniemi, and Karvonen Sakari, "Kohonen's Self-Organizing Map in Contextual Analysis of Data," in *Information Organization and Databases,* ed. K. Tanaka and S. Ghandeharizadeh (Helsinki and Boston: Kluwer, 2000).

13. The Raw Data Diet, All-Consuming Bodies, and the Shape of Things to Come

LYNN HERSHMAN-LEESON

For the past three decades, I have been fascinated with the construction of identity and how it affects culture: the symbiotic relationship between the real and the virtual, and how identity reacts and shifts when processed through manipulated time. Most of the "bodies" I have used in my work have been female. *Synthia Stock Ticker* (2000–4), *Agent Ruby* (1991–2004), and *DiNA* (2004) are my most recent cyber fatales/autonomous agents. These works are in a constant state of change. They morph by cannibalizing information and exist as shifting reincarnated feedback patterns. Their cumulative identities are also a networked trajectory of consumed information. In the context of the Web, these pieces reveal cultural obsessions. Information flow swallows itself live.

For example, *Agent Ruby* is a self-breeding, artificially intelligent Web agent that recognizes users and talks to them. Not only is she fed information from AIML (Artificial Identity Markup Language), but her brain is a search engine, allowing her to converse on any subject that has ever been entered on the Internet. Her memory system is shaped by encounters with these users. Existing on a multitude of platforms with the capacity for increased intelligence and flexibility, *Ruby* is a reactive communicator—a networked conduit between individuals and society, bodies to technologies, the real to the virtual, and, ultimately, fragmented human subjectivity. *Ruby* converses with users, remembers their questions and names, and has moods and emotional synapses. Her mood may also be affected directly by Web traffic. Users can interact with *Ruby* through both voice and text and can download *Agent Ruby* onto Palm Pilots and laptops, thereby extending her life cycle into one of continual replication and breeding. *Agent Ruby* is seeded to users' servers, as well as being downloadable to desktops or Palm OS handheld computers. She is multiplatform, integrating PC, MAC, and Palm systems. This Tamagotchi-like creature is an Internet-bred construction of identity that continually fleshes out through cumulative virtual use.

249

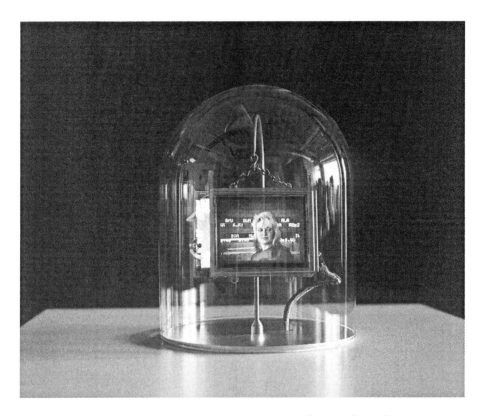

FIGURE 13.1. STILL FROM LYNN HERSHMAN-LEESON, *SYNTHIA STOCK TICKER*, 2002. INTERACTIVE NETWORK INSTALLATION. PHOTOGRAPH BY IRA SCHRANK.

Agent Ruby evokes questions about the networked potential of consciousness and identity, but through her interactions she also encounters both corruption and redemption. All of the double-sided mirroring and reflections are implicit in the resulting "double":

> In effect, they are a summoning of a contemporary golem. According to this interpretation, Hershman, as the artist, represents a modern version of the learned one, the devoted Talmudic disciple, who seeks to bring her own creation into the world. Furthermore, the golem is a form (or, shall we say, image) that is given life through a magical formula, such as the power of the letters of the divine name or the word for "truth" that according to some legends is inscribed on the forehead of the golem. What better description of a Golem than a "simulated" person?

There were two legitimate reasons for creating such a golem. One was to protect the community. In the case of Hershman's work, we could interpret community to mean the family. . . . The other legitimate reason to invent a golem was to achieve a greater understanding of the creative process.[1]

Synthia, also female, is the personification of the stock market. Her "drive" is composed of accumulated stock data that are compiled and then transferred to her response in real time. The market numbers are also on view in the piece and indeed become part of *Synthia*'s identity. Live online Internet information is transferred into the real space of a miniaturized stock ticker, modeled after Thomas Edison's original stock ticker. *Synthia* reacts in real time to changing stock data, which include the DOW, NASDAC, S&P, and Russell Small Cap, by exhibiting behavior that is guided by two percent changes in the market. Examples of how *Synthia* interacts with her own received data include:

- If the market is flat, she goes to bed.
- If the market is up, she dances.
- If the market is hot, she turns to fire and does back flips.
- If the market goes down, she chain-smokes.
- If the market is very low, she turns to water and becomes depressed.
- If the market goes up, she shops at Hermès or Dior.
- If the market goes down, she goes to Goodwill, takes a gun to her head, has nightmares, visits the zoo, goes to the stock exchange, checks her e-mail, or dances.
- When the market volume is up, her pet bull morphs into a bear and her fish swim fast.
- If the market volume is down, her fish go belly up.

There are sixteen base behaviors for the characters that are made in modules that correspond in real time to her compiled and compressed data. It is the data that define and defy this piece, just as we humans are programmed to act on the information we receive or the perceptions of information that filter through our own systems.

What is most interesting about *Synthia* is the attempt to give her a kind of life that is dependent on the virtual environment of the financial markets, but which is algorithmic and not fixed, and certainly independent of direct manipulation by either the artist or the viewer. In the "AD" era, this "animation" has

increasingly hinted at, both rhetorically and in the artwork, the notion of an
independent (but connected) existence of the artificially intelligent, virtual,
and cyborgian other.[2]

My newest work, *DiNA*, will use *Ruby*'s "brain" and the aesthetics of her
accumulated information, but she is more developed, autonomous, with a
specific programmed personality. She too enjoys feeding on the pulse of life
and information as it happens through her active internal search engine.
Ruby and *DiNA* talk with immediate lip-synched animation via a program
called the Pulse 3D Veeper System.

DiNA employs a global view of information garnered from several feeds.
What is significant about this work is that the data actually interact and
exist by modifying live Internet reactive data transmitted in real time.

Art produced in the second half of this century was often based in destruc-
tion, decomposition, and deconstruction, perversely and pervasively eroding aesthetic preconceptions. Art became not only live, but unstable. Form
merged with content to create an aesthetic of rupture, participation, and
interactivity. Delivery systems through which art reached its audience were
also shifting and became at least as subversive as the art itself. A new audience
emerged comprised of a broad community of receivers/participants, whose
interactions helped to shape a revolution of art capable of self-replication,
unstable and shifting content, and database information reconfigurations,
all processed in real time, creating reflections of our cultural obsessions,
such as privacy in an era of surveillance and personal identity in a time of
pervasive manipulation.

In an era of digital and human biological sampling, our relationship to
computer-based virtual life forms that are autonomous and self-replicating
is critical. The political as well as the psychic stakes are urgent, compelling,
and inescapable.

Notes

1. Ruby B. Rich, "My Other, My Self: Lynn Hershman and the Reinvention of the
Golem," in *The Art and Films of Lynn Hershman Leeson: Secret Agents, Private I*, ed.
Meredith Tromble, DVD ed. Kyle Stephan (Berkeley and Los Angeles: University of Cal-
ifornia Press, forthcoming).

2. Steve Dietz, "Animating the Network," in ibid.

14. Time Capsule: Networking the Biological [Biotech and Trauma]

EDUARDO KAC

New technologies culturally mutate our perception of the human body from a naturally self-regulated system to an artificially controlled and electronically transformed object. The digital manipulation of the appearance of the body (and not of the body itself) clearly expresses the plasticity of the new identity of the physical body. We observe this phenomenon regularly through media representations of idealized or imaginary bodies, virtual-reality incarnations, and network projections of actual bodies (also known as "avatars"). Parallel developments in medical technologies, such as plastic surgery and neuroprosthesis, have ultimately allowed the expansion of this immaterial plasticity to actual bodies; the skin becomes a site of continuous transmutation. As a result, a new problem emerges: the impact of biotechnologies that operate beneath the skin (or inside skinless bodies, such as bacteria) and therefore out of sight. More than making visible the invisible, telepresence and biotechnological art can raise the awareness of what firmly remains beyond our immediate visual reach, but which, nonetheless, affects us in a direct way. Two of the most prominent technologies operating under the skin are genetic engineering and digital implants. Both will have profound consequences in art as well as in our social, medical, political, and economic life in the future. In what follows I will first suggest that art on the Internet does not have to be confined to Web-centric approaches. Then, I will discuss the implications of my work, *Time Capsule*, which approached the problem of networking the biological, that is, the body as a literal Internet node from which digital information can be retrieved wirelessly.

BEYOND THE BROWSER

The Internet is not simply a means of storing, distributing, and accessing digital information. With digital literacy among the population at large increasing exponentially, the Internet has become an effective cultural force, affecting in tangible ways the reality outside cyberspace. Examples include, on the one hand, the commercialization of goods and, on the other, campaigns staged online to mobilize public opinion or special-interest groups to act publicly on a given issue. From the questioning of the white cube to street action, from environmental propositions to radio, video, videophones, television, and satellites, artists throughout the twentieth century have consistently sought to work in alternative spaces. Public spaces, in the form of urban settings and natural landscapes, as well as electronic media, have offered artists new challenges and possibilities.

In 1995, the general public started to think of the Internet as "the Web" as a result of the wide dissemination and the ease of use of Web browsers. In the spring of 1995, *Time* published a special issue under the title "Welcome to Cyberspace," and in its December issue, *Art in America* featured "Art On Line" on its cover. It is clear that most users and many artists consider the Internet and the Web one and the same thing. They are not. The Web is one among many protocols available online (to be accurate, the name of the protocol that makes the Web so user-friendly is "http" or Hypertext Transfer Protocol). In other words, the Web is a subset of the Internet. While several protocols are compatible with Web browsers, some standard and experimental protocols are not. Examples include CU-SeeMe and MBone, both used for real-time videoconferencing, and Napster and LimeWire, used for file sharing. If, on the one hand, the market constantly pushes for media convergence, leading us to believe that in the future more protocols will be integrated into common browsers, on the other, media research continuously develops new protocols that expand the reach of human agency online. Awareness that the Internet is not reducible to the Web is very important because it helps us understand the complexity of this network and its potential beyond the familiar Web browser.

The wide acceptance of the Web as a standard format since 1996 has led to a proliferation of "Web-centric" projects, self-contained hypermedia works that employ the Internet as a dissemination medium. While for the public the emergence of standard interfaces and communication protocols is productive because they facilitate accomplishing tasks, in art, conformation to standards runs the risk of imposing unwanted restrictions. In other words, artworks that require specific network topologies cannot adapt to Web-centric or Netless environments without severely compromising their meaning.

The ordinary use of interactive features of the Internet, such as chat and e-mail, might suggest that it is akin to the telephone and the postal systems, which basically enable the exchange of messages synchronically (telephone) and asynchronically (mail) between distant interacters. The Internet does incorporate aspects of television and radio by making possible the broadcast of video, audio, and text messages to small and large groups alike. At times, the Internet is a virtual catalogue or gallery, resembling a database. While some explore the Internet as a bi-directional medium, others integrate interactivity with hybrid contexts that incorporate physical spaces. Perhaps the most exciting feature of the Internet is that it is simultaneously all of the above and more. The Internet continues to grow and transform itself as we read e-mail on our cell phones.

The Internet produces a dense information landscape that shapes a particular sensibility. On the Net, one becomes capable of inhabiting multiple contexts at once and of absorbing large amounts of sensorial stimuli simultaneously. On the Net, one evolves strategies to manipulate large amounts of data and to move through fields of information. Most Internet users thrive in the exchange of chat and e-mail messages, in their participation in online communities, in the newly accessible body of knowledge they discover daily, and in the wealth of multimedia and interactive experiences available online. Further expanding the interest and the reach of the Internet are systems that provide high-speed access from home and work, IP telephony (the use of the Net as a phone network), mobile wireless connectivity via palmtops and cell phones, satellite delivery of Net traffic to remote geographic locations, and, in the conceivable future, microchip implants. These and other developments open up new opportunities for artists as well.

DIGITAL MEMORY INSIDE THE HUMAN BODY

The presence of digital information inside the human body, stored on an implanted microchip, is at the core of my artwork *Time Capsule,* realized on November 11, 1997, at Casa das Rosas, a cultural center in São Paulo, Brazil. The piece is a distributed work that links a local event installation, a site-specific intervention in which the site itself is both my body and a remote database, and a live simulcast on television and the Web. The object that gives the piece its title is a microchip that contains a programmed identification number, integrated with a coil and a capacitor, and all hermetically sealed in biocompatible glass. The temporal scale of the work is stretched between the ephemeral and the permanent, that is, between the few minutes necessary for the completion of the basic procedure, the microchip implantation, and the permanent character of the implant. As with other underground time capsules, it is under the skin that this digital time capsule projects itself into the future.

When the public walked into the gallery where this work took place, what they saw was a horizontal bedstead, seven sepia-toned family photographs shot in Eastern Europe in the 1930s, an online computer serving the Web, a telerobotic finger, and additional broadcasting equipment. I started (and concluded) the basic procedure by washing the skin of my ankle with an antiseptic and using a special needle to insert subcutaneously the passive microchip, which is, in fact, a transponder with no power supply to replace or moving parts to wear out. Scanning the implant remotely via the Net generated a low-energy radio signal (125 KHz) that energized the microchip to transmit its unique and inalterable numerical code (026109532), which was shown on the scanner's sixteen-character Liquid Crystal Display (LCD). Immediately after this data was obtained, I registered myself via the Web in a remote database located in the United States. This is the first instance of a human being added to the database, since this registry was originally de-signed for identification and recovery of lost animals. I registered myself both as animal and owner under my own name. After implantation, a small layer of connective tissue formed around the microchip, preventing migration.

Canal 21, a station based in São Paulo, produced the television broadcast and the Webcast was produced by Casa das Rosas. The TV-Web simulcast, which included interactive scanning of the implanted microchip via the Internet, was not realized as "coverage." Instead, it was deliberately conceived as an integral part of the work, as a disturbance in the predictable horizon of newscasting. The television broadcast was thought of as a way of creating art directly in the realm of mass media, as a means of intervening in a social realm by realizing the event in millions of living rooms simultaneously. The live *Time Capsule* television broadcast reached approximately seventeen million viewers, who routinely tuned in to watch the Canal 21 nightly news.

The transmission was divided into three parts. During the first segment, viewers were introduced to the main ideas that inform the work and were told what was about to happen. The second segment presented the process of implanting the microchip. In the last segment, viewers saw the interac-tive remote scanning of the microchip via the Internet and the subsequent database registration. Additional delayed television broadcasts by other sta-tions (TV Cultura and TV Manchete) extended the audience to more than fifty million. If the microchip was developed to identify and recover lost animals, in *Time Capsule*, before millions of viewers, the human animal was tagged, registered in a database as both a domestic animal and its "owner," identified, and "recovered" through the Web.

Not coincidentally, documentation and identification have been one of the main thrusts of technological development, particularly in the area of imaging, from the first photograph to ubiquitous video surveillance. Throughout the nineteenth and twentieth centuries, photography and its adjacent imaging tools functioned as a social time capsule, enabling the collective preservation of memory of our social bodies. This process has led to a global inflation of the image and the erasure by digital technologies of the sacred power of photography as truth. The representational power of the image is no longer the key agent in the preservation of social or personal memory and identity. We are able to change the configuration of our skin through plastic surgery as easily as we can manipulate its representation through digital imaging. We can embody the image of ourselves that we wish to become. With the ability to change flesh and image also comes the possibility of erasure of their memory.

Memory is a chip. As we call "memory" the storage units of computers and robots, we anthropomorphize our machines, making them look a little bit more like us. In the process, we mimic them as well. The body is traditionally seen as the sacred repository of human-only memories, acquired as the result of genetic inheritance or personal experiences. Memory chips are found inside computers and robots and not ordinarily inside the human body. Yet, in *Time Capsule,* the presence of the chip, with its recorded retrievable data inside the body, forces us to consider the co-presence of lived memories and artificial memories within us. External memories become implants in the body, anticipating future instances in which events of this sort might become common practice and inquiring about the legitimacy and ethical implications of such procedures in the digital culture. Live transmissions on television (during a primetime newscast) and on the Web were an integral part of *Time Capsule* and brought the issue closer to home. Scanning of the implant remotely via the Web revealed how the connective tissue of the global digital network renders obsolete the skin as a protective boundary demarcating the limits of the body.

THE FUTURE OF DIGITAL IMPLANTS

As electronic devices with embedded browsers and servers become pervasive, we will have access to the network in many new ways. For example, it will be common to browse and serve from cars and airplanes. Telephones, as well as photo and video cameras, will have IP addresses, numbers that enable them to be directly connected to the Internet without a desktop computer. This newly gained mobility, coupled with broadband access and future protocols, will open new possibilities for network art. It is conceivable that the human body will host embedded miniature servers in the future.

In research labs worldwide, there are clear signs of the future integration of computers, networking, and biology. Straightening the connection between digital technology and mental activity, memory in particular, Theodore Berger and his colleagues at the University of Southern California (a team of neurobiologists, computer scientists, physicists, and electronics engineers) developed a microchip in 1997 that reproduces the neural activity of a part of the brain involved in memory and learning: the hippocampus. The research is far from concluded, but the goal is to allow the chip to take information already within short-term memory and transfer it to long-term memory. Berger and his colleagues hope that computer chips implanted in the brain will replace the part of the hippocampus that is no longer functioning and thus, one day, benefit Alzheimer's patients, stroke victims, and people with brain damage.

Brain implants are also a form of neuroprosthesis that enable direct communication between the patient and a computer. In 1998, Emory University doctors implanted a device into a man's brain that amplified his brain signals and allowed him to move a cursor across a screen and convey simple messages such as hello and goodbye. The man was a paralyzed, mute stroke victim who used his brainpower to communicate with others through the computer. The signals were transmitted from his brain to a laptop computer through an antenna-like coil placed on his head.

In 1997, the U.S. Food and Drug Administration (FDA) approved the first implantable neuroprosthesis, the Freehand system. This device uses an implant to give individuals with quadriplegia the ability to grip and hold. Another application, a prototype bladder-control system, allows individuals with paralysis to control their bodies' waste schedule. NeuroControl developed both implants, and employs a wireless controller activated externally. The successful use of microchips in spinal injury surgery already opens up an unprecedented area of inquiry, in which bodily functions are stimulated externally and controlled via microchips. Experimental medical research toward the creation of artificial retinas, using microchips in the eye to enable the blind to see, for example, forces us to accept the liberating effects of intrabody microchips. Another example is the tiny transmitter that can be implanted in a mother's womb to monitor the health of an unborn child.

We are intrigued, and perhaps just as fascinated and terrified, by the notion that we are embodying technology. We are intrigued because of our innate and insatiable curiosity about our own limits; we are fascinated because of the new possibilities of an expanded body contemplating the notion of eternal life; and we are terrified because these technologies, originally developed to aid ill or physically impaired persons, are in fact not desirable for a healthy body and therefore renew our fear of confronting our own mortality.

Albeit for distinct reasons, contemporary art partakes some of the same concerns shared by fields conventionally seen as extraneous to the "fine arts," such as biology, computer science, digital networking, and robotics. On the one hand, art is free to explore the creative potential of these tools and fields of knowledge unconstrained by their own self-imposed limits. On the other, art can offer a critical and philosophical perspective that is beyond their stated goals.

Standard interfaces, both physical (keyboards) and virtual (Web browsers), enable a plethora of possibilities, but they also impose restrictions. The standard desktop configuration that requires us to pound a keyboard and sit behind a desk staring at a screen creates a physical trauma that amplifies the psychological shock generated by ever-faster cycles of technological invention, development, and obsolescence. In its most obvious manifestation, this physical trauma takes the shape of carpal tunnel syndrome and backaches. In its less evident form, interface standardization has led to an overall containment of the human body, which is then forced to conform to the boxy shape of the computer setup (monitor and CPU). It is almost as if the body has become an extension of the computer, and not the other way around. This, perhaps, only reflects technology's general outlook, since organic life is indeed becoming an extension of the computer, as vectors in microchip technology clearly point to biological sources as the only way to continue the exponential process of miniaturization, beyond the limits of traditional materials.

The human hosting of digital memory—as exemplified by *Time Capsule*—points to a traumatic, but perhaps freer, form of embodiment of alternative interfaces. The subdermal presence of a microchip reveals the drama of this conflict, as we try to develop social models that make explicit undesirable implications of this impulse and that, at the same time, will allow us to reconcile aspects of our experience generally regarded as antagonistic—such as freedom of movement, data storage and processing, biological interfaces, and networking environments. As art participates in the wider debate and circulation of ideas we witness in culture at large, it can help us develop new philosophical and political models, and influence the new kinds of synergies emerging at the frontier where the organic and the digital meet.

15. AESTHETICS OF *ECOSYSTM*

JOHN KLIMA

Commissioned by Zurich Capital Markets (ZCM), *ecosystm* was shown to the public for the first time in the exhibition *BitStreams,* curated by Larry Rinder at the Whitney Museum of American Art. The press release for the show provides an introduction:

> John Klima's *ecosystm* was commissioned by a leading investment bank to represent, artistically, real-time global stock market fluctuations, and currency volatility. Rather than indicate these dynamic economic forces with dry statistics, Klima has created an ecosystem in which market indexes are represented by branching trees, and currencies by birds that swoop and flock according to trading volatility. Connected to the Internet, Klima's digital projection simultaneously represents local weather conditions, reflected in the light and atmosphere in which this economic ecosystem unfolds.[1]

I was very pleased to discover that the title was correctly spelled and in lowercase in the *BitStreams* catalogue, as it has appeared elsewhere as *"Ecosystem," "Ecosystem2000,"* and *"ecosystem."* When I chose the title for the work, I followed the computer file-name convention of eight letters, all lowercase. This is my normal naming convention for software I have authored, and it reflects the requirement-turned-tradition of the "eight dot three" name space for DOS computer files. The file name thus becomes the title when the work is purely "screen based" software art. Screen-based works require no more than a computer and a monitor (or projection) to be experienced. However, my body of work also includes "true" installations, where substantial sculptural and mechanical components are working closely with "virtual" constructs on the computer. While these works have proper titles, they still cling to a "classical physics" of art. The continuing confusion around the title *ecosystm* emphasizes how digital constructs are at odds with the established rules of a brick-and-mortar world, not to mention conventional grammar and syntax. The computer has its own linguistic conventions appropriate to it, but increasingly these are more like spoken-language conventions (and this is a separate essay I'll leave to a better writer than myself).

Further, friction arose when I attempted to provide the "medium" for the obligatory catalogue and wall text; there is no established way to label new media artworks, particularly if they are software that the artist wrote. Though everyone picks up a paintbrush in kindergarten, the public has only vague notions of what the creation of "software art" is about. I insisted on the following for the catalogue entry:

> Title: *ecosystm*
> Date: 2001
> Medium: WorldUp Simulation
> Dimensions: 1024 × 768 pixels
> Courtesy Zurich Capital Markets

The medium, WorldUp, is the programming environment I used most frequently at that time. It is best described as a high-level Integrated Development Environment, or IDE. This is, in a very real sense, "the medium." To the average art viewer, this means nothing. However, if one executed a Web search on WorldUp, one could easily find the erstwhile stretcher, canvas, and paint (since the initial writing of this essay, the company that created WorldUp has gone out of business, like so many technological providers who were just a tiny bit ahead of their time). One could even go so far as to download a demonstration version of WorldUp and try it yourself. If one were to follow a sample tutorial, you could get a few balls and boxes spinning around. You would also get a sense of the challenge if you were to attempt something more complex. I find this much more useful than a medium listing that states: "Real-time 3D renderer, live data stream" or any other such descriptive. For the average viewer, this too is meaningless, or worse, misleading. Many people who possess some knowledge have just that—they are partially informed. I'd much rather the viewer have fewer assumptions about the work, experience it, and hopefully find it intriguing enough to read the brief catalogue text, and perhaps be so inspired as to have a go at "the medium."

For the dimensions, I looked again to the machine for assistance. When allocating memory in the BASIC programming language, one employs the directive "Dim," meaning dimension. The optimum screen resolution for *ecosystm* is 1024 × 768 pixels. These are its true dimensions; the image has been dimensioned in RAM to occupy a grid of video, 1024 × 768 pixels in size.

Some feel it is imperative that viewers have the whole back-story when apprehending a work of software art. I can't help feeling that this is not only impractical but also undesirable. Though for some works understanding the back-end is critical, often the very point of understanding the front-end, everything the viewer needs to know in *ecosystm,* exists within the work itself. Through interaction, or through the observation of others interacting, the back-story unfolds. In the case of *ecosystm,* the viewer can easily toggle a brief database entry for each visual element in the work, the entry appearing as an overlay in proximity to its visual element. An additional toggle will show all the data for the entire system as a screen overlay in conventional tabular format. Through the simplest of interactions (pressing one or another button on a game pad), the viewer is presented with every indication that a connection exists between the activity of the flocks and trees, global currencies, and markets. Why else would the data be there? In a painting, this connection would be conceptual and visual; in the case of the computer, it should be implicit that a functional, as well as a conceptual and visual connection, exists. Making the "real" world materialize in a "natural" (though highly aestheticized) computer representation is the breath of life in this virtual environment. Coming to this understanding through the work is optimal; this is the moment when an individual has a powerful aesthetic experience. The implicit understanding that functionality can directly connect conceptual and visual elements in a work of software art may not be a widely held belief in the general public at this point. However, computing has become ubiquitous and it will not be long before an art public with an interest in this medium will come to expect functional connections between all elements in a work—and, if connections are absent, the artist will be asked to explain why the connection is missing, rather than being asked to explain why the connection exists in the first place.

Once this state of implicit understanding exists, the inner workings of the connections can be of great interest in and of themselves. In *ecosystm,* these inner workings are best described by example: for instance, each flock of birds in *ecosystm* represents a global currency. For Thailand, the database overlay might read:

Thai bhat
Aggressing
Population Stable, 12 members

There are also treelike structures that represent global market indices. For the Japanese market, the entry might read:

Nikkei 300
Soil Condition Good

In the currency example above, the Thai bhat is "Aggressing." This means the daily volatility of the Thai bhat is at least three times its yearly volatility. This is an important figure for currency traders; it indicates a significant and rapid fluctuation in the value of a currency. In this state, the flock will attack a neighboring flock. The second value is a long-term measure of the currency's strength against the U.S. dollar. Although a currency may experience short-term volatility, the number of birds in the flock (the population) changes only when there is sustained increase or decrease in value. Similarly, in the example of the Japanese market index (Nikkei 300), advances and declines are expressed in terms of a soil condition, subsequently visualized by the tree structures growing or losing branches.

The bird flocking algorithm I authored is based on the following three rules of flock simulation established by Craig Reynolds, known as the "Boids" algorithm:[2]

1. All birds will try to fly toward the center of mass of the flock.
2. All birds will try to avoid collision with other birds.
3. All birds will try to match the speed of other birds.

Based on these three simple rules, a reasonably competent programmer armed with a vector math library can create convincing real-time bird-flocking, fish-schooling, or dinosaur-stampeding software. The keys to the algorithm's implementation in *ecosystm* are not the rules so much as the descriptive "will try." This "will try" degree of effort is an important parameter. Changing the birds' "will try" parameters directly modifies the behavior of the flock. In *ecosystm*, these parameters were simply "fed" from the real-time foreign-exchange data stream after passing through standard financial volatility calculations suggested to me by analysts at Zurich Capital. Although any kind of data expressed as a percent can be used to drive *ecosystm*, there is something directly evocative, appropriate, and meaningful in the use of global currency values, where one country's gain is another's demise. This is the kind of work Zurich Capital is engaged in on a daily basis; these are the data they use every day. However, no one in the company found the piece to be an indictment of their occupation. Quite the contrary, a number of ZCM employees expressed a desire for blood splatters and explosions, something I refused to provide.

I created a few additional state parameters to allow the flock to do things like perch, feed, strut, sleep, and breed. I also established a connection between a country's leading stock market index, represented by growing and shrinking trees, and its flock. The space in which the flock has to fly is directly proportional to the size of its tree. As the market index declines, the birds fly closer to it. When a country's market index declines at the same time that its currency value significantly fluctuates, the flock appears to swarm the tree in a feeding behavior. However, in a volatile currency bolstered by a strong market index, the flock has sufficient room to move around such that its condition does not appear as critical. A strong currency and a strong market index result in graceful, stately, and coordinated flock behavior.

When I sat down to create *ecosystm,* I had the sense that based on these rules, and how I implemented them, something interesting would naturally emerge. I had chosen to group the flocks according to their geographic region. This is how the data arrive from the data providers. I created a European region (before the adoption of the Euro), an Americas region, a region for Asia, and one for the Middle East. After running *ecosystm* for a few days (it requires a sustained twenty-four-hour connection for the math to begin working), I was stunned to discover that the Middle Eastern region was a swarm of aggression—flocks constantly attacking other flocks. At first I thought this must be an anomaly in the programming, but with some manual number crunching I quickly realized that all the figures were correct. Should it have been a surprise that the flocks in the Middle East were at one another's throats? Why would I expect anything different? Though hardly joyful with the result, I was nonetheless joyful that the result was so clear.

During the course of the *BitStreams* show, the Argentine peso collapsed. After a brief period of violence, the flock's population dropped to just two birds, the minimum number. I heard many reports from Whitney employees of Argentine nationals hovering around *ecosystm* with heads hung low, mourning the sorry state of their flock. Some months after the *BitStreams* show, *ecosystm* traveled to South Korea for an exhibition at the Daejeon Municipal Art Museum. To simplify the installation for the institution, rather than have a live data stream, I ran *ecosystm* on historical data. For the data set, I chose a two-week period, the first week before, and the last week following, the 1997 Hong Kong market crash. I chose this period specifically because I knew the data would be active, and I subsequently discovered that at the time, the Korean won had been officially stabilized and would not have changed. After the anticipated crash, the Middle East was brought to new heights of frenzy, the market trees around the world withered, and most bird flocks went into feeding and aggressing modes—yet the Korean won floated above it all, as if nothing happened. Critical to my appreciation of what I create is the moment when I step back and say, "It really works. It does what I claim it does."

I think *ecosystm* is visually stunning, but it was never my intent to dazzle. That path leads to a comparison of a "Hollywood" game release, where scores of programmers and graphic artists spend millions of dollars to create the next dazzler. Nobody would ever claim an independent film inferior to the Hollywood product because the production values are not as high. With real-time 3D rendering software, however, the artist will inevitably be compared to the gaming industry. Rather than fight the comparison, I choose to embrace the game, but repurpose its technology for my own aims. Critical within that repurposing is the ability to make the game function in any way I see fit. While Chinese artist Feng Meng Bo places himself in *Quake II Arena* and makes cinema, and Anne-Marie Schleiner, Joan Leandre, and Brody Condon patched weapons that shoot antiwar graffiti into *Counter-Strike* multiuser online death matches, I choose to build everything in my "games" from the ground up. I love *Quake II for You* and *Velvet Strike*. I love the universe of skinning and moding games. However, there is no way to drive *Quake II* or *Counter-Strike* with market data, and there is no way to make the characters in these games behave like flocking birds. Understanding this technological state enhances the understanding of the work. Unfortunately, a back-story can be appreciated only through familiarity with both the state of the game industry and at least a mild critical interest in the social impact of ubiquitous computing.

Regardless of my need to apologize for being one person and not Lucas Arts, it's the dazzle in a game that is the first element to look dated, ridiculous, or, at best, charming. The faded dazzle is normally most evident in the blood splatters and explosions. By contrast, *Tempest,* a classic of the "quarter arcade" era of video games, was built with nothing but monochrome line drawing on a cathode ray tube. Nonetheless, *Tempest* is the most sought-after arcade game for many collectors. It is not the dazzling graphics that set *Tempest* apart, but the unique space and unusual function of the game. In *Tempest,* a tunnel of lines are drawn converging on a single point of perspective, with a co-efficient that would scandalize a Renaissance painter. Game elements fly toward the player, clinging tenaciously to the lines. The input device is a "spinner," a palm-sized wheel with enough weight to retain considerable momentum when it spins. Although not necessarily easy to control, the spinner "feels" right. Spinning the wheel rotates the viewer's avatar around the tunnel. To me, *Tempest* is the essential, visceral "formula" for a good game—and it looks and plays just as well today as it did in 1981. When I look at *ecosystm* today (it was made in 2000 based on technology from 1995, ancient history to "the industry"), it too "holds up" viscerally. Though the geometry is simple, it is not crude. Though there are only a few environmental and atmospheric effects, they are rich and dynamic. The behaviors are as elegant now as when they functioned for the first time. In fact, I think it looks better than ever. When run on contemporary hardware, it can accommodate many more birds, and can achieve true cinematic frame-rates, resulting in a much smoother "ride." Although Barbara Pollack, a staunch critic, falsely stated in *Art in America* that the user pilots the birds through *ecosystm* with a game pad, the "input device" is actually the foreign-exchange market itself.[3] To control the birds in *ecosystm,* one must engage in foreign-exchange trading on the open market. It is entirely within the capability of major foreign-exchange traders to significantly affect the volatility of a currency, and thus its flock of birds. This happens all the time in the market and this is how you "play" *ecosystm.* The game pad *ecosystm* is normally displayed with allows only the observation of the aviary. It is immediately evident that the game pad has no influence on the birds whatsoever. By looking to *Tempest* for a historical model of timeless aesthetic computing, the aesthetics of a work of contemporary software art do not reach obsolescence when the technology on which they are based does. Ms. Pollack went on to remark sarcastically, "The thrill, if any, comes from finding a video game—gee whiz!!—in an art museum," without once asking the more important question, "Why this video game"?[4]

The geometric construction of *ecosystm* involved the creation of sixteen individual flock species and sixteen uniquely identifiable tree species, thirty-two models in total. Faced with this task, if I ever hoped to complete it, I would have to sit down and get it done with little fuss. There was plenty of behavior code yet to write, not to mention the data stream back-end and the volatility calculations—modeling was only one-third of the total project workload. The only way to proceed was to trust that the aesthetic "beef" would get into the models all on its own, without conscious deliberation of the contextual ramifications of each gesture. A decidedly modernist approach, I admit, but I think in *ecosystm* this modernist trust was well placed. The result was such that in *ecosystm* the Swiss species is small and tidy. The

Asian species have an Asian "feel" (for lack of a better word), and distinguish themselves from each other with decidedly regional features. The species hold an aesthetic that expresses my internalized image of the regions they represent. It is an internalization that I am sure other people can relate to. None of this was I fully conscious of while making the geometry. If I had been, in all likelihood I would have forced myself into the logical and conceptual trap of using a national symbol, a nation's flag or its mascot or favorite foliage, to represent the indicators. The result is, to my mind, a much less aesthetically complex, intriguing, and visceral experience. I have no idea what the state bird of New York is, or why and how it came to represent New York, though I have lived in New York for most of my life. Flags and symbols require a great deal of back-story to be anything but arbitrary representations. By contrast, an intuitive approach to a meaningful aesthetic representation has great potential to trigger evocative responses in a viewer similarly acculturated to the artist.

A differing, though interesting, view to the aesthetic in *ecosystm* was held by the critic Jerry Saltz in *The Village Voice*, who thought of the species as "origami pterodactyls."[5] If my work can inspire the words "origami" and "pterodactyl," I consider the job done. That a decidedly "brick-and-mortar" critic could inadvertently consider the 3D polygons and geometry expressed through metaphor to origami is a sign of hope for the future. Origami as a metaphor for 3D software modeling is apt, and serves as a strong indication that elaborate back-stories are not required because the piece itself conveys all the information the viewer needs. Equating the geometry to origami should (through the implicit understanding that functional connections exist) lead the viewer to an intuitive understanding of the medium and how an artist works with it—without the viewer ever touching brush and paint.

As a final addition to *ecosystm*, I connected the qualities of light and atmosphere to the real-world data stream of weather reports from John F. Kennedy Airport. These text-based observations of local weather conditions, provided in the METAR code, are constantly updated from more than six thousand weather stations around the world. Since a great deal of currency speculation occurs in New York City, it seemed appropriate to use local weather conditions. The work is permanently installed on a large plasma monitor on the forty-eighth floor ZCM's downtown office. Surrounded by large windows with breathtaking views, the display is also a window, but it opens onto a vista where wind speed and runway visibility are parameters to fog, cloud, and ocean-wave algorithms. Thus occurs a direct, visual similarity between the weather perceived in *ecosystm* and the real weather observed

from the windows of the office. Here the implicit understanding of functional connections is reflected in the data, by suggesting that the weather in
New York has an effect on the markets. I would expect data to confirm that,
on average, the markets close lower on rainy days. The weather represented
in *ecosystm* has no internal, functional connection to the behavior of the
birds and trees. That connection exists, if but evocatively, in the real world
itself. All I had to do was place the two together. The world is the code that
functionally connects them.

NOTES

1. Stephen Soba, press release by the Whitney Museum of American Art, March 2001.

2. Craig Reynolds, "Steering Behaviors for Autonomous Characters," http://www
.red3d.com/cwr/steer/.

3. Barbara Pollack, "Back to the Future with 'Bitstreams,'" *Art in America* 9 (September 2001): 61.

4. Ibid.

5. Jerry Saltz, "Byte Lite," *The Village Voice*, May 1, 2001, 71.

16. *POLAR*

MARKO PELJHAN

Polar was created during a two-year process at the Artlab Canon, beginning in 1998 at the *Artlab 10* exhibition, and was installed from October 28 to November 6 at the Hillside Plaza, Daikanyama, Tokyo.

Polar can be described as an immersive intermedia environment and architecture. At the start of the process, we had envisioned a 7m × 7m × 4m networked tactile space, which was defined as a tactile matrix interface that enables the visitor to experience the flow of data in the global and local networks in a completely immersive, yet cognitive, way.[1] The work was inspired by the notion of the cognitive "ocean" as described, respectively, in Stanislaw Lem and Andrei Tarkovsky's *Solaris*.[2] The initial conceptual equation was "Ocean = Matrix."

The outline of the work was based on the creation of two software and hardware "engines," the so-called Polar Engine (with the adjacent Pols, Polar Dictionary, and Knowledge Base modules) and the Change Engine (with the adjacent Traceroute Visualizer). The first was envisioned as the input, analysis, and construction zone, and the second as the output, synthesis, and experience zone. These zones were defined both in the conceptualization of the software and hardware architecture and systems, and in the environment and material space architecture. We have defined a "zone" as a specific space-time interval in which the biological and physical was networked with the abstract-immaterial.

The primary question posed in this process was how is it possible to construct a cognitive and tactile experience of the seamless and near-abstract matrix with the analysis, construction, and transformation of it included in the process. We sought to exteriorize and experience the equivalent of a "quantum," "Heisenberg" effect on the level of the networks and to create an interface between the human body, its senses and the matrix, which would, by the very presence and activities of the humans, transform the structure of the matrix that is being observed and experienced, and also that of the physical space that is being inhabited during this process.

THE SPACE

The *Polar* space was a 7m × 7m × 4m bright white three-dimensional translucent physical space, which included four projection surfaces, seven speakers, a 3D high-resolution tracking system, a micro-organism growth module, a wave-patterning water-vibration module, two field displays (touch screen input GUI modules), and seven Pol zones.

The environment architecture was modular and included the ceiling, where a system of thirty-two lights controlled by the main engine of the project played an active role in the tactile and sensorial experience. One of the primary experiential goals of the environmental design was to minimize the presence of clearly discernible technological elements within it, on one hand, and, on the other, to approach it from the pragmatic viewpoint of an all-encompassing "human-machine" interface.

THE SOFTWARE SYSTEMS

The software systems were divided into two primary zones. The first one served as the input and cognitive zone, the second as the output, sensorial, and tactile zone. To connect the two, a third routing module was created, named Solaris. Its purpose was to route and connect all the systems in the *Polar* network. To do so, a protocol to connect different software, hardware, and operating systems was created. This system was the most invisible, but also was the most important part of the software development, since it connected systems as diverse as the modified Canon Inc. *Advanced Intelligent Information Retrieval System* (AIIRS) and the Twosuns *Cartasia* and *Enclued* software workbench and 3D trackers. While the protocol was the language of *Polar,* the Polar Engine, Polar Dictionary, and Knowledge Base were the heart of the content systems and the connecting point of the work with the information matrix. The authors and curators built the Knowledge Base as the initial content part of the work. The database consisted of at least twenty text files of 100KB for each of the seven categories for each language (the whole work is bilingual, in English and Japanese) defined by the authors as the content categories of the Polar Dictionary. The seven categories are: (1) crystal-crystallization, (2) diagram, (3) stealth-stealthy, (4) machine-machinic, (5) wave-waveform, (6) symmetry-symmetriad, and (7) spectral-spectre-spectrum. Ten keywords were defined for each of the categories.

The seventy keywords in English and the seventy keywords in Japanese were the initial material for the Polar Dictionary that served for the database search options. The Polar Dictionary was enlarged during each session through searches of the Internet and proprietary databases, and from the distillation of keywords from retrieved texts and documents.

The Polar Engine consisted of three modules: the Keyword Distiller Module, the Knowledge Base Generator Module, and the Category Filter Module. These modules selected useful information from the retrieved texts, summarized it, extracted keywords, and categorized them. The system used for this operation was a derivative of the proprietary software, *Artificial Staff*, developed by the Canon Media Technology Laboratory. This is a multi-agent model suited for the architecture of an information retrieval system and it was used as the base for modification. *Artificial Staff* agents are autonomous, observe the users' patterns and other agents, and exchange the acquired information under a loose protocol. The flow-type information retrieved from the matrix is in turn processed and categorized. The Polar Dictionary grows autonomously, determined only by the pattern of the initial visitors' choices and the results of information retrieval and analysis. During this process, an immense amount of numerical data are created. This data were the blood flow of the system and were routed through Solaris to the tactile zone and systems. There, the physical and tactile interaction with the visitors was taking place.

The heart of the tactile zone was the Change Engine and the Traceroute, Data Flow, and 3D space visualizers. The Change Engine consisted of the *Enclued* and *Cartasia* software modules, which served as real-time, dynamic multimedia process generators and trackers. This was the output generator, which generated tactile and sensorial (light, space, sound) changes in the "ocean space." Along with them, a pair of displays showed real-time data flow within the system and the networking of the system with the matrix. The first one was a synthetic 3D display of the space, combined with data flow and database element processing visualization, so the displacement of data in the matrix, triggered by visitors' activity in the space, was visualized. The second was a two-level trace routing display, showing real-time trace routing of data from Japan on the top and from the world on the bottom. The software for the Data Flow display was based on an open GL Library simulating a large, fluid, latex surface behavior. This tactile zone was enhanced using other analog systems of interaction that did not include data exchange but only the triggering of processes.

THE HARDWARE SYSTEMS

The hardware systems consisted of a LAN network, a MIDI controller for light systems, two mobile wireless computing and sensor units (Pol), display systems, and analog electronics loop systems. The systems were connected through a TCP/IP protocol and also by analogue I/O lines. They included a micro camera filming the process of growth of the human cell culture in a physiological fluid whose growth was triggered by the temperature changes connected with the usage of the space, and a system of an analog input of sound into the video inputs of two projectors. The third analog system used was the wave-patterning water-vibration module, which consisted of a specially fitted pool of water, adjacent to two subwoofer bass speakers. The different frequencies and modulations were visualized in the water-wave patterns. For the connection between the LAN machines and some of the output analog systems, sound signals were used as the main trigger. The four projectors used in the system showed the data flow and 3D real-time space trace routing, analogue output, and changes of a test-pattern video system triggered by sound inputs, and the magnified picture of the growth of a human ear skin-cell culture during the two weeks of operations.

The other hardware elements of the system were the two field displays, which were the graphical user interfaces with the Polar Dictionary and the Pol units (two mobile wireless sensor packages that collected and relayed temperature, acceleration, sound, and visual data of the space and movement within it). The Pol units generated the first string of numerical data collected in space by the visitors that triggered the power-up of the field display and the initial generation of the keyword list on each monitor. During the exhibition, a controllable Web camera was placed within the architecture of the system so that network users could observe the activities in the space and the visitors' exploration and behaviors.

The Pol was the user's primary interface during the initial exploration of the "ocean space." It included a sensor package measuring outside and inside temperatures, a 3-axis accelerometer, a still camera, and a sound-recording system. With it, the visitor explored the space and recorded its environmental parameters. The Pol consisted of a Sony Vaio PCG-C1VN Transmeta Crusoe-based computer, a wireless LAN card, and a proprietary sensors package. It was envisioned as the first encounter of the visitors with *Polar* and the "ocean space," and as a tool that would generate a code sequence for the start of the change processes in space through its physical readout (the multisensor package). When the Pol was placed in the right position in the space (on one of the seven Pol zones), the spatial change processes began.

The 3D high-resolution tracking of the visitors and the Pol units was done through a motion-tracking system, consisting of six computers and twelve IR cameras, tracking four IR sources. The system constantly relayed positioning data back to the main Solaris router and the Change Engine. These data were included in the main routing and, accordingly, the changes in the visual, aural, and tactile spaces were generated.

EXPERIENCE FLOW

In this section, I will try to convey the experience flow of a series of dynamic and interactive processes within the artwork from two perspectives—that of the visitors and that of the data packet. It is an attempt to define a method for describing this kind of work in writing and is meant to be descriptive and not analytical.

Visitors

The visitors first receive the main rules of interaction with the "ocean space." The hosts also explain the functioning of the Pol, the graphical user interface, and the functionality of the field display. After that, they don a jacket, which includes a visitor's infrared ID badge, and are each given one of the Pol units. With that, they are ready to enter the "ocean space," which is filled with a constant low hertz hum. Its frequency changes immediately after the visitors enter as the system senses the Pol and the visitors' actions. Light patterns start to slowly change the sound and the temperature in the space as well. These processes of space-time change are based on a random generation of data from the random generators on the real-time data flow from the 3D tracking system and the Pol data output. The visitor has two to three minutes for this initial exploration and environmental data gathering, then a specific sound marks the point when the Pol must be placed on one of the seven Pol zones. When the visitor chooses the right zone, the environment reacts with a very bright and quick flash of light and a very different high-pitched sound. This indicates that the Pol is in the correct position. Then the random keyword extracting sequence is generated from Pol sensor data, the field displays turn on, and the visitors can start using them. First, the visitor chooses the language of interaction, then the first list of seven randomly selected keywords displays, and the Solaris sends a message to all modules that the change processes have started. When one of the visitors chooses a keyword and places it in the system, the Solaris sends the keyword to the Polar Engine. Exactly what happens with this keyword will be explained in the data packet path description that follows. For the visitor, the time lag between the involvement of the keyword in the matrix and the first results is the time in which the visitor has to explore the "ocean space." This exploration changes the position of sound fields within the three dimensions of the physical space, and the initial numerical results from the Pol data (which are now combined with results from the search processes) are reflected in the different sound pattern levels and other environmental and sensorial activity. Because of this interrelation, no two experiences in the space are alike. Visitors can observe the changing wave patterns, a result of their movement, and the movement of data through the system, in the water module. They can observe the cell organism live and projected (the temperature in the cell module also fluctuates according to data generated through movement and the search-and-extraction process). Of course, only a visitor on the first and last day could see the difference in the actual growth of the cell, but that long time span is crucial for understanding the extended time component of the work.

The data flow and 3D tracking combined wave display made the visitors aware that the space they inhabit is not only physical but also is a data space. The data-flow patterns are interwoven with the patterns generated by the visitors' position and the position of the Pols in space. When the trace routing display starts (very late in the process, because of the large amount of data from the trace routing that needs to be processed and parsed), the field display is ready for another keyword input. The list of keywords grew in the process if the search and extraction were successful and a new keyword list was generated. The visitors had a chance to involve two to four keywords in one session, depending on the keyword and the result base. This was due to the limited ten minutes of time for the exploration of the "ocean space," which was programmed in the system because of the limitation of the exhibition context, designed to process as many visitors as possible. Of course, longer times can be set and more changes in the space-time data-space could be observed. After the clock runs out, the system automatically turns the lights on to maximum and the process of "cooling down" begins. This process enables the visitor to understand that the change process is over. The visitors are also reminded that the process is over through the field display (GUI) and can thus exit from the environment.

Data Packets

The experience of the data-packet flow in the processes of *Polar* is as hard to describe as the experience of the visitor, since there are many parallel processes in the network and database architecture, but the basic pattern can be described as follows:

- Pol acquires environmental data, acceleration, temperatures, visual data, and sound.
- When Pol is in the space, the 3D tracker starts to track the Pol and the visitor and relays the tracking data to Solaris.
- This tracking results in the light-pattern and sound-pattern changes in space. The space is full of light/sound positions that are constantly shifting according to the data input form the tracking system.
- The system has a time limit and Pol stops collecting data after two to three minutes, depending on the buffer.
- The tracking system waits until the Pol is put into the right, randomly chosen position (all random operations are processed on sensor-gathered data).
- The whole packet of the Pol data is sent to Solaris.
- Solaris sends start commands to other modules.
- The field displays start up and wait for the language input.
- After the language choice, the Polar Engine selects a list of seven keywords from the Polar Dictionary.
- The keywords are displayed on the field display (GUI).
- The visitor chooses a keyword and the keyword is sent to Solaris. In parallel, Solaris relays the space-positioning data and the data-flow information to the Data Flow visualizer.
- Solaris sends the chosen keyword to the Polar Engine, which then sends the keyword to fifteen different search engines for each language and to proprietary databases connected to the system.
- The results/pages from the search are put into a temporary data pool. Then they are analyzed, compared to the Knowledge Base, and the new possible keywords are distilled.
- The results are also analyzed according to the URL and trace routing. Each URL of a positive sample (a text from which a new keyword was extracted) is trace routed and the result is sent to the trace-route visualizer.

- All numerical data generated in this process are sent to the Change Engine by using the protocol. The space-time-sound activity in the environment is constantly shifting and changing accordingly.
- After the keyword is added to the Polar Dictionary, the Solaris sends a message to the field display that another session can be opened.
- The process could continue indefinitely, but a timer in the Solaris can be set to a time limit, at which the processes of one session end.
- The systems and the modules power down and wait for the new session initializing.
- The transformation is completed and the data representation in the space is changed.

When we designed Polar, our goal was to construct a cognitive and tactile experience of the seamless and near-abstract matrix with the analysis, construction, and transformation included in the process.

Polar tried to answer this question and the Ocean from Solaris was the inspiration for it, with its complexity and cognitive elementarity. For us, one of the primary goals was that each interaction of human visitors with this data and physical space would result in its being different than before the interaction—transformed in size, shape, and content. Sounds, sound, and light-trigger positions within the data space shift. New keywords are generated in the process, and the dictionary, based on the seven basic categories set up by the authors, grows as well. Everything is shifting and changing, some things are growing (cell), some physically changing (water). *Polar* had a life of its own, without any human interpretation, because it was a system that could primitively think.

Polar Personnel

>   Authors: Carsten Nicolai, Marko Peljhan
>   Engineering team: Artlab Canon, Twosuns
>   Curators: Yukiko Shikata, Kazunao Abe

Project Team

>   Mizuuchi Yukiharu, Manager Artlab
>   Kimura Hiroyuki, Manager Factory Team
>   Tamai Shun-Ichi, Operations Pol
>   Shindo Yoshinori, Operations, Pol Sensor Package, HW Systems
>   Akisada Hirokazu, Solaris, protocols
>   Bessho Hiromi, Routing Display, Polar Engine, Multi Search Engine

Bohn Andreas, Enclued Authoring, Cartasia-Polar Operations
Goto Hironori, Polar Engine Dictionary, Knowledge Base
Isonuma Tomoyuki, Polar Engine Display
Sugiyama Shinko, Field Display
Titel Olaf, Enclued Post-Development, Solaris Enclued protocols
Tenno Shin-Ichi, Artlab Operations, Project Website

NOTES

1. The word "matrix" as it is defined in John December's Cybermap landmarks. See http://www.cybergeography.org/atlas/december_cyberland.gif.

2. *Solaris* (1972), directed by Andrei Tarkovsky, screenplay by Andrei Tarkovsky and Fridrikh Gorenshtein.

PUBLICATION HISTORY

Parts of the Introduction were previously published as the Introduction to a special issue on database aesthetics in *AI & Society* 14, no. 2 (2000): 155–56.

Parts of chapter 1 were previously published in different form as "Databases Are Us," *AI & Society* 14, no. 2 (2000): 157–75.

Chapter 2 was previously published as "The Database," in *The Language of New Media* (Cambridge: MIT Press, 2001), 218–43; and as "Database as a Genre of New Media," *AI & Society* 14, no. 2 (2000): 176–83. Reproduced with permission from The MIT Press and from Springer-Verlag London Ltd.

Chapter 3 was previously published as "The Ocean, the Database, and the Cut," in Christina Lammer, ed., *doKu/Kunst und Wirklichkeit inszenieren im Dokumentarfilm* (Vienna: Verlag Turia + Kant, 2002). Reprinted with permission from Turia + Kant.

Parts of chapter 8 were previously published as "Collaborative Systems," *AI & Society* 14, no. 2 (2000): 196–213.

Chapter 9 was previously published as "Artificial Intelligence and Aesthetics," in Michael Kelly, ed., *Encyclopedia of Aesthetics* (New York: Oxford University Press, 1998). Copyright Oxford University Press. Reprinted with permission of Oxford University Press.

Chapter 10 was previously published as "Manufacturing Agency: Relationally Structuring Community In-Formation," *AI & Society* 14, no. 2 (2000): 184–95.

Chapter 13 previously appeared as "Raw Data Diet," in *Identity in the Digital Age* (Hamburg: Hoffmann und Campe Verlag, 2004). Copyright 2004 Hoffmann und Campe Verlag, www.hoffmann-und-campe.de. Reprinted with permission.

Chapter 14 was previously published as "Time Capsule," *AI & Society* 14, no. 2 (2000): 243–49.

CONTRIBUTORS

Sharon Daniel is an artist working with technology for social transformation. She is an associate professor of film and digital media at the University of California, Santa Cruz, where she teaches courses in digital media theory and practice, and a member of the University of California's Digital Arts Research Network.

Steve Dietz is artistic director of ZeroOne: The Art and Technology Network. He curates contemporary art exhibitions and festivals, as well as speaking and writing extensively about the art formerly known as new media. His interviews and writing have appeared in *Parkett, Artforum, Flash Art, Design Quarterly, Spectra, Afterimage, Art in America, Museum News, BlackFlash, Public Art Review,* and *Intelligent Agent.*

Lynn Hershman-Leeson has worked extensively in photography, film, video, installation, and interactive and Net-based media. She is a recipient of the prestigious Golden Nica Prix Ars Electronica and a Daniel Langlois Foundation Fellowship, the Alfred P. Sloan Prize, and, in 2007, the first ZeroOne Award for "Media that Matters." She has completed five feature films, more than two hundred international museum exhibitions, and nine interactive installations. She is emeritus professor at the University of California, A. D. White Professor at Cornell University, and chair of the Film Department at the San Francisco Art Institute.

Eduardo Kac is internationally recognized for his telepresence work and his bio art. The first human to implant a microchip, Kac is the creator of "GFP Bunny" (Alba, the green bunny). His work can be seen online at www .ekac.org.

Norman M. Klein is a cultural critic, media historian, and novelist. His most recent book, on scripted spaces and the "electronic," is *The Vatican to Vegans: The History of Special Effects.* He is a professor at the California Institute of the Arts.

John Klima employs a variety of technologies to produce artwork with hand-built electronics and computer hardware and software. He has exhibited his works internationally, including *BitStreams* at the Whitney Museum of American Art, the 2002 Whitney Biennial, Eyebeam, the New Museum of Contemporary Art, PS.1, and the Brooklyn Museum of Art, the Museum for Communication in Bern, Switzerland, the NTT InterCommunication Center in Tokyo, and the Daejeon Municipal Museum in Korea. Klima was recently a research scientist at the Courant Institute, New York University, and is currently adjunct professor of digital media at the Rhode Island School of Design. He also teaches an extensive course in game design theory and production at the Polytechnic University of Brooklyn.

George Legrady is professor of interactive media in the Media Arts & Technology Doctoral program at the University of California, Santa Barbara. His contribution to the digital media field since the early stages of its formation has been in intersecting cultural content with data processing as a means of creating new forms of aesthetic representations and sociocultural narrative experiences. His digital interactive installations have been exhibited internationally, most recently at ISEA 06, San Jose (2006), 3rd Beijing New Media Festival (2006), Frankfurt Museum of Communication (2006), and BlackBox 06 at ARCO, Madrid (2006).

Lev Manovich is the author of *Soft Cinema: Navigating the Database.* His book *The Language of New Media* was hailed as "the most suggestive and broad ranging media history since Marshall McLuhan." Manovich is a professor of visual arts, University of California, San Diego and a director of the Lab for Cultural Analysis at the California Institute for Telecommunications and Information Technology. See www.manovich.net and visarts.ucsd.edu.

Robert F. Nideffer researches, teaches, and publishes in the areas of virtual environments and behavior, interface theory and design, technology and culture, and contemporary social theory. He is associate professor in the departments of Studio Art and Informatics at the University of California,

Irvine, where he also serves as codirector of the Arts Computation Engineering (ACE) graduate program, and director of the Game Culture and Technology Lab.

Nancy Paterson is an electronic media artist working primarily in interactive installations. She is an instructor at the Ontario College of Art and Design and artist in residence at the School of Communications Arts, Seneca@York, Toronto.

Christiane Paul is adjunct curator of new media arts at the Whitney Museum of American Art and the director of Intelligent Agent, a service organization and information resource dedicated to digital art. She has written extensively on new media arts and is the author of *Digital Art*. She teaches in the MFA computer arts department at the School of Visual Arts in New York and the Digital+Media department at the Rhode Island School of Design and and has lectured internationally on art and technology.

Marko Peljhan founded the arts organization Projekt Atol, which works within the performance, visual arts, situation, and communications fields. He is associate professor in art and media arts and technology at the University of California, Santa Barbara, director of Projekt Atol, and founder of the Interpolar Transnational Art Science Constellation I-TASC.

Warren Sack is a software designer and media theorist who explores theories and designs for online public space and public discussion. He is on the faculty of the Film and Digital Media Department at the University of California, Santa Cruz. His work has been shown at the ZKM I Center for Art and Media, Karlsruhe, Germany; the New Museum of Contemporary Art, New York; the Walker Art Center, Minneapolis; and the artport of the Whitney Museum of American Art.

Bill Seaman explores emergent meaning through interface, text, image, object, and sound relationships. He is head of the graduate digital media department at Rhode Island School of Design.

Victoria Vesna is an artist who explores how communication technologies affect collective behavior and how perceptions of identity shift in relation to scientific innovation. She has exhibited her work internationally in twenty solo exhibitions and more than seventy group shows in the last decade. She is the recipient of many grants, commissions, and awards, including the Oscar Signorini award for best Net artwork in 1998 and the Cine Golden Eagle for best scientific documentary in 1986. She is a professor and chair of the Department of Design I Media Arts at the UCLA School of the Arts.

Grahame Weinbren creates interactive cinema installations, which have been exhibited internationally since 1984. *The Erl King* (collaboration with Roberta Friedman), one of the first works to combine interactivity with cinema, was recently acquired by the Guggenheim Museum. He teaches in the graduate program of the School of Visual Arts and was a visiting artist in the Department of Visual and Environmental Studies at Harvard University.

INDEX

Abelson, Robert P., 207n.34, 208n.50
absence, data as, 89–93
abstraction of information, 18–19
Academy of Machinima Arts & Sciences, 227
äda'web, 112
Adorno, Theodor, 202
Advanced Intelligent Information Retrieval System (AIIRS), 270
Advanced Research Projects Agency (ARPA), 237
aesthetic common sense, 192, 193, 196
aesthetics: artificial intelligence and, 187–91; information and, 27–28; intersection of ethics, 142–43; social, 159–64. *See also* database aesthetics; dignity, aesthetics of; network aesthetics
Aesthetics of Care?, The (Menezes), 157
Agent Ruby (Hershman-Leeson), 249–51, 252
Agre, Philip E., 207n.41
Ahearn, John, 165
AI. *See* artificial intelligence (AI)
AIML (Artificial Identity Markup Language), 249
Albers, Joseph, 37n.20
algorithm(s): bird flocking, in *ecosystm*, 263–64; computer game, 42; in database as meta-narrative, 104, 105–6; data structure and, 41–44, 45; Kohonen

self-organizing (Self-Organizing Map), 104, 245–46
Ali, Muhammad, 25
Alice in Wonderland, TextArc's reading of, 101–2
Amazon.com, 44
Amis, Martin, 75
Andrews, Larry, 181n.58
Andújar, Daniel García, 113, 116, 120n.10
animal database, xviii
Anna Karenin Goes to Paradise (Lialina), 118
Another Day in Paradise (Vesna), 36n.15
Apollo (spacecraft), 30
apple metaphor, 72
Arabesque (Whitney), 53
Arabian Nights, 166; *Medea Project: Theater for Incarcerated Women* as contemporary, 167–68
Aragon, Louis, 89
architecture: absence in, 90; artists as "information architects," xiii–xiv, 28; discourse, xvii–xviii; recombinant, 140n.13; virtual, 135
archivist, artist as reliable, 118–19
Aristotle, 202
Aronowitz, Stanley, 177n.9
ARPANET, 237
Ars Electronica, 157
art: creative potential of biology, computer science, digital networking,

Xanadu (Nelson), 28

Yang, Shenglin, 141n.30
Yates, Francis A., 140n.9
Young, Annie Mae, 164
Youngblood, Gene, 53, 59n.21

Zimbardo, Phillip G., 230n.12
Zimmerman, Philip, 9
ZKM in Germany, 130
Zorns Lemma (film), 69–70
Zurich Capital Markets (ZCM), 260,
    263–64